Deliberate Conflict

Argument, Political Theory, and Composition Classes

Patricia Roberts-Miller

Southern Illinois University Press
Carbondale

Publication was partially funded by a University Cooperative Society Subvention Grant awarded by the University of Texas at Austin.

Library of Congress Cataloging-in-Publication Data

Roberts-Miller, Patricia, 1959–
    Deliberate conflict : argument, political theory, and composition classes / Patricia Roberts-Miller.
        p. cm.
    Includes bibliographical information (p.) and index.
    1. English language—Rhetoric—Study and teaching. 2. Rhetoric—Political aspects—Study and teaching. 3. Report writing—Study and teaching (Higher). 4. Persuasion (Rhetoric)—Study and teaching. 5. Political science—Study and teaching. I. Title.

PE1404 .R525 2004
808'.042'071—dc22
ISBN 0-8093-2566-7 (alk. paper)
ISBN-13: 978-0-8093-2766-9
ISBN-10: 0-8093-2766-X   2003023972

CONTENTS

Preface

But we lean forward to the next crazy venture beneath
the skies.

—Jack Kerouac, *On the Road*

Sometimes it seems that teaching first-year writing has the place in the
academy that sex had in the Victorian era—the language surrounding
it is one of duty and distaste, but the simple presence of a younger generation demonstrates that people are engaging in it, or did it at some
point in their lives. The accepted explanation is that we participate in it
because it is the means necessary to attain our true ends of security, pres-
tige, and legitimacy. Our real interests are somewhere else, but we are
willing to lie back and think of tenure. Once we have paid our dues, we
move on to the higher and better things that we really enjoy, leaving
others to such "service." As with Victorians, there are some people who
do enjoy the activity, and there are even books that tell one how to do it
better, but we treat them as pornography, as texts serving impulses far
baser than the intellectual pursuits that we really admire. Of course, there
are some people who have no other pursuits, who have no responsibilities other than teaching first-year writing, but we see their existence as
the result of vice and cupidity and pass them without acknowledgment.
In a perfect world, we think, they would not exist.

But me, I love teaching first-year composition. That is an odd admission for someone like me—who does not have to teach it—to make, and
I have seen people physically recoil at the statement. For reasons obscure
to me, this admission is always taken to mean that I do not love other
kinds of teaching. Yet I see no reason to think that one must choose
between graduate seminars, upper-division topics courses, and lower-

division writing courses, perhaps because, for me, the project is much the same: considering the place of rhetoric in democracy.

As James Thurber says, even the best job in the world (which he identifies as hitting baseballs through the windows of the RCA building) would eventually get boring, and I don't claim that I love every moment of teaching first-year composition (or any other course, for that matter). My long-term scholarly interests in deliberative forms of rhetoric, in fact, come out of certain recurrent frustrations—students committed to the notion of argument as aggression (whether they opt for participating in the aggression or staying out of it entirely). My intermittent responsibilities for supervising and training first-year composition instructors have also sometimes led to frustrating conversations about teaching writing, especially when trying to work with someone who seems committed to hating the course.

There is a conversation I occasionally have with first-year composition instructors: They tell me how much they hate the course (often focussing on the teaching of argument) and what an intellectual wasteland it is. When I respond by seeing if we can come up with assignments, texts, or a course arrangement that might make the class more interesting for them and their students, they get visibly frustrated with me, as though I am completely missing the point. And, in a way, I am. My premise (validated by my experience) is that the course can be great fun, and student papers can be genuinely enlightening. For those instructors, such a premise demonstrates the smallness of my mind; I might as well have announced to a Victorian drawing room that I look forward to bedding my husband. Their premise (validated by their experience) is that student papers vacillate between incoherent and predictable and that neither they nor their students will learn anything intellectually challenging from the course. This disconnect, I have come to believe, happens because we are talking about pedagogy, but we really disagree about the place and nature of argument in democratic society. Hence this book.

Most instructors, of course, are not so cynical about first-year composition, and I have been lucky in my career to have had teachers, colleagues, and students who were deeply committed to teaching. As a graduate student in the Berkeley rhetoric department, I had faculty mentors who enjoyed talking about teaching, especially William Brandt, Bridget Connelly, Fred Antzack, and Arthur Quinn. It was my fortune to take a position at UNC-Greensboro, which has a faculty I will always admire for its dedication and sheer quality. The English department at the University of Missouri at Columbia is made up of teachers who indicate no tension between high-quality teaching and impressive scholarly productivity. Were I to do the department justice, my acknowledgements would include the entire faculty roster. Mizzou has the added distinction of being a place where I could pick up the phone and talk to Ted Tarkow, an associate dean, or Ruth Wright, head adviser, in order to have time-consuming conversations about individual students. I am also indebted to the University of Missouri for allowing me a semester's research leave and to Howard Hinkel for being such a wonderful department chair. The devotion of University of Texas to undergraduate teaching is demonstrated in the fact that the Division of Rhetoric and Composition is an undergraduate teaching unit. I am also grateful to the University of Texas for having given me a research leave, to Heather Grassmick for aid in the completion of this book, and to the UT Co-op for a very generous subvention grant.

I have also been aided by people who have to be acknowledged individually. Kenn Barry, Linda Harmann, Tony Quirke, Jim Roberts-Miller, and Tom Stroik argued with me about portions of this book. Doug Hunt, David Read, and the two SIU Press readers engaged in extraordinarily careful and helpfully critical readings of it. Gary Chapman, Elisabeth Coughlan, and Jon Elster pointed me toward important readings at crucial moments. Heather Grassmick tracked down lost quotes and confirmed citations. Dana Kinnison took over administrative responsibilities, giving me time. The generous praise of my earlier book by Davida Charney, Greg Clark, Michael Halloran, and Tom Miller was important in the long, dark nights of persistence. Mike Bernard-Donals, Rosa Eberly, Lester Faigley, and Jeff Walker sent encouraging e-mail at the exact right times. Cathy Roberts very helpfully sent along readings from legal journals on hate speech. I am deeply indebted to several people in ways that are difficult to define, for something along the lines of intellectual companionship—modeling a teaching life or simply sharing insights that have stuck with me: Kylo Ginsberg, Elaine Lawless, Pat Okker, Catherine Parke. Chester Burnette, Hubert Sumlin, and Jacob Roberts-Miller did their best to help me keep the project in perspective. And, most importantly, my undergraduate writing students continually reminded me why it mattered.

There are certain books whose influence is pervasive. These include Hannah Arendt's *The Human Condition,* Wayne Booth's *Modern Dogma and the Rhetoric of Assent,* and Thomas Farrell's *Rhetorical Norms.* I am also indebted to the following journals in which portions of chapter 4 were first published: "Fighting Without Hatred" appeared in *JAC* 22 ([2002]: 585–601). "Post-Contemporary Composition: Social Constructivism and Its Alternatives" appeared in *Composition Studies* 30 ([2002]: 97–115). "Communitarianism and Communities of Discourse" appeared in *College Composition and Communication* 22 ([2003]: 585–601).

Deliberate
Conflict

INTRODUCTION

> The thing that strikes me more and more . . . is the extraor-
> dinary viciousness and dishonesty of political controversy in
> our time. I don't mean merely that controversies are acrimo-
> nious. They ought to be that when they are on serious
> subjects. I mean that almost nobody seems to feel that an
> opponent deserves a fair hearing or that the objective truth
> matters as long as you can score a neat debating point. *touché*
> —George Orwell, *As I Please*

Everyone knows what it means to teach public argumentation in writing classes. It means that the instructor brings in examples of public policy writing on various topics, pointing out various formal qualities.
Then the instructor gives an assignment something like the following:

> Pick a topic about which you care deeply, and write a letter of 1,000–1,250
> words to your congressperson arguing for or against some specific policy con-
> cerning that topic. You should make certain that, at some point in your pa-
> per, you consider the opposition's argument. You must use at least four sources.

The instructor then grades a set of completely unrelated papers, on topics
ranging from financial aid to gun control. Susan Wells has aptly called
this kind of assignment "generic public writing."

> In such assignments, students inscribe their positions in a vacuum: since
> there is no place within the culture where student writing on gun control
> is held to be of general interest, no matter how persuasive the student, or
> how intimate their acquaintance with guns, "public writing" in such a con-
> text means "writing for no audience at all." (328)

Wells goes on to argue that there are several ways that we can go about
teaching public writing, each of which is a reasonable proposal, but each

of which depends upon her audience's perceiving that the formalistic approach to public discourse is a problem that needs solving, and I'm not sure that's true. While I share Wells's hostility to that kind of assignment, the project of this book turns on a slightly prior question: In what model of politics, the self, and knowledge does that formalist approach to public writing make sense? My answer is that it is transparently sensible in the liberal model of the public sphere, and that the liberal model is not the only model available.

book's focus

This book concerns the relation—and sometimes lack of relation—between writing pedagogies and models of argument in a democracy, between, in other words, composition theory and political theory. That is a complicated topic for a book, for several reasons, not least of which is that I am not pointing to something that people in rhetoric and composition already recognize as a problem. While argumentation is often central to the practice of composition, it is not central in our theorizing with one another about the teaching of writing. Rhetoric and composition has nothing comparable to speech communication's *Argumentation and Advocacy,* a journal devoted to argumentation. Richard Fulkerson has pointed out that the major resources for composition instructors fail to provide any discussion of argumentation, and he infers from this silence that "A knowledge of argument/logic and its relationship to composition is not regarded as significant for composition teachers. It isn't part of the pedagogical paradigm of our discipline" (*Teaching the Argument* 1). This gap is, most likely, the result of the sense that argumentation is not really an issue. We know what it is, and we know how to teach it, or we know why we avoid teaching it.

I agree w/ Fulkerson!

Yet we also know that the teaching of argumentation can go terribly wrong. Dennis Lynch, and Diana George, and Marilyn Cooper describe the frustrating but common result:

> In their writings, our students fall easily into one of two camps: for or against. They cling to their original positions as if those were sacred to home, country, and spiritual identity. Too frequently absent from these debates is any real knowledge of the issue at hand as anything more than a pointless argument among people who do not care very much about the outcome—except that it is always better, in the classroom as in many other arenas, to be on the winning rather than the losing side. (390)

Given these problems (and more discussed below), it is no wonder that many programs and instructors simply avoid teaching argumentation.

A classic (even classical) argument for teaching argumentation is that it is necessary for the life of the polis, that, as Gregory Clark has said,

> the classroom, particularly the writing classroom, is primarily a place where students can be guided and protected as they learn to perform rhetorically in the variety of roles required of them as they participate in a variety of discourses where the shared beliefs and actions are determined cooperatively. (387)

As old as Aristotle and as recent as the latest edition of Ramage and Bean's popular textbook *Writing Arguments,* this defense may seem both obvious and straightforward to people like me who promote rhetoric, but rhetoricians' continued reliance on this topos is actually rather odd in a couple of ways.

First, its constancy should raise suspicion—there have been profound differences among political communities in Western history, such that the very sense of what is (or should be) a polis has shifted. It should seem odd to assume that a skill developed in a homosocial and slave-based polis like Athens, which put a premium on uniformity, would have the same value in a heterogeneous and postmodern polis, which claims to value difference, such as the United States. The assumption seems to be that rhetorical theory can be disconnected from political context, that one can interweave strands from theorists of any era or place—a little Aristotle, a little Cicero, a little Kant, a little Mill, a little Arendt, a little Burke, a little Berlin, and so on. But what has Athens to do with Pittsburgh?

Second, rhetoricians—of all people—ought to be attuned to the effectiveness of an argument, so we ought to be troubled that this defense of rhetoric is obviously unpersuasive to so many of our colleagues. And yet it often is. Entire programs simply avoid it, and I've often worked with instructors whose response to the teaching of argument seems modelled on "Bartleby the Scrivener." This is not to say that composition journals are filled with arguments against argumentation; in my experience, opponents of argument, appropriately enough, do not argue about why it is wrong but simply evade it.

Just as we think we know what teaching argument is, so we think we know what it means to engage in public argument. Argumentation textbooks typically say that skill at argument is important in a democracy, but they do not make clear which model of democracy they imagine; in fact, very little (if any) of the current discourse regarding the teaching of argument indicates awareness that there are different models. This lack of debate is not a sign of consensus; it is not the case that instructors and theorists of teaching fail to discuss the sort of public sphere for which we imagine we are preparing students because we all agree on the nature of democratic discourse. On the contrary, much of our disagreement about pedagogical practices is disagreement about what it means (or should mean) to participate in a democratic public sphere.[1] We are arguing about pedagogy because we disagree about political theory, and my point in this book is that we would do well to make the nature of such participation the subject of deliberate conflict.

To explain how composition studies could be enriched by paying closer attention to differences among models of the public sphere, I first need to set out a rough taxonomy of the kinds of public spheres that will be discussed at greater detail through the book. I divide them into six categories: liberal, technocratic, interest-based, agonistic, communitarian, and deliberative.

By the term "liberal model," a form explored in chapters 1 and 2, political theorists (and I) mean something that is only historically related to what is popularly called "liberal" politics or a "liberal" education. A product of the Enlightenment, the liberal model theorizes a public space where people rely on rational discourse in order to determine what is in the universal best interest. At the same time that they have the ability to ignore their own particular situations and needs, interlocutors remain fundamentally (even profoundly) individual—able to resist the pressures of conformity, to think critically about their own traditions, to stand above and away from the crowd. This model is explicitly utopian, as both advocates and critics of the Enlightenment model describe it as a vision that has never existed, except as a goal.

Technocracy (briefly discussed in chapter 2) assumes that policy questions are fundamentally technical questions and are best solved either through letting technical experts make the decisions, or through using the public sphere for the dissemination of technical information that can then inform the decisions of the general public. Either way, the public sphere is not a realm where people deliberate together to make decisions; all rhetoric is technical rhetoric. This model is of little interest to current political theorists (dependent as it is on subsuming all reasoning to instrumental reason) and not explicitly advocated by composition theorists, but it is implied in some pedagogies.

The interest-based model of discourse (discussed in chapter 3) assumes that people can and should look to their own self-interest in regard to public policies; the conflict among them should not be settled through argument, as much as through bargaining, relying on market forces, and/or advertising. Closely related to what Wayne Booth calls "motivism," the underlying model of rhetoric is what Thomas Conley calls "motivis-tic." The second most prevalent model in popular discourse, it has been out of favor among political theorists since some time in the 1980s. Although I'm not aware of any pedagogy that explicitly advocates it, there are sometimes bits and pieces of it interspersed with advice based on mutually exclusive models, (such as saying that students should use rational argument *and* that they should analyze their audience in socio-economic terms).

The interest-based model is often described as a degradation of the liberal model (e.g., Habermas's *Structural Transformation of the Public Sphere*), but it is as likely to have come from the agonistic tradition in rhetoric (briefly discussed in chapter 3). Sometimes categorized as part of the communitarian approach to public discourse, agonism is more conflictual than communitarian or liberal discourse but not quite the verbal free-for-all of interest-based discourse.

Communitarianism, sometimes called neo-Aristotelian (discussed in the chapter 4), takes issue with liberal theory on two counts. First, it rejects the liberal model's aspiration for transhistorical foundations for democratic practice, instead arguing that democracy depends on a sociohistorically constructed ethos that must be consciously enriched. Second, it rejects the liberal model's privileging of the autonomous individual, arguing that this model of the self means that the liberal model necessarily ends up enacting the interest-based model.[2]

The deliberative model (the subject of the chapter 5) is similar to the liberal model in that the main goal of this model of democracy is to articulate a system in which issues would be settled by who makes the best argument, not who has the most power. It is different in that proponents of this model tend to assume a much broader notion of argument than is present in the liberal model—one that includes narrative, attention to the particular, sensibility, and appeals to emotion.

Even with this brief explanation, one can see that some of the conflict over the place and nature of argument in writing classes is based on different models of public discourse. As Susan Jarratt says, teachers often opt for writing assignments and pedagogical approaches that put a premium on collaboration, cooperation, and individual expression. In consequence of this resistance, composition courses "spend too little time helping students learn how to argue about public issues" (121). But there are strong criticisms of teaching argumentation. Some argue that it requires reinforcing masculinist views of language as combat and domination (see Daümer and Runzo). Others have said that argument is a form of coercion at worst and bargaining at best—both types of action that privilege those who enter with more power (see Lassner). If it does not require the adoption of an aggressive approach (see Connelly), then it seems to require an equally dishonest neutrality (see Clifford; Ohmann). If not a passionate invocation of the high style, then it seems to be an excessively dispassionate and hyperrational discourse (see Brody).

My summary of attacks on argument may make them seem contradictory—how can argument be both neutral and aggressive, hyperrational and impassioned?—but, in a sense, these characterizations are all right. The liberal model of public discourse does put a tremendous amount of emphasis on neutrality and rationality, while the interest-based model makes argument a form of bargaining and coercion, and the agonistic model rewards and requires a potentially masculinist aggression. Thus the different critiques of argument are contradictory insofar as they result from different assumptions about the ideal form of public argument.

For instance, John Clifford ridicules *The St. Martin's Guide to Writing* for stressing the importance of thoughtful writing and good reasons; he says,

> I can just imagine my students using cogent reasons and cold facts to persuade Jesse Helms to support abortion rights or funding for AIDS patients, or perhaps students could use logic and statistics to persuade their professors to give up tenure or to convince the tobacco industry to make the ethical gesture of switching its crops to bean sprouts. (44)

Clifford's criticism comes from his assumption of an interest-based model—his examples presume that people's political stances are the result of their socio-economic status and interest. *The St. Martin's Guide,* however, partially (but not completely) assumes the liberal model, which presumes that rhetors can and will transcend their particular socio-economic interests in pursuit of the common good. Clifford proposes a different practice because he assumes a different model.

But *The St. Martin's Guide* (along with other composition texts) only intermittently presupposes the liberal model, and that is a problem. The liberal model is (and always has been) explicitly utopian. Theorists of the liberal model have never claimed that rational-critical discourse actually persuades everyone, or even most people; they claim that it does persuade a certain sort of person—the ideal Enlightenment citizen—and they hope that teaching how to persuade that sort of person will transform political practice. The ideal Enlightenment citizen is, if not hostile to religion (as defined by, for example, Karl Popper in *The Open Society*), then deeply suspicious of religious enthusiasm (see, for instance, Stephen Holmes' list of the qualities of "the ideal-typical liberal citizen" in *Passions and Constraints* 14–15). Jesse Helms is not that sort of person; his political positions are explicitly and emphatically religious positions he is proud to hold with enthusiasm. The presence of people like Jesse Helms is not a problem for political theorists who advocate the liberal model since they do not describe that approach to discourse as the most effective—the hope is that requiring students to behave like ideal Enlightenment rhetors will cause them to demand "enlightened" behavior in the public sphere. Thus, students who have been so trained will not be like Jesse Helms, they will not be persuaded by someone like him, and they will not vote for him. Also, they will not try to persuade him—thus, whereas Clifford says that *The St. Martin's Guide* "asks writers to believe that by adopting and carefully orchestrating an objective, rational argument, they can win the day and bring Jesse Helms to his senses" (44), in fact the text makes no such claim. On the contrary, composition texts that implicitly adopt the liberal model typically recommend that students avoid trying to persuade their opposition, reaching instead toward some kind of hypothetical neutral or mildly skeptical audience. *The Bedford Guide to Writing* says, "Your readers, you can assume, are people who may be familiar with the controversy but who have not yet taken sides" (Kennedy 190). *The Informed Argument* recommends that students write to a "skeptical" audience (Robert Miller 5). *Elements of Argument* rather confusingly says that students should write to "persuade the unconvinced, to acquaint them with good reasons for changing their minds" (Rottenberg 4).

Such texts are and are not correct to recommend that students not try to reach an informed, intelligent, and committed opposition. Certainly, the kind of advice typically given in those texts will not work with such an audience—to that degree, this recommendation is accurate. But such limitations should cause us to rethink that advice; this is a kind of rhetorical fatalism, and like many forms of fatalism, it is self-fulfilling.

Not all pedagogies avoid conflict altogether; some restrict it to a late stage in the writing process, so that one comes up with one's argument in a supportive environment (what political theorists call an enclave). Conflict at an early stage, while one is still doing the thinking, is assumed to be paralyzing; once one's position is already determined, then considering a hostile audience can help one think about issues of effectiveness in arrangement and style. In contrast to agonists like Wayne Booth who say that good writing is audience-attentive from the moment of conception, Elbow insists that good writing "comes from the writer's having gotten sufficiently wrapped up in her meaning and her language to forget all about audience needs" ("Closing My Eyes" 55). After saying that "there are some occasions when we benefit from keeping a hostile audience in mind from the start" and that there are some audiences who are so inviting that imagining them helps us write better, he says: "*Most commonly,* however, the effect of audience awareness is somewhere between the two extremes: the awareness disturbs or disrupts our writing and thinking without completely blocking it" (52, emphasis added). While Elbow uses the language of middle ground, it is actually a very strong claim—that our writing and thinking are "most commonly" disturbed and disrupted by considering audience. Similarly, his solution to this problem presented by audience is to consider audience not as part of invention but revision:

> We can ignore that audience altogether during the *early* stages of writing and direct our words only to ourselves or to no one in particular—or even to the "wrong" audience, that is, to an *inviting* audience of trusted friends or allies. . . . *After* we have figured out our thinking in copious exploratory or draft writing—perhaps finding the right voice or stance as well—*then* we can follow the traditional rhetorical advice: think about readers and revise carefully to adjust our words and thoughts to our intended audience. (53, emphasis in original)

This strikes me as an extraordinary claim—and yet one that is quite common in teaching practice (as when, for instance, students are told to develop a thesis and then do research).

Pamela Annas and Deborah Tenney, citing Elbow, insists that students must form their positions in a situation in which they have "the freedom to explore without being criticized, either by their own internalized critics or by critics external to them" (137). Annas and Tenney emphasize writing as "exploration" of one's own position, with a need for "privacy and freedom from judgment" (138); it is also a freedom from conflict. The exploration in which students engage is of their own reactions to the course texts, texts that are themselves selected for their ability to show how "powerfully convincing" writing can be when "authentically voiced and grounded in one's own specific reality" (137). Annas and Tenney say,

> critical assessment comes later and is an essential part of argument—but in the beginning it can silence a neophyte voice simply because the demands of argument (owning a position, understanding the requirements of taking a stance, being willing to speak in support of that stance) are so great. (138)

For the most part, such approaches describe conflict and opposition as unpleasant and destructive, albeit possibly a kind of necessary evil. In this regard, they fit well into the liberal public sphere tradition that similarly searches for ways to have public discourse without public conflict.

Elbow's discomfort with conflict is explicit; a large number of composition theorists simply ignore argumentation altogether because they do not see college as education in or for citizenship. Erika Lindemann's "Three Views of English 101," for example, does not even mention the view that first-year composition is a course in public discourse, in argumentation oriented toward participation in a public sphere. In her essay "Freshman Composition," she simply asserts that first-year composition courses are pre-academic writing courses: "Freshman English does what no high school writing course can do: provide opportunities to master the genres, styles, audiences, and purposes of college writing" (312). Neil Daniel and Christina Murphy say, "The place to learn writing is in the context of a discipline or a profession" (233), thereby assuming that the teaching of writing is pre-academic or preprofessional training. When Jeff Smith insists that we pay attention to "larger enterprise known as college" and students' own reasons for being in college, he writes entirely in terms of their careers; there is no mention of their roles as citizens. Smith expresses concern for future clients of our students, but not for fellow citizens (see especially 312–13).

To raise the issue of imagining our students as citizens is to invoke the specter of the "politicized" classroom, the hobgoblin of attacks on academia. The politicized classroom debate, while often apparently about pedagogy (e.g., whether a teacher should openly advocate a political agenda, what texts should be taught as canonical, the extent to which students should be allowed to criticize traditional texts), is, I will contend, so acrimonious because it too reflects different models of public debate. I don't mean this in the conventional sense—that stances regarding the postmodern turn in academia result from one's relationship to a leftist political agenda (on the contrary, I will argue that postmodernism is not necessarily connected to any particular political agenda and has been quite cheerfully coopted by the very people on the right who condemn it as immoral). Instead, the "debate" about pedagogy is a conflict about the very nature of democratic discourse (and, to some degree, whether we want a democracy at all). Debate is in quotation marks because, as Michael Berubé has said, this "'debate' is conducted by rules that most academics—and most responsible citizens—don't recognize" (19). Certainly, the number of jaw-dropping errors in polemics like Lynne Cheney's apparently ironically titled *Telling the Truth* or Dinesh DeSouza's *Illiberal Education* make one wonder about the authors' rules for public controversy.

But not all attacks on the above movements in academia are politically reactionary or untruthful; some of the criticisms come from within academia (Allan Bloom's *The Closing of the American Mind*), or from within the left (Todd Gitlin's *The Twilight of Common Dreams,* Terry Eagleton's *The Illusions of Postmodernism,* Christopher Norris's *What's Wrong with Postmodernism*). Jean Bethke Elshtain's *Democracy on Trial* is from the perspective of a liberal feminist, and Martha Nussbaum (who is, somewhat bizarrely, included in Cheney's gallery of poststructuralists) has numerous essays arguing against what she considers the re-emergence of sophistry (see especially "The Sophists Are among Us" in *Love's Knowledge*). Roger Kimball's *Tenured Radicals,* while from a politically conservative non-academic, is, as Berubé says, grounded in Kimball's having read the material he attacks (71); Kimball has taken the time to listen to the people with whom he disagrees. Berubé rightly criticizes Kimball for the internal contradictions of the argument (69), and they are striking: While Kimball describes the traditional humanist education he champions as elitist, he condemns new methods of scholarship for being elitist; he repeatedly asserts that texts in the canon are recognized as universally valid, while he is outraged that tenured radicals fail to recognize their validity.

Of most importance for this project is that he says that tenured radicals should be condemned for thinking of education as political at the same time that he repeatedly asserts that there are political consequences to educational practice (see, for instance, 58). This argument (with its apparently contradictory premise) continually comes up in regard to critical pedagogy. Maxine Hairston, Louise Wetherbee Phelps, Jeff Smith, and other critics of liberatory pedagogy advocate a practice supposed to be apolitical at the same time that they claim political benefits for such practices (for more on this point see Lynch's "Teaching Rhetorical Values"). To dismiss this argument because of the contradiction is to miss the fact that the distinction between a politics of an avowedly disinterested inculcation of certain skills (critical reading, clear writing, logical reasoning) and an openly impassioned advocacy of certain policy arguments seems obvious to many people. It seems so because the liberal public sphere—especially in its most popular forms—depends upon and reinforces the dichotomies that make sensible the notion of an apolitical grounding for politics.

Hence, both within and about academia, an often unarticulated part of the arguments about classroom practice concerns the very nature of public argument: how one engages in argument, how (or whether) one addresses the arguments of one's opposition, what counts as good evidence. Quite possibly, some of the specific public issues in which academics sometimes find themselves enmeshed—concerning hate-speech codes, the "politicizing" of composition, Ebonics—will never be resolved unless there is more debate about argument itself, unless we at least can talk with one another about how we want to go about disagreeing.

The point of this book is to do just that, to explore the premises and consequences of the several most promising models of democratic public argument. The very logic of a book structure—the need for a chapter-based organization—means that the options are presented as different categories, but that's misleading. In fact, it's more accurate to think of them as falling in sundry places on a matrix with two axes. One axis measures the degree to which one considers ideal speech to be oriented

ement (agonistic). The other axis ublic sphere is a place where indi- expressive—or a place where groups licy—deliberative (see fig. 1).[3]

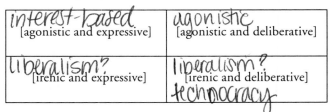

interest-based [agonistic and expressive]	*agonistic* [agonistic and deliberative]
liberalism? [irenic and expressive]	*liberalism?* [irenic and deliberative] *technocracy*

Fig. 1. Role and desirability of conflict in democratic public argument

This is not the conventional way of categorizing speech, as most domi-nant theories (e.g., Bain, Kinneavy) put expressive speech at the other end of a continuum from argument, but these theories ignore that there is such a thing as expressive argument. In addition, most taxonomies obscure that there is considerable difference of opinion as to just what makes an argument good. In an irenic public sphere, a productive argu-ment results in the interlocutors reaching agreement on the issue about which they originally disagreed (or one about which there was never disagreement in the first place). An irenic public sphere does not have very much conflict. In an agonistic sphere, a productive argument leads to appropriate policies, raises interesting questions, brings up injustices, or draws attention to points of view that had been obscured. By the first definition (an irenic public sphere), the debate between Federalists and Anti-Federalists was a failure because the two sides never reached agree-ment; there is no indication that the major proponents of either view shifted position. From an agonistic point of view, however, the debate was very productive, both in the sense that it led to a thorough discus-sion of the constitutional principles (one that influenced Supreme Court decisions and political theory), and in the very pragmatic consequence that the debate led to the Bill of Rights.

The second axis concerns the function of discourse—whether the par-ticipants are trying to settle policy questions. Thus, one might have a fundamentally irenic group (such as a support group) that has two dif-ferent kinds of meetings: ones in which people describe their experiences and express their feelings, expecting support, and ones in which the group is trying to determine policy, still with a sense that people should be supportive of one another.

These are axes, not dichotomies. The U.S. Congress is less agonistic than the British Parliament, more agonistic than the community association meetings I've observed. And, of course, any particular group will engage in a range of practices, at moments becoming more or less agonistic and deliberative, and so on. My intention here is not to drop practices into boxes, but to point to tendencies. And a strong, albeit completely unintentional, tendency of an irenic public sphere is to foreclose criticism.

A guiding assumption of the Enlightenment project and democratic theorizing is that, as my son says, talking is better than hitting—as a community, we are in a better situation if we can reach decisions through discourse rather than violence. It is assumed that this talking must be critical, at least at times, that people must have the opportunity to say negative things about popular and/or dominant practices, mores, institutional arrangements, and so on. If public discourse loses that critical function, then systemic injustices cannot be discussed. They are either left in place or brought to the public's attention violently. Because it is difficult, if not impossible, to have agreement and criticism at the same time, the more that a culture values an irenic public sphere, the less critical the discourse.

My project involves persuading my readers that argument (and the lack thereof) is a problem, and there are two very popular perspectives from which argument is not a problem. There is what one might call a prerhetorical approach, which assumes a stable and transparent relation among self, knowledge, discourse, and reality. For the prerhetorical approach, which might be connected to a religious standpoint (as among the New England Puritans) or antireligious (as within popular versions of positivism), argument is not a particularly complicated project. One announces one's thesis and list one's reasons. Logic, reason, self, and argument are straightforward terms with stable meanings and privileged positions. In what one might call the postrhetorical approach, such terms are equally straightforward but because they are objects of derision. Sometimes attributed to poststructuralist attacks on positivism, which are occasionally asserted to have proven that there is no such thing as proof, it can also result from a kind of crude Freudianism (one that assumes that the libido provides our "real" motives and that everything else is just a front), popular versions of behaviorism, sociobiology, sentimentalism, transcendentalism, and a variety of other sources. Because people are not persuaded by reason, argument is more or less a waste of time, and all one can do is to express one's point of view.

While they seem to be opposed, both views accept the rational/irrational split, with the prerhetorical privileging the rational and the postrhetorical privileging the irrational. Binary oppositions tend to function by one term's being carefully defined and the other one's operating as the catch-all for whatever is left over. In regard to the rational/irrational split, this usually means that "rational" is the carefully delimited term, signifying instrumental reason. Hence, all beliefs not the result of (or at least defensible through) instrumental reasoning are necessarily irrational, and irrational beliefs are "mere preferences"—random, arbitrary, likely the result of leaps of faith, cultural norms, or sheer superstition. Irrational beliefs, it is assumed, are not susceptible to reason and are therefore not things that can be changed by argument.

To mix my metaphors, the rational/irrational split is one of the ways that popular versions of reason saw off the branch on which they are standing. Enlightenment thinkers like John Locke and Immanuel Kant described issues of religion, aesthetics, and morals as subject to "rational" discourse because they had a fairly broad notion of what it meant to be rational, and that notion was not the materialist/instrumentalist notion that pervades current popular (and even some scholarly) discourse. A. J. Ayer summarizes the logical positivist view on this point. He says positivists, following Russell, divide propositions into two categories: logical ones that are tautological (e.g., mathematical ones) and factual ones.

> These classes were supposed to be exhaustive: so that if a sentence succeeded neither in expressing something formally true or false nor in expressing something that could be empirically tested, the view taken was that it did not express any proposition at all. It might have emotive meaning but it was literally nonsensical. (10)

This dismissal of nonmaterial propositions was intended to keep philosophy from dealing with metaphysical questions, but if a culture adopts the logical positivist view of rationality, then it will look on instrumental reason or scientism as "rational," and on ethics, metaphysics, and religion as "irrational."[4]

The more that one assumes that anything not empirically demonstrable is irrational, the greater the number of issues of common concern that fall into the irrational category, thus seeming to make public discourse incapable of resolving public controversies—a situation described with considerable eloquence in Wayne Booth's *Modern Dogma and the Rhetoric of Assent.* As long as one thinks of rationality as materialist and instrumental, and makes the assumption that ideas are rational or they are "nonsensical," then fairness, justice, and democracy itself look like propositions with nothing more than emotive meaning, or like "mere preferences." Liberal political theory thus loses one of its main virtues: It can no longer identify and rouse outrage about structures of oppression because the desire for justice is no less a "mere preference" than the desire for injustice.

The rational/irrational split is so pervasive in popular culture and its narrow definition of rationality so seductively simple that some very important (and very unreasonable) slippages pass unnoticed. There is a tendency for this notion of rationality to equate formal logic and scientific method, though the two are quite different. The scientific method is only appropriate to a materialist philosophy, and it can only be used to answer specific kinds of questions. The same is not true of formal logic. For example, there are some, but not many, religious questions that can be effectively answered through a materialist approach (such as dating the books of the Bible); but Christian, Jewish, and Muslim theologians have long used formal logic to debate religious issues.

Ian Barbour, in an unusually balanced discussion of the relation of theology and science, summarizes the conventional dichotomy of the two: "In the popular stereotype, the scientist's theories are tentative hypotheses that are continually criticized and revised, while religious beliefs are unchanging dogmas that the faithful accept without question" (130). Barbour goes on to discuss the ways that science and religion are, on the contrary, quite similar. In fact, the notion that religion is a nonintellectual process is a recent development (primarily nineteenth-century) and has frequently been identified as heretical. Despite the post-Enlightenment notion that religious faith is a random hodgepodge of dicta, numerous religious virtues depend upon conceptions of consistency.

After all, the very accusation of hypocrisy (a central concern of Christianity going all the way back to Jesus's condemnations of the Pharisees) depends upon the assumption that religious people should be consistent in their beliefs and actions—that it is unreasonable for a Christian to slash the tires of a student who objects to school prayer, for example, or that it is illogical for Christians to lie in order to attack evolution. The notion that religious faith is necessarily and entirely irrational is only true insofar as one equates "rational" and "subject to materialist scientific proof."[5]

This is not to say that all religions are logical (although many make a virtue of being systematic and internally consistent) but rather to say that dumping everything nonscientific into the category of irrationality means that we have trouble distinguishing among degrees of reasonableness. It means, for example, that we cannot distinguish between a religious person who believes in a God who set up a universe that includes evolution and one who thinks that God put fossils into the ground to test our faith. Since neither proposition can be proven through a scientific and materialist process, they both seem equally irrational, or, by the same token, equally rational. The difference between the two is merely preference.

The rational/irrational split exacerbates unproductive views of conflict insofar as it suggests that all public questions are to be resolved by relying on scientists (who must be in perfect agreement); if that avenue is not open, then we stagger down the path of mere preference and arbitrary faith. This was never what the Enlightenment philosophers intended or imagined, nor is it even what philosophers like Rawls or Jürgen Habermas mean when they use terms like "reason," but it is an unhappy inheritance from logical positivism—a school of thought whose general discrediting has done nothing to end this legacy. To reiterate, I am not saying that science and religion are equally logical. I am saying that trying to divide all systems into rational (subject to materialist scientific proof) and irrational (based on arbitrary preferences not subject to proof or disproof) is precisely what paralyzes the science versus religion discussion (and, by implication, all policy discussions that impinge on that one). Rather than think in terms of categories, we need to think in terms of degrees and kinds of support, something the rational/irrational split precludes.

This issue merits so much detailed discussion not because the rational/irrational split is the central topic in the book, but because it is a synecdoche for the kind of argument I will be making. For many, rationality is not an issue: Those who take the prerhetorical stance assume that the term has a stable and unproblematic definition; those who take the postrhetorical stance assume that the term has a stable and discredited definition. My point is that the issue is not settled and that the very definition of the term is up for argument. And the same is true for many other terms crucial in our discourse—autonomy, argument, community, discourse, neutrality, universality. One criterion we should use for deciding on our definition of these terms is pragmatic—does the definition facilitate a model of public reason that can enable people of different points of view to come together in deliberate, thoughtful, and considered conflict? Does it promote a public sphere of communal inquiry?

While it will become clear that I find the deliberative democratic model most persuasive, it is not the only appropriate basis for argumentation. On the contrary, it seems to me that students can benefit from a writing course consciously grounded in any of the various models and permutations I discuss (with the possible exception of the interest-based model); the harm (both to instructors and students) comes from the unreflective grounding of teaching practices in muddled combinations of different models, or the assumption of a model that has implications with which the instructor is deeply uncomfortable, or practices that entangle moments of unconsidered utopianism with equally unconsidered cynicism.

1

POLITICS WITHOUT ARGUMENT

> Liberalism will always remain an aspiration. It can never be
> fully realized or institutionalized. But it can provide a guide
> and stimulus to action. A liberal nation is a nation that keeps
> the worthier aims of liberalism steadily in view.
> —Stephen Holmes, *Passions and Constraints*

The liberal model of the public sphere is not the first or oldest model
of democracy (the agonistic model long predates it), but it is the
most common in political theory and public discourse. Like current-traditional pedagogy (which is, in many ways, the pedagogical enactment
of liberal political theory), it is grounded in Enlightenment values of
civility, rationality, neutrality, and autonomy. While current-traditional
rhetoric is—if mentioned at all—an object of derision in composition
theory, my own observation of classroom practice would suggest that it
remains common, if not predominant (as is also suggested in Hillocks's
Ways of Teaching). The pedagogical tenacity of current-traditional rhetoric
may well be the result of people's desire not to abandon the goal of a rational, critical, and inclusive form of policy discourse that respects the
privacy of individuals.

As will be discussed later, liberalism (both as a political agenda and a
theory of democracy) is under attack from many directions. Hannah
Arendt begins her critical discussion of Marx with what almost amounts
to an apology, saying that she does not want to be understood as joining the people she calls "professional anti-Marxists" (*Human Condition*
79). I hesitate to criticize liberal political theory because I do not want
to be understood as joining in, or even approving of, the attacks on
political liberals by the professional antiliberals. I am, ultimately, criti-

cal of the liberal public sphere, but even I will grant that many attacks on it are not entirely fair insofar as they rely on attacking liberal political theory for its use of concepts like autonomy, the public-private split, neutrality, rationality, and universality because those terms are used by liberal political theorists in ways significantly more complicated than many criticisms imply—a point to be pursued in the next two chapters. That is not to say that the attacks are entirely wrong, and that liberal political theory is right, but simply that the argument is not over.

The ideal public sphere of Enlightenment theorists is one where intellectually autonomous interlocutors judge one anothers' arguments purely on the basis of how well they are presented, rather than who presents them. A good argument is presented in a rational, decorous, impartial manner, and appeals to universal principles. Defenders of this vision argue that it is inclusive in that it is open to all people—regardless of gender, race, class, and so on—who can make their arguments in such a way. Proponents of this theory do not claim that everyone has equal competence at such a discourse, but that everyone could were they properly educated. Thus, liberal political theory is always entwined with arguments about education. A liberal education is supposed to provide the skills of critical thinking and argumentation (as well as the knowledge base), which open the door to the liberal public sphere. The empirical fact that this sphere has always been populated primarily by white men from the upper and upper middle classes is not taken as indicating that there is something wrong with the standards of discourse, but rather with the preparation of women, minorities, and the lower classes. It is taken as a flaw in liberal education (or in the willingness of some groups of people to become educated), and not as a flaw in the liberal public sphere. Were all people adequately prepared for liberal discourse, then the liberal public sphere would be liberatory and inclusive.

The objection to such a line of argument is familiar to compositionists: that the standards are not themselves impartial, that the public sphere is liberatory and inclusive only to the extent that all participants adopt the ethos of a European white male. The familiarity (and fundamental justice) of that criticism means that we fail to look more at the complexities within Enlightenment theories. My intention in the next two chapters is to articulate those complexities because, as much as composition theorists may try to ostracize it and its brother current-traditional rhetoric, we are still left with the problem liberal political theory was trying to solve: How can we create and maintain a genuinely inclusive discursive realm where people can deliberate as equals?

And we are left with the terms that liberal political theorists used to answer that question. Because of the centrality of liberal political theory, because so many of the models of democracy are responses to it, and because of the ways those terms are interwoven into discussions of public argument, I will spend the next two chapters on liberal political theory. My intention is to define and critique the central concepts in liberal political theory, but in a way that acknowledges the complexities and attractions of the concepts. This chapter focuses on the concepts of the public-private split, universality, neutrality, self-evidence, and rationality. The next chapter discusses autonomy, individuality, objectivity, and the deontological versus traditional-universalist models of liberalism.

One of many problems with talking about political theory is that, as Donald Lazere has said, Americans have an impoverished notion of the political spectrum ("Teaching the Political Conflicts"). In consequence, we imagine that all political views can be laid out on a one-dimensional continuum from extreme left to extreme right (ignoring that political views are rarely one-dimensional). Leftists are at one end, with liberals next to them, moderates in the middle, conservatives to the right of them, and reactionaries at the far right. Laid onto this already problematic schema is a description of political stances (*not* philosophies): One's tolerance for political correctness (such as hate speech laws) is commonly assumed to be determined by how far to the left one is, as is one's willingness to resort to governmental intervention to engage in social engineering (such as affirmative action). Meanwhile, it is assumed that people are more religious the more to the right they are, more supportive of capitalism, more suspicious of government, and (yet?) more willing for the government to engage in strict enforcement of law and order.

But such a model becomes a hash once one thinks about how people actually behave: the large number of people who oppose the death penalty (thus on the left) for religious reasons (hence, on the right); organizations like the ACLU that are suspicious of big government and hostile to hate speech laws (supposedly a right-wing tendency) yet equally hostile to governmental promotion of religion (a position identified with the left); people who support affirmative action for athletes or children of alumnae but oppose it for underrepresented minorities. The very issue of political correctness exemplifies the muddled political categories of American culture. Generally used to mean attentiveness to language use, such as insisting on the term "people with disabilities" rather than "disabled people," political correctness is supposed to be a vice of those left of center. Yet, it is easy to come up with examples of such delicacy on the part of those who would hardly consider themselves leftist, such as parents who force publishers to remove the word "witch" from popular children's tales, or who object to Mr. Rogers's "land of make believe."

In short, in general parlance, the term "liberal," as a category describing political agenda or policies, is nearly meaningless. Some historians use the term to denote a political tradition with certain specific values: a sense that equal opportunity (rather than strict equality) is and should be a major goal of public policy; a desire to protect the intellectual and moral independence of individuals, and to encourage critical thinking; a belief that protecting such independence means ensuring that the government permit public expression of unpopular beliefs and private enacting of unpopular practices; and an assumption that the solutions to the most pressing problems are not likely to be radical reshapings of existing constitutional and institutional arrangements, but new ways of operating within them (adapted from Diggins's *Rise and Fall of the American Left*). Once defined this way, the term is more meaningful, in that it defines a set of premises many people and groups (such as the ACLU) do follow. When referring to this political agenda, or set of policy desiderata, I will use the term "liberal political agenda."

The liberal political agenda is not, however, what political theorists (or I) mean by "liberal political theory" or the "liberal tradition." The relation between the liberal political agenda and liberal political theory, as David Held has said, is historically complicated and very nearly random. I want to emphasize this point, as it is easy for my general argument to be misunderstood, and for people who identify themselves as advocates of the liberal political agenda to feel that my (and political theorists') criticisms of liberal political theory are misrepresentations of their political beliefs. My point is that they are not *mis*representations because they are not even attempts at representation: the liberal political agenda and liberal political theory are only grammatically related.

And, in fact, advocates of the liberal political agenda do not necessarily offer good examples of liberal political theory. Thus, were one to look for a journal or magazine that best represented the liberal political *agenda*, one might look to the *Nation* or *Mother Jones*, but, were one to look for one that represented liberal political *theory*, the *Economist* or even the *National Review* (both politically conservative) would be better examples. This is not to say that liberal political theory is necessarily conservative but simply that it does not necessarily enact the liberal political agenda. When it comes to applying liberal political theory principles in education, for instance, one can find political liberals like Maxine Hairston, E. D. Hirsch, and Stephen Fishman, as well as political conservatives like Allan Bloom, Roger Kimball, and William Rice.

Most writers in political science and theory use the term "liberal" in something closer to the British sense, one that is as easily associated with a conservative position as with a leftist one. This sense of the term is exemplified in Stephen Holmes's definition of liberalism's "core practices":

> religious toleration, freedom of discussion, restrictions on police behavior, free elections, constitutional government based on a separation of powers, publicly inspectable state budgets to inhibit corruption, and economic policy committed to sustained growth on the basis of private ownership and freedom of contract. (*Anatomy* 3–4)

The models of public discourse discussed in this book are all friendly amendments to liberal political theory or extensions of some part of it. Thus, with the possible exception of the assumed connection between "freedom of contract" and democracy, these core practices are shared with all the models discussed in this book.

As Stanley Weintraub and Krishan Kumar have said, the liberal model is "dominant in most 'public policy' analysis and in a great deal of everyday legal and political debate" (7). Its prevalence in popular culture is obvious in political movements like those for English Only, a movement that asserts a necessary connection between violent separatist movements and the failure of some groups to assimilate fully, but also in groups like the ACLU or People for the American Way that insist on personal autonomy. Politically conservative attacks on recent movements in academia often appeal to liberal theory principles. Roger Kimball, for example, lists the tenets of his credo: "the notions that reality is not an invention and that the human mind is capable of apprehending truths that exist apart from the perturbations of subjective fancy" (58) [what might be called rationality]; "that the aspiration of the humanities [is] to speak to the concerns of all men and women" (56) [the assumption of human universality]; "the traditional ideal of disinterested intellectual inquiry" (15) [impartiality]; and the assumption that a liberal education should focus on the canon, "the best that has been thought and written" (56) [universality]. Appeals to liberal political theory principles are certainly common in composition studies. When, for instance, Maxine Hairston bemoans the politicization of the classroom, or Stephen Fishman and Lucille McCarthy assert that the best stance for the instructor is to remain neutral on the topics students are discussing, or textbooks insist upon a stark division between personal narrative and policy argument, they invoke central assumptions of the liberal public sphere.

Initially, the liberal model was almost notorious for making critical discourse so important, and established orders found themselves threatened by its emphases on equality, individuality, and popular education. There are substantial differences among the theorists. Michael Sandel distinguishes deontological (exemplified by Rawls) from procedural (exemplified in various Supreme Court decisions); Bruce Ackerman distinguishes contractarian (e.g., John Locke, Rawls) from utilitarian (e.g., John Stuart Mill); David Held has eight different types of liberal political theory. I distinguish deontological (e.g., Rawls) from what I call traditional-universalist (exemplified in the above quotes from Kimball) because that is the distinction with the greatest differences in pedagogy. What is shared among all these versions is that they are, in Chantal Mouffe's (not entirely critical) terms, rationalist, universalist, and individualist ("For an Agonistic" 2). They are also utopian.

The liberal model is utopian in that advocates do not claim it has, or even can be, achieved, but that does not make it inconsequential. Stephen Holmes, one of the most eloquent current defenders of liberalism, ends his chapter "The Liberal Idea":

> Liberalism will always remain an aspiration. It can never be fully realized or institutionalized. But it can provide a guide and stimulus to action. A liberal nation is a nation that keeps the worthier aims of liberalism steadily in view. (*Passions and Constraints* 41)

In *The Structural Transformation of the Public Sphere*, Habermas insists that the rational-critical sphere of the *philosophes* was never achieved yet still had important consequences. Like Holmes, he points out that it functioned as a norm against which actual practice could be compared. There is a strong case to be made that this does happen. *The Universal Declaration of Human Rights* is a perfect example, with its emphasis on autonomy, rationality, and universality. Kofi Annan has described the *Universal Declaration of Human Rights* as a "yardstick by which we measure human progress" (qtd. in Ignatieff), and Brian Urquhart has pointed to the connection between that declaration and highly effective groups like Amnesty International and the Helsinki Rights Watch. Urquhart concludes, "The Universal Declaration of Human Rights initiated an immensely important revolution in human affairs" (34). Utopian, rationalist, individualist, and universalist, it has had real consequences.

Liberal political theory arose both as a continuation of and a reaction against Reformation religion (see Taylor's *Sources of the Self*, 234–47; David Zaret). It branched from its religious root when it began to downplay the significance of mystery, divine revelation, and original sin. Charles Taylor describes this divergence as occurring most obviously among a kind of second-generation Lockean liberal who tries to have the Enlightenment ideals without any basis in Deism. This kind of liberal theorist, the one probably most clearly influential in the Anglo-American tradition, is centrally committed to three "life goods": a "self-responsible reason" with its attendant "freedom from all authority"; the value of everyday life; "the ideal of universal and impartial benevolence" (*Sources of the Self* 322). Hector St. John de Crevecoeur's "American Farmer" typifies this ideal Enlightenment citizen—rejecting the authority of religion and European tradition, he attends to his homely agricultural tasks while considering political questions in the light of the common good. This character is what Henry Nash Smith identified in American letters as the yeoman farmer, and he is perfectly described in Stephen Holmes's paean to the ideal liberal citizen. "Simultaneously anticlerical and antimilitaristic," an advocate of literacy, a believer in social mobility and political equality, he is suspicious of religious enthusiasts but a champion of religious freedom, with a "selective but still warmly welcoming attitude toward commercial society" (*Passions and Constraints* 14–15).

Anne Phillips has remarked that the current tendency to condemn liberal political theory for being blind to diversity and difference "is distinctly odd, for notions of diversity and difference have been central to liberalism from its inception and to liberal democracy throughout its formation" ("Dealing with Difference" 139). Many of the things for which the liberal model is currently criticized—such as universalism, neutrality, and autonomy—were originally intended to allow different people to reason together in ways that did not require deference to traditional authorities:

> Hence the search for a contractual basis for political authority that would bind these different individuals into a contractual whole; and hence the concern with rights and autonomies that would allow them to pursue part of their lives under their own steam. In these and subsequent developments, difference remained politically significant and theoretically important: a driving force, indeed, in the separation of public from private affairs. ("Dealing with Difference" 139–40)

So the question is not whether or not the liberal model acknowledges difference, but what kind of difference(s) it can accommodate and how it does so.

It is important to remember the virtues of liberalism, and one can see the attraction of those virtues by considering examples of this character in American letters. When John Proctor denies the authority of the court, even at pain of death, when Huckleberry Finn rejects much of what he has been taught about slavery, even believing he is risking eternal damnation, when Henry David Thoreau refuses to support the Mexican-American War, even spending a night in jail, they behave like the ideal liberal citizen. Ideal-typical liberal citizens—like their ancestors, ideal-typical Christians—feel the call of the truth, and that call is stronger than authority, tradition, patriotism, or clan.

It is no coincidence that these examples are all male and white (nor that Stephen Holmes always uses "he" when talking about the "ideal-typical liberal citizen").[1] The ethos of the ideal liberal citizen is one that has only recently been made available to women and nonwhites, and its application remains problematic. Proponents of the liberal public sphere grant that it has not long been open to women and minorities; their response is that it is a system in progress and that its recent extension to women and nonwhites should be counted as an argument in its favor because it shows a system capable of change. Stephen Holmes describes four "classically illiberal arrangements": "autocracy, aristocracy, theocracy, and collective ownership" (*Passions and Constraints* 16) and asserts that liberals condemn three of these threats to freedom whenever they arise: "To the extent that autocracy, aristocracy, and theocracy are decried, liberal rhetoric, at least, has triumphed" (17).[2] It is notable that he does not claim that liberal political theory has created an egalitarian and open society; instead, he describes its triumph as having created a set of criteria—a rhetoric—that can be used to try to persuade people to propose and apply remedies against oppression. This is the sense in which the utopianism of the liberal model is consequential; its advocates can point to major documents of liberation—the Declaration of Independence, the Seneca Falls Declaration, Thoreau's *Civil Disobedience,* Frederick Douglass's *Autobiography,* the writings of Susan B. Anthony, Martin Luther King Jr.'s "Letter from Birmingham Jail," Betty Friedan's *The Feminine Mystique,* Supreme Court rulings on freedom of speech, segregation, and freedom of religion—and see their reliance on liberal model rhetoric. While I have found myself ultimately persuaded by critics of the liberal model of the public sphere, these triumphs strike me as both important and admirable. And they point to an appropriate standard by which to judge other models: Do they provide a rhetoric that enables people to identify, be outraged by, and persuade one another to change structures of oppression? Can one have "Letter from Birmingham Jail" without the liberal model of public discourse? In regard to teaching argumentation, does abandoning the liberal model mean that we are abandoning the goal of liberatory discourse?

The best way to be fair to liberal political theory is to work through the centrally contested terms, describing the various meanings they have. The most obvious of these is the public/private split, manifest in composition pedagogy in the strict distinction between public and personal writing. Liberal political theory restricts "public" discourse to the realm of governmental policy, thereby moving both familial and economic activities out of the range of policy. Habermas summarizes this view: "the state is conceived of as an apparatus of public administration, and society is conceived as a system of market-structured interactions of private persons and their labor" ("Three Normative" 239). Keeping this distinction in mind can help prevent conflating liberal political theory and political liberalism. The conventional stereotype of advocates of the liberal political agenda is that they support Big Government, but, as Held says, central to liberal political theory is the idea that individuals must be protected from the power of the state:

> [T]he state exists to safeguard the rights and liberties of citizens who are ultimately the best judge of their own interests; the state is the burden individuals have to bear to secure their own ends; and the state must be restricted in scope and restrained in practice to ensure the maximum possible freedom of every citizen. (299)

The state, then, is an evil necessitated by human frailty; Thomas Paine says that the "origin and rise of government [is] a mode rendered necessary by the inability of moral virtue to govern the world" ("Common Sense" 68), and that "Society is produced by our wants, and government by our wickedness; the former promotes our happiness *positively* by uniting our affections, the latter *negatively* by restraining our vices" (*Common Sense* 66, emphasis in original). As Popper puts it, "the state is a necessary evil; its powers are not to multiplied beyond what is necessary" ("Public Opinion and Liberal Principles" 155).

Because government is seen as the main danger, critical discourse focuses on governmental behavior: "The thrust of liberal arguments is directed against the disruptive potential of an administrative power that interferes with the independent social interactions of private persons" (Habermas, "Three Normative" 247). As a result of limiting public discourse to governmental policy, the rhetoric of liberal political theory functions most effectively when injustice results from unjust laws (as opposed to business practices, family relations, etc.). But, as historians of the Civil Rights movement have argued, the liberatory power of liberal political theory becomes more problematic when the source of the injustice is in the "private" sphere (such as racist covenant restrictions).

The problem is that there is something to the distinction. When communitarians argue that the state should actively promote marriage, or when spokespersons for the religious right argue for laws prohibiting sexual practices they consider abhorrent, the most sensible response does seem to be to assert something along the lines of a distinction between behaviors that are appropriately regulated by the state and ones that are not. In contrast to people who insist that the state should require assent to metaphysical principles (such as people who say that the state should actively promote Christianity in public schools, or that politicians must all be Christian), liberal political theory assumes and asserts that the state can be neutral in regard to "competing worldviews or 'comprehensive doctrines'" (Habermas, "'Reasonable' versus 'True'" 75).

As Seyla Benhabib has said, "The most significant conversational constraint in liberalism is *neutrality*" ("Models of Public Space" 81, emphasis in original). But a major criticism of the liberal public sphere is that the government's "neutrality" (essentially, refusal to legislate) regarding a specific issue actually benefits one set of interests. So, for instance, the government's refusal to pass labor legislation benefited employers. "Neutrality," then, simply means preserving the status quo.

For instance, Herbert Wechsler famously argued that the Supreme Court decision in *Brown v. Board of Education* was not "neutral" because it failed to treat as equally valid blacks' desire to attend schools with whites, and whites' desire not to attend school with blacks (qtd. in Sunstein, "Neutrality" 5). According to Wechsler, the Court should have seen them as equally valid private preferences. As Cass Sunstein says, Wechsler's understanding of neutrality has "an otherworldly quality" because it ignores the "system of racial segregation that reflected and helped create and perpetuate those desires" ("Neutrality" 5). This is one meaning of the word "neutral"—not activist.

I will suggest that neutrality is not inherently incompatible with critical debate, that one might aspire to a neutral public discourse without necessarily paralyzing the possibility of calling attention to injustice, depending on one's definition. By this definition, aspiring to neutrality necessarily means preserving the status quo and seriously hindering, if not entirely preventing, any criticism of the current system. This is the sense of "neutral" (and, as will be discussed below, related terms like "objective" and "universal") in what I am calling the traditional-universal strand of liberal political theory. It treats tradition as the rockshelf of experience, beyond which one cannot go without losing ground entirely. Because tradition is neutral, anything that preserves that tradition (or returns to it) is also neutral. One can see this assumption in the argument about education—that a traditional education (which is always defined differently) is neutral, and one that is critical of traditional values or texts is politicized. In political discourse, the same distinction is behind the tendency to call some behaviors "judicial activism"—they are no more active than the decisions of judges who are actively trying to dismantle certain kinds of tendencies—but they are not seen as traditional and so can be characterized as not neutral.[3]

But that is not what everyone means by the term. For Kant, Rousseau, and Rawls, one is neutral to the extent that one's stance would not change were one's situation to change; thus, one makes assertions to which one sincerely believes all people would assent. This definition can imply very different practices. It might mean that rhetors look for statements with which no one can disagree, a goal that leads to the dream of politics without argument. Or it might mean that one is forbidden from thinking only in terms of one's particular self-interest, thereby precluding argument as bargaining.[4] Or it can mean that rhetors only make arguments with which they believe everyone *should* agree. While the latter is what Rawls, for instance, means, and this approach is almost certainly intended to open up debate, it can turn into a hidden prescriptive, which shuts debate down.

Two points about all of these definitions are worth noting. First, a neutral argument is one not particular to one's interests—if one is making an argument that pits one's interests against others, it is not neutral. Thus, the notion that segregation was "neutral" is impossible to maintain, as one's attitude toward it would change were one to change positions. Second, as will be discussed at greater length later (in regard to the term "objective") a "neutral" argument is not necessarily true, at least not by this definition; it is simply not particular to one's own perspective.

There is another meaning to the term "neutral": unemotional, or, more accurately, dispassionate. The assumption is that passions disrupt one's reasoning processes. Hence John Quincy Adams insists that the good rhetor will not speak in the midst of such passions:

> Let no man dare to undertake the guidance of reason in others, while he suffers anger or vanity, the overflowings of an inflated or an irritated mind, to intermingle with the tide of his eloquence. When the ebullitions of passion burst in peevish crimination of the audience themselves, when a speaker sallies forth, armed with insult and outrage for his instruments of persuasion, you may be assured, that this Quixotism of rhetoric must eventually terminate like all other modern knight errantry and that the fury must always be succeeded by the impotence of the passions. (1:365.)

"Neutrality," then, is defined by the absence of the corrupting passions (which include outrage).[5] Alcoff points to the troubling political consequences of this sense that outrage is epistemologically and discursively corrupting—it disenfranchises certain groups of people (74).

Canonical American documents of protest like the Seneca Falls Declaration and "Letter from Birmingham Jail" express a muted outrage.

Texts that tend toward a higher style and more prophetic stance (such as Henry's "Give Me Liberty or Give Me Death" or Bryan's "Cross of Gold" speech) exemplify enclave-based rhetoric, in that they are not "crimination of the audience themselves" (in Adams's terms); they express outrage at someone other than the audience. I have seen that students become extremely uncomfortable when other students get angry (especially, I think, when women get angry), so much so that a persuasive relationship dissipates at that moment. This aversion to angry rhetors is not true of all cultures—one need simply think of Demosthenes, Cicero, or Adams's hero Edmund Burke—but it does seem true that, even when Americans find outrage entertaining, they (we) do not find it persuasive. Making neutrality a virtue, especially as long as neutrality is implicitly or explicitly defined as not being impassioned, means that people who have suffered grave injustice must either adopt the tone of someone like King, or be excluded from the community of discourse. By adopting a rational tone, though, one necessarily diminishes the gravity of the injustices—as Arendt says, there are moments when outrage is a very rational response (*On Violence* 63).

Like the sense that traditions are neutral, this sense that passions like outrage are forbidden in "neutral" discourse hinders the ability of discourse to uncover injustice because people are likely to be outraged by injustice. One can see the troubling consequences of this view in the topos in antebellum America that freed slaves could not become part of the American community because they would be too angry. When explaining his failed attempt to put an end to slavery in Virginia, Jefferson says: "Nothing is more certainly written in the book of fate than that these people are to be free. Nor is it less certain that the two races, equally free, cannot live in the same government" (*Autobiography* 44; see also "Letters" 1434). Jefferson's assumption is that ex-slaves' rage (with which Jefferson does not even appear to disagree) with whites is too great to allow them to get along, and that whites would be made too uncomfortable by continually being presented with victims of their injustice. Thus, the collective guilt of whites and the collective rage of freed slaves necessitates the exclusion of the latter (for more on the importance of this line of argument in antebellum discourse on slavery, see Freehling 123–30).

An older notion of neutral, and one present but already fading in the Enlightenment, is that one has no direct economic interest in the issue.

John Lind, in his hostile response to the Declaration of Independence, says that the king was not acting out of his interests because the king's actions neither increased his power nor provided him with new revenues, the only two ways that a man can "advance his own separate interests" (8). Hamilton's *Federalist* 1 asserts that one of the major obstacles of the new Constitution is "the obvious interest of a certain class of men in every State to resist all changes which may hazard a diminution of the power, emolument, and consequences of the offices they hold under the State" (34). Hamilton is here using "interest" in the same way as Lind. Such a usage makes sense within a vision of a community that imagines that some people have the ability not to have economic interests (because, presumably, they are not in trade), and that makes a clear distinction between economic and political issues. But the more that one assumes that man is an economic man, always trying to maximize power (the notion of human nature behind, for instance, the interest-based model of the public sphere), the less sense this notion of some people being disinterested makes.

The second definition of neutral—that one would adopt a neutral position regardless of one's situation—is problematic in fairly obvious ways, but it could certainly enhance critical thinking. It would imply a pedagogy heavily reliant on role-playing, or on writing papers from various perspectives. The first definition of "neutral"—the sense that the status quo is neutral—is behind the arguments over politicizing the classroom. This tendency to treat the status quo as neutral is exactly what Sunstein identifies as one of two "strands in contemporary legal and political thought" ("Neutrality" 1). This strand distinguishes between neutrality and partisanship "by treating existing distributions of wealth, opportunities, preferences, and natural endowments as the baseline against which assessments of neutrality and partisanship will be made" ("Neutrality" 1). Thus, for people like Kimball, Cheney, and Bloom, traditional methods of teaching are apolitical *because* they are traditional.

This use of the word explains what must strike many readers as odd about the argument over politicizing literary texts (at least those aware of the history of "the" canon). When Kimball lists the authors whom he thinks are inappropriately politicized by postmodern literary critics, he includes writers like Dante, Milton, and Aristotle. My impulse is to say that it boggles the mind to try to imagine a depoliticized Dante—

would one simply ignore the political figures who people the Inferno?—but it can be done by taking the underlying political situations and agenda as givens, rather than as topics for argument.

It is not simply that Kimball wants these texts taught, but that he wants them taught in a fundamentally uncritical fashion, as "better and more important than others" (3). There are two points I want to emphasize about this notion of education. First, it aspires to an irenic education; to the extent, then, that education is preparation for the public sphere, this is preparation for an irenic one. The purpose is not to introduce students to traditional texts so that they can think critically about them (as in, for instance, Arendt's "The Crisis in Education"), but so that we can have perfect agreement. Second, this is a circular argument, appealing to a false universalism, asserting as a common culture one that is, and always has been, shifting and transient. The tradition is not very old, and certainly not universal.

Kimball's very argument about the canon ought to have alerted him to the problem with asserting that certain texts are obviously superior—clearly, the people arguing for changing the canon do not see the texts in the currently constituted canon as obviously better and more important. A cursory glance at the history of literary criticism would also show that there has never been much agreement regarding what works an undergraduate should read, or even what kinds of texts are of literary significance; the notion that anything other than Greek and Roman texts might have value is far from a timeless notion (it dates from the nineteenth century). Kimball universalizes from a consensus among a small number of people at a particular moment in the history of literary criticism. All of this is captured in his slips regarding "a country of immigrants" and the tradition "we" hold in common, and the slips exemplify a problem in liberal political theory, especially when applied in education. Kimball, in his defense of a monocultural canon, refers to "the social fact that America, a country of immigrants, has always been a multicultural and multiethnic society" (218). He thereby universalizes to all "Americans" the European experience, ignoring the millions of people who did not immigrate, but were enslaved, or whose presence on the continent long predates "America," or who were forcibly made part of the United States. Similarly, Kimball is genuinely dismayed at attacks on the Western canon, on the idea of a common culture, the idea that, despite our many differences, we hold in common an intellectual, artistic, and moral legacy, descending largely from the Greeks and the Bible, supplemented and modified over the centuries by innumerable contributions from diverse lands and peoples. (221)

The problematic term in this passage is "we." To what extent do Native Americans share an intellectual, artistic, and moral legacy descending largely from the Greeks and the Bible? To the extent that they are educated to do so. As a descriptive, Kimball's passage is nonsense; it is an implied prescriptive, describing a situation that he believes (but does not argue) *should* exist. By taking the majority experience for the universal one, he precludes his being able to understand how other people might read what are, for him, canonical texts. He fails to see his own perspective as a particular one, shaped by time and culture.

Linda Alcoff summarizes the problem with the implicit epistemology (and ontology) in arguments like Kimball's:

[T]his struggle has been framed as a conflict between the (correctly) apolitical and the "politically correct." Only the latter group, which includes disproportionate numbers of scholars who are working-class, white women, and/or persons of color, is said to have a politics, which is then said to disqualify them from the academy. This notion of objective inquiry, then, continues to have significant political effects in censoring certain kinds of voices and obscuring the real political content of others. (74)

This argument regarding universality and governmental neutrality is subtly circular. Government is supposed to remain neutral regarding the good (a vague term meaning something like metaphysical assumptions, religious beliefs, or what Rawls calls "transcendent backing"); it is assumed that the deepest disagreements concern such issues. But, if those are bracketed out of public discourse, then we cannot argue about the things about which we most disagree and which, presumably, serve as the grounds for all of the positions we take.[6] Such differences are private because they are defined as private, so the public self is or should be a uniform and undifferentiated self. In Kimball's words, "our identity as human beings transcends our membership in a particular class, race, or gender" (222).

The hope is that, if individuals effectively transcend our own transient particularities and look toward the public good, we will all agree as to what it is. This assumption is most clearly exemplified in Rousseau, whose goal, as Sandel has so eloquently put it, is for a state that collapses "the distance between persons so that citizens stand in a kind of speechless transparence, or immediate presence to one another" (Sandel *Democracy's Discontent* 320). For Rousseau, there is an absolute distinction between private and common interest (see especially 150, 162). The common interest is "what these different interests have in common" and "it is utterly on the basis of this common interest that society ought to be governed" (153).

Given its tradition of strong support for freedom of expression, one would expect liberal political theory to recommend that one determine this "common interest" through public debate, but liberal political theorists are often surprisingly ambivalent about public *argument*, as is indicated in Sandel's phrase "speechless transcendence." Rousseau sees debate as destructive to determining the common interest:

> If, when a sufficiently informed populace deliberates, *the citizens were to have no communication among themselves,* the general will would always result from the large number of small differences, and the deliberation would always be good. (156, emphasis added)

This is public policy without public disagreement. Locke, in *Some Thoughts Concerning Education and of the Conduct of the Understanding,* discusses the importance of considering the opposite possibility or proposition, but he does not make it clear that public argumentation is necessary for achieving this goal (184, 189). In fact, when Locke says that reading is not adequate for understanding, he does not go on to say that one must discuss the things one has read; instead he describes a solitary process:

> Reading furnishes the mind only with materials of knowledge; it is thinking makes what we read ours. We are of the ruminating kind, and it is not enough to cram ourselves with a great load of collections; unless we chew them over again, they will not give us strength and nourishment. (193)[7]

Pace Arendt, Kant's definition of thinking does not specifically require argument with others (see *Logic* 71, discussed at greater length later). Hence one has an expressive public sphere, and people talk of freedom of expression as though it were the same as freedom of speech.

Although it is not intended to do so, the assumption that the ideal situation is a polis where there is perfect agreement about the common good means that the liberal public sphere often ends up demanding conformity. Jefferson's argument regarding the preferability of increasing population in early America through "our actual stock" versus immigration exemplifies this tendency. He sets out the premise that "It is for the happiness of those united in society to harmonize as much as possible in matters which they must of necessity transact together" (*Notes* 84). Because people from countries with absolute monarchies are unlikely to understand the "peculiar" set of ideas central to American civil government—which he defines as "a composition of the freest principles of the English constitution, with others derived from natural right and natural reason" (*Notes* 84)—those people constitute a threat to democracy: "They will infuse into [legislation] their spirit, warp and bias its direction, and render it a heterogeneous, incoherent, distracted mass" (*Notes* 85). This argument was not restricted to Jefferson and became—in a sense, remains—a central principle regarding immigration quotas. As Craig Calhoun says,

> The language of the liberal public sphere is used to demand that only English be spoken in Florida, for example, or that Arabs and Africans conform to certain ideas of Frenchness if they wish to stay in France. And for that matter, many other arguments—for example, that only heterosexuals should serve in the military—have much the same form and status. They demand conformity as a condition of full citizenship. ("Nationalism" 87).

It appears to proponents of the liberal model that English must be spoken in Florida because a situation in which people are speaking different languages seems to be one in which participants remain engulfed by the particularities of their situations—they have not yet transcended differences to the universal values and experience that are assumed to be the rockshelf of identity. Dennis Baron, in his study of the English Only movement, says that "The motives for laws privileging English are often simply practical or patriotic: proponents of official English assume that a nation functions best if its citizens share a common language" (4). This is the sort of tendency that critics of the liberal public sphere refer to when they argue that it depends upon a denial of difference. It would, however, be more accurate to say that the liberal model tends to assume or assert that difference is destabilizing, and that it must be transcended.

So, for example, Kimball grants that our country is multicultural but asserts that these differences must be subordinated:

> Indeed, it is our country's singular political achievement to have forged a society in which vast religious, ethnic, and racial differences are subordi-

nated to the higher unity of national identity. Hence the once-defining image of America as a "melting pot." (218)

Once one has reached past one's own particular situation toward the rock-shelf of universal experience and identity, one is assumed to have reached the place of objectivity and neutrality. This is the process Kant describes, in which one pays attention to other perspectives, not in order to adopt them, but in order to use them (in an almost dialectical fashion) to see past the limitations involved in any specific perspective (see, for instance, *Logic* 73). The liberal privileging of neutrality in public policy argument results from the idea that private differences neither can nor should be the objects of argument because they neither can nor should be the objects of public policy. A major function of education then becomes the promulgation of the monolithic culture presumed to be the basis of democratic practice. This education may be politically liberal and even potentially multicultural, as in Hirsch's *Cultural Literacy,* or conservative (even reactionary) as in Bloom's *Closing of the American Mind.*

There is, then, a depoliticizing impulse to politics implicit in what I am calling the traditional-universalist strain in liberal political theory. This move may take the form of Rousseau's (or, for that matter, Thoreau's) assumption that a populace might be informed without engaging in argument. Or it can take the form it does in Kimball, Cheney, and Bloom, in which education serves to inculcate a uniform (and uniformly admired) culture. Or it can take the form of something other than argument being made the foundation of public decision-making. Arendt argues that this is exactly the process that transpired in the nineteenth century, in which the discourse of politics (i.e., rhetoric) was displaced by the discourse of the market and bureaucracy (i.e., profit); she describes this as the era when "businessmen became politicians and were acclaimed as statesmen, while statesmen were taken seriously only if they talked the language of successful businessmen and 'thought in continents'" (*Origins* 138). The transition Arendt saw has advanced to the point that success in business is considered an indication of competence for governance.[8] This partiality for an unfettered capitalist model is not the answer all liberal theorists reach regarding the problem of governmental neutrality, but it is the one asserted in the sort of textbook advice attacked by Ohmann and Clifford, and it would lead one to technocracy.

By "technocracy," I mean any form of government in which public discussion is replaced by information provided by people with technical knowledge. The most extreme (and most extremely undemocratic) form is one in which experts make the decisions (what one might call "strong technocracy"); at the less extreme end is a form in which the general public makes the decisions after listening to information from the experts—the public sphere functions for the dissemination of expert information (what one might call "weak technocracy"). Neither form encourages discursive deliberation on the part of nonexperts—in strong technocracy, nonexperts have no role in the decision-making process at all (except to be objects of the decisions); in weak technocracy, nonexperts may make the decisions on the basis of information that they get from experts, but they vote without having themselves engaged in argument. Neither model imagines a public sphere where people argue with one another on matters of principle in order to determine the best course of action.

Technocracy acknowledges that people do have different opinions but assumes that we can ignore such differences for one of several reasons. First, we can assume that the differences result from ignorance on the part of some group; we resolve this problem through having a public sphere where experts inform others. Second, we can assume that experts have access to some body of knowledge (such as econometrics, cost-benefit analysis, constitutional law) that enables them to remain neutral while mediating the competing views. The dream of technocracy is that one could forgo the vicissitudes of impassioned public debate on the part of a minimally informed populace in favor of some process assumed to be beyond politics—expert opinion, quantitative analysis, time-motion studies, cost-benefit analysis, and so on. It is, sometimes implicitly and sometimes explicitly, an attempt to have policies without politics.

The arguments for technocracy have always had two parts—the negative case (the attack on the ability of the common person to make intelligent political decisions) and the affirmative case (the argument that some other group can make the right political decisions). The role of scientists in Nazism, the environmental consequences of unbridled technology, and the policy blunders made by supposed experts have all contributed to the unpopularity of strong technocracy and have more or less silenced the affirmative case. But the negative case remains persuasive to many people, and its acceptance is at least suggested in pedagogies that make the teaching of writing a technical or purely preprofessional task.

When I was teaching in Berkeley, I generally had students read material on homelessness, as the issue was deeply pressing in the Berkeley area. It was, in fact, impossible to get to class without being confronted by someone who at least claimed to be homeless, so that certain philosophical and ethical questions (Should one give money to the homeless? Should one instead give money to institutions that serve the homeless? Does supporting such institutions actually worsen the problem by enabling other communities to foist their homeless onto Berkeley? Should one be kind to such people, or does any human contact risk inciting a mentally ill person?) were not abstract policy or philosophical questions but decisions the students had to make simply in order to get from one place to another. Each semester, graduate student instructors were observed by a faculty member, and I happened to be observed by a faculty member who wanted to shift the program away from argument toward a current-traditional modes-based approach with heavy emphasis on correctness. After observing a rollicking class discussion on homelessness, he asked me if I did not think that discussion had been a waste of time. "After all," he said, "we can't teach them anything that will solve the homelessness problem, but we can stop them from making comma splices."

My response, then as now, was that this argument represents an abandonment of one of the major arguments for public funding of education: that it prepares students to participate in the political life of their communities. Whether or not students solve homelessness is not the point; the point is that they try to articulate their own answers to the questions posed, and that they understand how those answers fit (or do not fit) with the answers that other people pose. But his answer was based on the perception of first-year composition as a kind of technical training—we should be giving students technical competence. What I did not understand then was that his perception was firmly grounded in another of the major arguments for public funding of education: that it prepares students to participate in the economic life of their communities by making them more productive and effective employees. In composition studies, one sees this attitude when theorists assume that the sole or primary purpose of first-year composition is to enable students "to develop as writers in ways that will be relevant to their college education and relevant to their professional lives" (Bazerman, "Interview" 23; for a similar assumption, see Peterson; Gross; or Lindemann, "Freshman"). Such theorists simply ignore the role that first-year composition plays in teaching students how to think through issues of public policy.

Such a preparation is not necessarily as low-minded as slapping students who make comma splices; it might involve taking a writing-in-the-disciplines approach, or emphasizing professional and technical writing, or any one of several other intellectually challenging approaches. And there are strong arguments for engaging in it. S. Michael Halloran criticized such approaches for their evasion of issues of public concern, and I largely agree with that criticism. Even I will grant, however, that such criticism is partially off the point in that—if one sees the public sphere as a place that should be reserved for technical communication—one might see oneself as teaching students how to communicate more or less technical information to the general public. That is, there are two ways to see the relation of writing in the disciplines and the public sphere. One is to make the liberal model assumption that there is such a thing as apolitical training in discourse, and that explicit politics can be avoided. The other is to assume that public discourse *is* technical discourse; that is, to assume technocracy.

Not all writing-in-the-disciplines approaches amount to preprofessional writing, of course, but they may still implicitly promote a technocratic public sphere. The work of Charles Bazerman, for instance, with its careful attention to how knowledge is constructed in different fields, does not suggest that one should teach writing in the disciplines merely as a question of adopting different formal conventions (see, for example, *Shaping Written Knowledge*). Such pedagogies promote teaching technical discourse as texts that can be analyzed, and, as such, can be seen as helping students participate in a public sphere where they will have to evaluate the discourse of experts. It may even be seen as something that will help students should they find themselves identified as experts having to make a case in front of a general public. Either way, though, there is no attention paid to students *qua* citizens, unless one assumes that political discourse is professional discourse. Kenneth Cmiel has criticized such a view as derailing the possibility of nonexperts engaging in argument with one another on matters of principle; instead it enriches "the illusion of civic discussion void of debate" (262).

I am, consciously, trying to be very fair to advocates of first-year composition as writing in the disciplines by imagining how their arguments *might* be applied to civic discourse; on the whole, as indicated above, civic discourse and the role of students as citizens is not even imagined by such writers. Radical pedagogues have argued, with considerable force, that the preprofessional pedagogical focus instrumentalizes students, with the consequence, if not goal, of smoothing the workings of advanced industrial capitalism by ensuring that students will be round pegs for the round holes they will face in their lives as workers and consumers. James Berlin, for instance, criticizes the work of Linda Flower and John Hayes because they never "question the worth of the goals pursued by the manager, scientist, or writer" ("Rhetoric and Ideology" 685). For James Berlin, this means that Flower and Hayes take the goals of students as "self-evident and unquestioned" ("Rhetoric and Ideology" 686; see also 685), but I would suggest instead that he take Flower at face value when she makes comments like "whatever your goals" (qtd. in "Rhetoric and Ideology" 685,696). Her intention is to remain neutral on the question of students' own ends, providing them with a means of writing that is, she assumes, universal. She is making the liberal model assumptions about the possible relations of discourse and the public.

Jeff Smith acknowledges that teaching is instrumental to certain ends, focusing exclusively on the career goals of students, and ignoring that public universities have the explicit end of preparing people to be effective citizens in a democracy. His focus almost certainly results from his insistence, repeated throughout the piece, that we take as a given the ends with which our students enter our classes, as when he says, "I don't think it's my job to tell them their aims are wrong" (318). This attitude perfectly exemplifies liberal political theory's ideal of remaining neutral on the question of ends; Smith, like the government, will simply act as gatekeeper. Smith's piece also exemplifies something that Arendt criticized so eloquently (the ways that business models and values creep into all areas) by noting that his metaphors are almost exclusively business metaphors. It's his job, students are his clients, and so on. Thus, Smith's use of metaphors and ignorance of civic discourse belie his claim to neutrality; he has a strongly probusiness and anticivic orientation.

Smith distinguishes good from bad gatekeeping, between standards that keep students out of some realm on an arbitrary basis (bad) and standards that students choose (or do not choose) to accept (good). Smith's ostensible respect for students' own ends depends upon seeing those ends as autonomously chosen (an assumption rejected by radical pedagogues). His distinction between good and bad gatekeeping presumes some kind of neutral standards; he is not opposed to exclusion in principle. And any gatekeeping has a problematic relation to the liberal political sphere's goal of perfect inclusion; the people who have passed through the gate are alike in that they have all met the same standards. The more comprehensive the standards, the more likely the result is uniformity; one has then not a place of rational-critical argument (in Habermas's terms) but an enclave.

As Mansbridge says, an enclave is a place where people speak only to people who share their values—it is a place of perfect agreement:

> First come the dangers that arise when members of any group speak only to one another. When white supremacists speak mostly to white supremacists, Serbs to Serbs, feminists to feminists, and political philosophers to political philosophers, they encourage one another not to hear anyone else. They do not learn how to put what they want to say in words that others can hear and understand. The enclaves, which produce insights that less protected spaces would have prevented, also protect those insights from reasonable criticism. ("Using Power/Fighting Power" 58)

As is clear from her last sentence, Mansbridge is not entirely critical of enclaves—a political system needs to have places where people can engage in discussions that might be prohibited by the larger public sphere—but she insists that people *must* engage in critical discourse outside of enclaves as well.

It is difficult to determine at what points enclaves are necessary and at what points they have become over protective. A recurrent criticism of the politics-of-difference movement is that it creates a public sphere made up entirely of enclaves because it encourages sexual, ethnic, and economic minority groups to speak only to one another (see, for instance, Elshtain), but Iris Marion Young has discussed the historical complexities of this accusation (see especially "Difference as a Resource"). As she notes, the politics-of-difference movement arose because members of certain kinds of groups felt that the political sphere was, despite its claims to universality, an enclave (just a very large one). Todd Gitlin points out that the desire to have women represented in politics (a "much excoriated emphasis") is "in one sense, an extension of the normal pluralism of American politics—the practice of balancing tickets, for example, be-

tween North and South, urban and rural, Protestants and Catholics"
(*Twilight* 159–69). While generally critical of identity politics, Gitlin
notes that it is not new or unique to ethnic minorities:

> The Republican tilt of white men is the most potent form of identity poli-
> tics in our time: a huddling of men who resent (and exaggerate) their rela-
> tive decline not only in parts of the labor market but at home, in the bed-
> room and the kitchen, and in the culture. Their fear and loathing is, in part,
> a panic against the relative gains of women and minorities in an economy
> that people experience as a zero-sum game, in which the benefits accruing
> to one group seem to amount to subtractions from another. (*Twilight* 233)

In *The Company We Keep*, Wayne Booth describes the outrage that he
and other English professors felt when an African American colleague
criticized *The Adventures of Huckleberry Finn*. Until this colleague confronted them with his own reaction to the book, Booth could remain
satisfied that a highly aestheticized reading was the universal and correct one (3–5). There was nothing ill-willed about it; he simply had never
imagined the book from the perspective of an African American man.
Proponents of the "universality" of a certain reading are in the logically
odd position of asserting the universality of something not universal (as
in Kimball and Bloom); the logical problems of this position can be ignored as long as one speaks only (or even primarily) to people whose
particular reactions to the text are the same as their own. Their experience can *seem* "universal" because it is shared by everyone they know;
but once academia started to have more and more African American
scholars, for instance, the "consensus" on texts like *Huckleberry Finn*
became more difficult to maintain. As the enclave of white male scholars opened up, so did the arguments. This is the process Young describes:

> Too often those in structurally superior positions take their experience,
> preferences, and opinions to be general, uncontroversial, ordinary and even
> an expression of suffering or disadvantage. Having to answer to those who
> speak from a different, less privileged perspective on their social relations
> exposes their partiality and relative blindness. ("Difference as a Resource"
> 403)[9]

One can also make this argument about minority enclaves. My interest
in the problem of democracy, difference, and argument arose when I had
a frustrating experience writing about environmental issues as an undergraduate. I had trouble predicting, let alone responding to, the opposi-

tion arguments, and the writing processes of the class (which had emphasized class discussion, group work, and peer review) had not helped. I was well within a group of classmates and friends who shared experiences, preferences, and opinions regarding environmental protection. While we were in a minority compared to the general culture, it was enough of a majority within the subculture of a rhetoric classroom in Berkeley in 1980 to constitute an enclave. As such, it was difficult for me to see my own partiality and relative blindness for what it was.

There is a tendency, thus, to assert that a particular viewpoint is universal simply because everyone to whom one speaks espouses it. Mouffe points to the unfortunate and unintended irony that results from the aspiration for the universal:

> In the end, the rationalist defense of liberal democracy, in searching for an argument that is beyond argumentation and in wanting to define the meaning of the universal, makes the same mistake for which it criticizes totalitarianism: the rejection of democratic indeterminacy and the identification of the universal with a given particular. ("Democracy, Power" 254)

This is essentially the same criticism of teaching argument made by, for instance, Elisabeth Daümer and Sandra Runzo when they argue that argument requires that everyone adopt the same ethos:

> The language advocated by composition texts not only suppresses the feminine, but a student's achievement in a composition course will depend upon how well she can further bury other, more feminist values in her language and in her writing. (53)

Argument in the liberal public sphere does, in fact, make exactly that demand—rhetors should be impersonally aggressive, rely heavily on certain rules about relevance and fairness, use one dialect, avoid personal experience, refrain from expressing outrage, and appeal to "universal" (i.e., majority) premises.

The problem of universals is so familiar that, for many authors, simply pointing out that a theorist is universalist is presented as sufficient grounds to dismiss his or her work. While it seems to me a self-contradictory argument for critics of universalism to assert that universals are universally false, the term is certainly sometimes used in ways destructive to a critical debate. The prescriptive use is the one that most troubles theorists, especially when it appears to be an empirical claim, but is, in fact, a logically closed system structured to deny the possibility of counterexamples. As Henry Giroux says, "Universalism is denounced because it demands reverence rather than skepticism, recognition rather than critical engagement, and transmission rather than suspicion" (114). The liberal public sphere aspires to facilitate rational-critical discourse, but if, as Giroux says, universalism brackets off certain topics from criticism, then it inhibits the very goal of liberalism. The more that the standards are bracketed out of discussion, the more likely that they represent not a neutral and apolitical set of criteria, but the particular standards of the most privileged.

Because of such uses of claims to universality, universalism has been discredited, but without universality, we seem to be lost in particulars, with potentially troubling political consequences. Gitlin has argued that the shift to particularism can inhibit social justice movements because it ensures that people whose oppression is systemically related fail to see their common interests *(Twilight)*. The more that minorities see themselves as disconnected from one another, he says, the less they are able to see the political forces that oppress them all. His argument is that if universalism is easily coopted for a reactionary political agenda, it also provides powerful grounds for thwarting that agenda.

In the liberal model, universally true statements are "self-evident"; that is, they must be granted *a priori* and without argument. The concept of self-evident truths is complicated, and so problematic that the *Oxford Dictionary of Philosophy* begins its definition of the term: "Not a very useful philosophical term, since what is evident by itself to one person, may not be so to another" (345). As with "universal," the problem is whether calling a proposition "self-evident" is a descriptive, prescriptive, or proscriptive statement. The extent to which the attribution of self-evidence inhibits inclusive deliberation depends upon exactly what one means by "self-evident."

As Thomas Reid pointed out in his surprisingly modern discussion of the term, it is used in at least four different ways: to mean propositions to which people immediately assent, ones that are logically first principles (e.g., in geometry), ones present in all languages (e.g., causality), and ones to which all reasonable men assent. While the first and fourth look different, in practice, they often end up the same—when confronted with an individual who will not grant that a particular statement is self-evident, the tendency is to say that there is something wrong the person, and not the statement (e.g., Locke's discussion of people who do not grant the existence of God). These different definitions have different consequences for public discourse.

Reid's second meaning involves propositions that are themselves first principles and which, hence, "do not admit of proof" (although one might find examples that illustrate them) (152). One can, for example, illustrate the premise that all lines have at least two points, but all proofs of it will be essentially circular (such as showing that beginning with other premises necessitates self-contradiction). Reid distinguishes this kind of self-evident proposition from the first, as it functions differently epistemologically and rhetorically. The first meaning of "self-evident" says that one cannot (is not permitted to) deny the proposition; for this second kind of self-evident proposition, however, one might well deny it, as in cases when it is difficult to understand. Also, it is possible "that what is only a vulgar prejudice may be mistaken for a first principle" (152), so something might be identified as a self-evident proposition that is not even true.

A third kind of "self-evidence" involves propositions "wherein we find an universal agreement, among the learned and unlearned, in the different nations and ages of the world" (156). It is striking that, unlike so many of his forebears, contemporaries, and even descendants, Reid does not exempt the unlearned and the savage in order to determine the universal. For Reid, "universal" is not a prescriptive statement, but a descriptive one; one might test the claim of self-evidence through looking for a culture that did or does not grant the statement. Anticipating Noam Chomsky, Reid says that they include the "general rules of syntax common to all languages. This uniformity in the structure of language shows a certain degree of uniformity in those notions upon which the structure of language is grounded" (157). The abstract nature of the resulting statements means that they are of little use in political argument— they enable one to notice that there are universal conceptions of time, cause and effect, and such concepts. While this usage avoids the problems of exclusion and hidden prescriptives of the first use of "self-evident," it does not enable one to identify a lot of specific topoi one might use to resolve policy debates. That is not to say it is useless—as I will discuss later, Habermas's latest work relies on such concepts—but rather that one could never, for instance, assert the self-evidence of the aesthetic value of Beethoven. Restricting "self-evidence" to these kinds of propositions leaves a tremendous amount that must continually be argued and re-argued, something that makes some proponents of liberal political theory and liberal education uncomfortable.

Reid's final definition of self-evident propositions is much closer to how the term is used throughout Enlightenment discourse: "such facts as are attested to by the conviction of all sober and reasonable men, either by our sense, by memory, or by human testimony" (158). Unlike the other types, this kind of self-evident statement can serve as the foundation of argument, but only if one restricts the audience of the connected argument to those who agree with the proposition. Reasonable men are ones who assent to the propositions, so that simply disagreeing becomes a sign that one is not qualified to participate in the argument. In this case, to identify something as self-evident is to exclude rather than establish common ground with someone who disagrees.

The assertion of self-evidence is generally seen as an epistemological claim, and it is. But it is also a claim about rhetoric. In Locke's usage, to say that something is self-evident is to make an assertion about how it *should* function in argument. Because it has a certain epistemological force, it should have a similarly powerful rhetorical force—people should assent to it immediately. Not only in popular but much philosophical discourse, to say that something "cannot" be argued is a normative posing as a descriptive; it seems to be an epistemological claim but is actually a claim about discourse rules. Of course, the statement in question *can* be argued, in that even the most self-evident proposition has been disputed (and, in fact, a statement that something cannot be argued is generally said in response to it having been argued). Such a statement is simply asserting that the principle in question *should not* be argued. Reid explicitly rejects the idea that first principles are beyond argument: "We do not pretend that those things that are laid down as first principles may not be examined, and that we ought not to have our ears open to what may be pleaded against their being admitted as such" (158). Because self-evident propositions "openly lay claim to the character, and are thereby fairly exposed to the examination of those who may dispute their authority" (158), people do not simply accept them. This is very nearly the opposite of how Locke says such statements should function in discourse;

for Locke the assertion of something being self-evident simply moves it out of argument, whereas Reid suggests the assertion should highlight its argumentative nature.

Would that Reid were right. Despite his claim, one can see the rhetorical consequences of invoking self-evidence in what is probably its most famous American instance, Jefferson's assertion that "we hold these truths to be self-evident." There is considerable dispute as to the origin of Jefferson's notion of self-evident, whether he is drawing on Locke (Becker), Duncan (Howell), or Reid (Wills), but scholars almost universally cite Jefferson's 1825 letter to Henry Lee to explicate Jefferson's rhetorical intention in regard to the Declaration:

> When forced, therefore, to resort to arms for redress, an appeal to the tribunal of the world was deemed proper for our justification. This was the object of the Declaration of Independence. Not to find out new principles, or new arguments, never before thought of, not merely to say things which had never been said before; but to place before mankind the common sense of the subject, in terms so plain and firm as to command their assent, and to justify ourselves in the independent stand we are compelled to take. . . . All its authority rests then on the harmonizing sentiments of the day, whether expressed in conversation, in letters, printed essays, or in the elementary books of public right, as Aristotle, Cicero, Locke, Sidney, &c. (1501)

Clearly, Jefferson is claiming rhetorical self-evidence (i.e., making a claim about how the propositions should function persuasively), closer to Locke's meaning than Reid's in that he is asserting something in order to push it beyond argument. Just prior to this passage in the letter, he refers to everyone on this side of the water being of one mind, a statement that is patently false, as it casts a shroud over the sizable loyalist as well as apathetic populations. But of course Jefferson did not mean the loyalists, let alone the slaves, Amerindians, or settlers outside of the thirteen Anglo colonies (just as Kimball does not mean descendants of slaves, Amerindians, or inhabitants of Hawaii and Mexico when he refers to "a nation of immigrants"); Jefferson meant the people who agreed with him. The others simply did not exist or did not count.

John Lind, a pamphleteer for the North administration, reacted with sneering hostility to Jefferson's "self-evident" truths:

> "All men," they tell us, "are created equal." This surely is a new discovery; now, for the first time, we learn, that a child, at the moment of his birth,

> has the same quality of *natural* power as his parent; the same quantity of *political* power as the magistrates. ("An Answer" 120, emphasis in original)

Jefferson's self-evident truths were far from self-evident, and they certainly were not universally applied. Lind argues that government necessarily alienates some of those rights Jefferson calls inalienable, especially the pursuit of happiness, simply by passing laws (see especially 122). Lind mentions the glaring example of slavery (107), as well as rebels' treatment of loyalists; he points to the destruction of property of any printers who published loyalist tracts (6–7, 121), the invasion of Canada (121), and other pieces of evidence that rebels were perfectly willing to alienate the rights of some people to life, liberty, and pursuit of happiness. What these self-evident truths amounted to, Lind argued, was that the rebels wanted the freedom to rebel without having to grant to loyalists the freedom to remain loyal. And this is an important criticism of the accuracy and consequences of trying to base political discourse on self-evident truths: as in Jefferson's attitude toward loyalists and their arguments, it is associated with universalizing from one's own experience, and dismissing criticism or disagreement.

The rhetoric of self-evidence is closely connected (probably causally connected) to the expressive public sphere, seeing the public sphere as a place where people express their points of view rather than deliberate with one another. Robert Dahl describes democracy as "a political system in which all the active and legitimate groups in the population can *make themselves heard*" (*Preface* 137, emphasis added). The function of the public sphere, he continually asserts, is "the expression of preferences" (see especially *Preface* 63–70). This is essentially what I mean by the expressivist model of discourse; Jefferson expresses (or declares) certain ideas. In the argument for those ideas, he does not make any attempt to interweave a fair discussion of the views of his opposition. There is no attempt to explain why the King or Parliament would have done the things they did—on the contrary, there is every attempt to make those actions as completely unreasonable as possible. So this "mankind" to whom Jefferson is writing does not include loyalists, Parliament, the king, or anyone who sees their side of the question; they have suddenly been removed from humanity.

This exclusion of the opposition is an unfortunate, but logical, consequence of the rhetoric of self-evidence; if one is positing the self-evidence of one's position, then how is one to explain the existence of people who dispute it? One can simply deny or ignore their existence (as does the "Declaration"), or one can assert that those people are deluded by "prejudice" (used by *Common Sense* and Lind 10), or one can say that such people are looking to "their own private ambition" (as with the above, exemplified both in *Common Sense* and Lind 10). Thus, as is typical in an expressivist democracy, one does not try to persuade one's oppositions (since they are deluded at best and greedy at worst), but some hypothetical construct (who, not coincidentally, grants one's premises).

This tendency of the liberal public sphere to exclude people who will not grant "self-evident" (i.e., dominant) premises explains why it is so commonly criticized as denying difference. While Phillips is right that there is something slightly odd about the criticism, there is also something very apt about it. An expressivist public sphere both does and does not incorporate difference. In terms of sheer artifacts, one can see instances of very different arguments, and they may be responses to one another—in that sense, there is difference. On the other hand, especially if connected to the assumption that good arguments have universally accepted (or self-evident) premises, each of these expressions is just that—an expression. The public sphere has a variety of arguments that conflict with one another, but almost like bumper cars bouncing against each other. They are not changed by interacting with one another; contact with one another is arbitrary (if not random), hostile, and hard on the neck.[10]

The notion that there are propositions that can serve as reliable foundations for certain knowledge is a central tenet in Enlightenment philosophy. Isaiah Berlin remarks that what struck him about the seventeenth- and eighteenth-century philosophers was that they shared certain assumptions. The first is that "all genuine questions must have one true answer and one only"; the second is that "there must be a dependable path towards the discovery of these truths"; and the third is that all true answers—that is, to different questions—must be compatible with one another ("The Pursuit of the Ideal" 5–6). True answers are compatible because there are universal principles underlying all questions of nature, aesthetics, and ethics. While Berlin's comment is not unfair, it can obscure that Enlightenment philosophers did not agree as to the best path for reaching those true answers: moral sentiment (e.g., Rousseau); empirical observation (e.g., Locke); self-interest (e.g., Bentham); rational discourse (e.g., Kant).

The belief that moral sensibility is a universal and reliable foundation for knowledge of nature, ethics, and aesthetics is most strongly associated with the Scottish Enlightenment, a philosophical tradition with a strong influence on nineteenth-century rhetoric (see Clark and Halloran; Horner; Nan Johnson; or Thomas Miller). It also exerted a strong pull in the American literary tradition, and, it has been argued, on American political behavior (see Burstein's *Sentimental Democracy*). The Lockean tradition has a tendency to be fairly hostile to emotions (although Locke himself did not assert that all emotions distort the reasoning process), but the moral sense philosophers are quite friendly toward many emotions.

The Lockean tradition—virtually synonymous with the traditional-universalist theory—best exemplifies the assumption that empirical observation is the most reliable foundation of knowledge. Such a foundation necessarily means that science (or, more accurately, the process of looking for material and quantifiable tests of falsifiable hypotheses) becomes the queen of knowledge, as when Popper begins his essay "Knowledge and the Shaping of Reality" by "declaring that I regard *scientific knowledge* as the best and most important kind of knowledge we have" (3, emphasis in original). One can see a similar deference to the scientific method in other liberal theorists such as Dewey. This sense that only empiricism is valid certainly informs the intermittent hostility within rhetoric between empirical and other approaches (which seems to operate with more animus in speech communications than within composition), the division between political science and political theory, and the preferences many public policy analysts have for econometrics.

But not every approach equates rational discourse and materialist/scientific discourse. The Kantian tradition (not until recently as influential in Anglo-American philosophy as the Lockean) has no such empirical/materialist prejudice. Kant lists the "general rules and conditions of avoiding error," which are to "think [by] oneself, (2) to think oneself in the place of another, and (3) to think consistently with oneself" (*Logic* 63). Thinking consistently with oneself means following the "universal laws of the understanding and of reason" (*Logic* 56); that is, logic. As argued above, "universal" is a confusing and confused term, no less so when applied to logic. Reid, as mentioned before, points to the grammatical structures of language as indicating certain universal conceptions, but these are quite abstract (such as causality and temporality); one would not thereby reach agreement on the nicer points of logic. One might, as in *Meno,* mean that they are universal in that one could enable any interlocutor to agree to them, if one had a sufficiently able teacher and sufficiently willing student. This is typically, when pressed, the preferred meaning, but it amounts to a hidden prescriptive, since "sufficiently willing" ends up being defined by whether or not the person assents to the proof. Were this truly a descriptive, then the existence of students who fail logic classes would be evidence that the rules of logic (at least as taught in logic classes) are not universal. I have yet to hear an advocate of the universality of formal logic reach such a conclusion.

Similarly, the popularity of certain lines of argument would be taken as evidence of their validity, a notion rejected by people who want to equate logic and formal (i.e., mathematical) logic. These issues become more problematic the more that one equates "logic" and "formal logic," and this is not a necessary equation (as will be discussed in regard to the Kantian tradition). There is, then, an issue of degrees—the more that one equates logic and formal logic, the more terms like "universal" and "self-evident" slide into prescriptives and proscriptives, and the more likely they will be ultimately oppressive because they will enable the exclusion of crucial issues.

A more common kind of exclusion results from the public-private split, in that, as Nancy Fraser, Seyla Benhabib, and others have noted, it was part and parcel of exempting certain practices—such as wife-beating—from the realm of public argument, critique, and policy. The liberal sphere assumption that private and public are obviously divided along certain lines, and that certain topics are not appropriate for public discourse, means that people with a minority viewpoint on that distinction—such as those who wanted to say that child labor was not a private contractual arrangement between the child's parents and the employer—can have their very right to make the argument questioned. Once again, as with universalisms and self-evident propositions, the conflict is simply distributed out of discussion.

If people cannot argue about our disagreements, then we are left with essentially three options. First, there is always the possibility of a naked show of force. Once that has happened, there is no longer even a pretense that this is a democratic system. Second, interlocutors can simply vote—an option discussed in more detail in the final chapter. Third, people can bargain. One of the central principles of the liberal public sphere is that one's ability to participate should not be a function of one's economic status or social position; this principle serves as the single most important criterion behind what Stephen Holmes identified as the rhetoric of liberalism. And it no longer operates once the decision-making is bargaining. Mansbridge remarks that in bargaining situations,

> each group marshals the resources available to it and tries either to subdue the other entirely or to achieve a compromise based on comparative potential coercion. In this compromise the amount that each party concedes to each other depends on its ability to inflict harm on the other parties by withdrawing from the bargaining session. ("A Deliberative Theory" 36)

Jon Elster, after discussing the importance of threats to bargaining situations, summarizes this aspect of bargaining theory:

> Modern, post-1980 bargaining theory asserts that the outcome, although constrained by the outside options, will be determined by the inside options of the parties, i.e., by the resources available to them while the negotiations are going on. . . . Both outside and inside options matter for the credibility of threats. A[n] agent can credibly threaten to break off cooperation (forever) if he can get more on his own than the other offers him. And he can credibly threaten to suspend cooperation (temporarily) if he can afford to hold out for a better offer. ("Arguing and Bargaining" 21)

So agents who enter a bargaining situation with more power (in terms of ability to make and enforce threats) can get a more favorable outcome. Marginalized people, who tend to have fewer resources, are disadvantaged twice over. Likely to be more dependent upon the outcome (as they have fewer resources should the bargaining be broken off), they are also likely to have less ability to influence it in their favor. Thus, while emphasis on compromise can appear to be pragmatic, it can shift the public sphere toward discursive forms of coercion. If rational-critical discourse is the goal of liberal political theory, then bargaining precludes that goal. It is not rational, in that successful bargaining depends upon one's ability to marshal credible threats, not good reasons. It is unlikely to be critical, since bargaining favors the powerful and the status quo.

Proponents of the liberal public sphere are well aware of the problems presented when participants treat it as a common space to be grabbed. Specifically, the distinction between the universal and the particular was intended as a solution to the problems presented by a public sphere understood as a forum for vicious competition. Dewey, in response to the view that he calls "'natural' economy"—that "commercial exchange would bring about such an interdependence that harmony would automatically result" (*The Public and Its Problems* 155)—paraphrases Rousseau: "interdependence provides just the situation which makes it possible and worth while for the stronger and abler to exploit others for their own ends, to keep others in a state of subjection where they can be utilized as animated tools" (155). Sometimes, as will be discussed later, this exploitation is defended as a natural consequence of competition; at other times, however, the exploitation can be invisible because people are within an enclave from which the victims of injustice have been excluded.

Throughout this book, I argue for inclusion of difference as a partial response to the problem of enclaves, but I do not mean to suggest that it is, therefore, a relatively simple problem with a straightforward solution. It is not merely the point that Mansbridge makes—that enclaves are sometimes good—but that exclusion of some form is absolutely necessary. Mansbridge criticizes Habermas's attempt to define a coercion-free public sphere:

> I would emphasize that in the real world—as Foucault reminds us and Habermas grants—there are no conditions free from the threat of sanction or use of force. The ideal of coercion-free deliberation resembles many important and useful democratic ideals in being impossible to achieve fully, although possible to approach. ("Using Power/Fighting Power" 51)

Democracy demands allegiance to procedures; a democracy is necessarily an enclave of people who will behave democratically. The dilemma for political theorists is how to define the rules for participation without thereby creating a destructively exclusionary enclave. It is *the* dilemma for teachers of argumentation that—as will be discussed later, in an area of "free" expression (i.e., one where no authority figures enforces deliberative practice)—not everyone is, in fact, equally free to participate, and minority views are easily silenced. Yet, trying to establish a situation in which minority views can be heard may necessitate restricting other views.

The liberal sphere can promote enclaves in a slightly more subtle way. For some liberal theorists, difference is a necessary evil—Dahl suggests that "we have glorified a historic inevitability as a virtue" (*Preface* 78); for others, it is an evil that results from people pursuing their own self-interest, and sufficiently broad-minded people are capable of seeing beyond those things that apparently divide us (Rousseau; *Federalist* 10). For still others, like John Locke, difference generally results from incompetence in thinking and speaking:

> And here I desire it may be considered, and carefully examined, whether the greatest part of the disputes in the world are not merely verbal, and about the signification of words; and whether, if the terms they are made in were defined, and reduced in their signification (as they must be where they signify anything) to determined collections of the simple ideas they do or do not stand for, those disputes would not end of themselves, and immediately vanish. (*Essay* 2:151)

This sense that there is something wrong (even if inevitable) about difference puts pressure on interlocutors to move as quickly as possible away from disagreement and toward agreement, with the unfortunate consequence that communities will try to evade or deny conflict. Mansbridge and others have discussed the ways this pressure to agree can encourage people with a minority viewpoint to remain silent or even ignore their own perceptions (see especially *Beyond Adversary Democracy*). Arendt has written eloquently about the extraordinary tyranny that can be exerted by groups, and not necessarily through any malevolent conspiracy; it is simply difficult for many people to resist pressures to conform (see especially *Eichmann in Jerusalem,* "The Crisis in Education," *Human Condition*). Describing her experience in the early years of the feminist movement, bell hooks writes:

> Solidarity between women was often equated with the formation of 'safe' spaces where groups of presumably like-minded women could come together, sharing ideas and experiences without fear of silencing or rigorous challenges. Groups sometimes disintegrated when the speaking of diverse opinions led to contestation, confrontation, and out-and-out conflict. It was common for dissenting voices to be silenced by the collective demand for harmony. Those voices were at times punished by exclusion and ostracization. (65)

In *The Sixties,* Gitlin describes a similar process in the development of the SDS 1963 manifesto, *America and the New Era*. Gitlin says that the workshop on foreign policy could not agree on a statement regarding American imperialism; "in the end, with no consensus in sight, we decided not to write a report at all. Better agnosticism—or ambivalence—

than division" (130–31). He goes on to say that this evasion of conflict marked the beginning of a sense in the organization that "consensus was best preserved by smothering conflict. . . . In a small but significant way, SDS proceeded to muffle itself, to slip toward precisely what it criticized in smooth, orthodox America" (131; for more on how consensual decision making uses imprecision to "blur potential disagreements" see Mansbridge, *Adversary Democracy* 165–67).

Stephen Holmes, for instance, asserts that one of the benefits of freedom of religion and group worship is that "they help keep divisive issues off the political agenda" (*Passions and Constraints* 31). This distribution of divisive topics "helps make public discussion and majoritarian decision making more effective. . . . Separation of church and state unclutters the democratic agenda and creates an opportunity for collaboration across sectarian lines" (31). This is a distinctly odd argument, even if it is common, because it rests on an assumption that ought to strike any proponent of a lively public sphere as false: that divisive conflict is something that should be avoided. That assumption is one proponents of liberalism often—at least at points—reject. Holmes, only two pages after praising liberalism for distributing off topics of disagreement, refers to the "interconnection between liberalism and democracy. This is the radically untraditional idea that *public disagreement is a creative force*" (33, emphasis in original). So divisive issues should be avoided *and* disagreement is a creative force.

This ambivalence toward conflict is quite common. The Federalists' argument for the particular construction of the constitution is that it preserves deliberation (for more on this point, see Fishkin, *Voice of the People*). Yet, they do not engage in deliberation with the Anti-Federalists. Although the Federalist Papers were written over a period of time, during which the Anti-Federalists were also writing pamphlets, Hamilton and Madison do not modify their line of argument in ways that would indicate the debate made them rethink any ideas. Berubé refers to the recurrent line of argument that "because American society (Western thought) is the locus of freedom, and already enables dissent from within, it is unnecessary to engage in actual dissent" (25). And Sacvan Bercovitch famously identified the "American Jeremiad" as a recurrent form in American letters, one that paradoxically presents an instance of dissent as conformity: American literary texts that condemn the status quo try to do so from a position of claiming to be speaking for the "true" American tradition. It is the status quo that is, in a sense, dissenting. Bercovitch suggests that this rhetorical move has a strangely inhibiting quality for American public discourse, in that it both causes and reinforces a tendency to see genuine disagreement as bad.

Jane Mansbridge's study of a 1970 town meeting in a small town in Vermont describes the difficulty that people have with deeply divisive conflict, and in ways that are troubling for a teacher of argument: She quotes a sizable number of citizens who either do not attend or do not speak at the town meeting because there is conflict, and they take that conflict personally. While Mansbridge notes that the tendency to take conflict personally is always a problem, the face-to-face quality of the town meeting makes this identification of people and their ideas more likely to occur and more likely to make people want to avoid the meetings altogether:

> Even in a representative democracy, many nonvoters avoid politics because it involves conflict. Face-to-face confrontation increases the tension dramatically: Jamie Pedley acquires a splitting headache. An older man claims he stopped going because he is afraid for his heart. A man in the next town tells how his hands shake for hours after the meeting. Altogether more than a quarter of the people I talked to suggested without prompting that the conflictual character of the town meeting in some way upset them. (*Beyond Adversary Democracy* 65)

One can easily imagine the same reactions on the part of students to class discussions that involve a lot of conflict. This description certainly echoes what teachers who avoid argumentation have said to me about their reasons.

The tendency to see all conflict as necessarily unproductive is self-fulfilling. Mansbridge observed a cycle in regard to the town meetings. Having previously had bad experiences with public argument, people tried to keep themselves from speaking at all; however, things that other people said so outraged them that they could not stop themselves. At that point, when speaking *because* one has lost one's temper, it would be a rare person who could engage in a noncombative form of conflict. The unpleasantness of the experience (trying not to talk, getting mad at what other people say, talking while in the midst of that rage, regretting the entire incident) confirms the sense that participating in public argument is uncomfortable at best and enraging at worst.

Amy Gutmann and Dennis Thompson mention the argument that certain kinds of public issues—particularly moral issues—should not be publicly discussed because people do it so badly. Gutmann and Thompson respond, "The trouble with this argument . . . is that the argument may be self-fulfilling. If citizens do not try to deliberate about issues such as sexual harassment, homosexual rights, or racial injustice, they may never learn how to do so responsibly" (109). This is, in general, my argument about the teaching of argumentation: Avoiding it because people do it badly means that they (we?) will never learn to do it responsibly.

People experience conflict as difficult because it is difficult. Young says, "The public is not a comfortable place of conversation among those who share language, assumptions, and ways of looking at issues" ("Difference as a Resource" 401). Yet, as Young suggests, that very discomfort can be pleasurable. She compares the ideal public sphere to a city, where there is an actively erotic energy from meeting people and things strikingly and even unproductively different. A world without any enclaves at all, in which one could never find a comfortable place of agreement, would be exhausting, but a world where people really disagree, where our central assumptions are questioned, can be exciting. The task for any democratic theory is to describe a city where difference is productively challenging, and to persuade people to spend much of their lives there. It is not clear that either the deontological or traditional-universalist version of the liberal model fulfills that task.

2

Autonomous Selves, Liberally Educated

> Like Dewey, Fishman's ideology is liberal. In other words, at
> the core of Fishman's teaching is a respect for the integrity of
> each student and a commitment to defend that student's right
> to think for him or herself. In the classroom this means he
> wants to grant each student as much liberty as is commensu-
> rate with granting similar liberties to every one of that stu-
> dent's classmates. He aims to be tolerant about pupils' deeply
> held beliefs and to profess a neutrality which encourages the
> critical and constructive skills which he and Dewey hold dear.
> As a consequence, Fishman tries to intercede in student debate
> only when he believes someone's liberties and opportunities to
> make up his or her own mind are being transgressed.
> —Stephen M. Fishman and Lucille Parkinson McCarthy,
> "Teaching for Student Change"

As described in the previous chapter, the most common criticisms of
the liberal public sphere focus on: the public/private split; the assumption of universality; the notion of the autonomous individual; limiting public discourse to rational argument. The discussion centered on
political theory, but those same criticisms trouble teachers of argument.
Should we restrict topics to public issues? What place should personal
writing have in a writing course? What sorts of generalizations can we
make about writers and readers? What models of writing processes falsely
posit an autonomous individual? What sorts of standards do we apply
to arguments without imposing our own more or less arbitrary value
judgments on people from different cultural backgrounds? How can we
be both critical and inclusive? And, of particular importance to liberal
political theory, is the notion of autonomous individuals a help or a hindrance in nurturing critical discourse?

At least since Kant, the notion of the autonomous individual has been central to liberal theory. Held says,

> Contemporary liberal thinkers have in general tied the goals of liberty and equality to individualist political, economic, and ethical doctrines. In their view, the modern democratic state should provide the necessary conditions to enable citizens to pursue their own interests; it should uphold the rule of law in order to protect and nurture individuals' liberty, so that each person can advance his or her own objectives while no one can impose a vision of the "good life" upon others. (299)

Initially, the term "autonomous" applied to city-states who were able to set their own nomos, their own laws. As will be discussed later, it now means everything from a sense that individuals can and should be completely independent of one another and their larger communities—particularly in the formation of their value-systems—to a sense that, whatever the origin of those value-systems, individuals have to take responsibility for them. The concept of autonomous individual is under attack in political theory and composition theory, but, as I will suggest, it isn't always clear *which* version is meant.

Particularly since the critical reactions against cognitivist and expressivist theories, it has become a commonplace in rhetoric and composition that it is inaccurate and politically problematic to talk about writers as autonomous individuals striving for originality and authenticity. David Bartholomae's critique of Peter Elbow's idea of "writing without teachers" (which really is, as Bartholomae says, a good example of the autonomous writer) is that "there is no writing that is writing without teachers" ("Writing with Teachers" 481). For Elbow, writers are empowered by freeing themselves from thinking about how their writing is situated; they benefit by seeing writing as something "which, even if someone reads it, doesn't send any ripples back to you" (*Writing Without Teachers* 1), by seeing it as operating within a vacuum (7). For Bartholomae and many similar critics of expressivism, Elbow's decontextualized space of writing is "part of a much larger project to preserve and reproduce the figure of the author, an independent, self-creative, self-expressive subjectivity" ("Writing with Teachers" 482). This project is not liberatory, as Elbow contends, but disempowering because it hides "the traces of power, tradition and authority present at the scene of writing" ("Writing with Teachers" 481). Elbow has objected that this criticism is not entirely fair; he, too, wants students "to see the act of writing as an act of finding and acknowledging one's place in an ongoing intellectual conversation with a much larger and longer history than what goes on in this classroom during these ten or fourteen weeks" ("Being a Writer" 495). Yet Elbow's defense just slightly misses the point of the criticism. It is not simply that there is a context outside of the student papers, but that those papers are determined by that context. For Bartholomae, Berlin, Giroux, and other critics who have made similar arguments, the students cannot be freed from those determining factors without seeing their presence and influence. To ignore them does not reduce their power to distort our thinking.

Elbow does acknowledge that he might be focussing too much on the individual; he acknowledges that he invites

> first year students to fall into the following sins: to take their own ideas too seriously; to think that they are the first person to think of their idea and be all wrapped up and possessive about it . . . ; I invite them to write as though they are a central speaker at the center of the universe. ("Being a Writer" 496–97)

There is a paradox here; Elbow wants students to see themselves as part of a larger conversation, but he invites students to do nearly the opposite. He grants that the almost narcissistic individualism of his teaching approach (as opposed to his desires) is a kind of fiction, but Elbow thinks it helps students write. One might dispute, as do Bartholomae and James Berlin, whether this fiction is genuinely liberating, but to argue that it is untrue seems off the point—Elbow does not claim it *is* true. Each side in this debate just slightly fails to engage the other. Elbow's granting the existence of the larger context does not answer Bartholomae's concern regarding just what that context does; Bartholomae's criticism of the existence of the autonomous writer just slightly misses that Elbow grants it is a fiction.

Political theorists also criticize the notion of the autonomous individual for the inaccuracy of the concept, and, as in the debate in rhetoric and composition, each side just misses engaging the other. Charles Taylor, Michael Sandel, and others have argued that this model of the self is false because it ignores the extent to which our ideas and identities are shaped by our personal and cultural histories. Others have pointed to the harm that can result from the myth—the emphasis on individual achievement can obscure systemic injustices, by falsely assuming that failure is always the result of the individual's inadequacies; it can also mean, paradoxically, that we deny our own responsibilities for the systemic injustices, or the ways that we might even benefit from them. Etzioni has argued that this model of the self leads to an isolated populace who pay little attention to one another, let alone to the issues that face us as a polis.

Henry Giroux has said that poststructuralism has replaced "the notion of an essentialized and fully transparent identity" with "one that is partial, decentered, and grounded in the particularities of history, place, and language. From this perspective, there is no subject or identity fashioned outside of its own history and contingency" (113). But one might wonder just who put forward the notion poststructuralism is replacing. Who has argued for an essentialized and fully transparent identity? And on what grounds did they do so? It is conventional to answer "Locke, Kant, the positivists," and not without reason—each of them does posit an individual who is in some sense(s) autonomous—but that assertion is usually made without actually quoting from those authors.[1]

This is not to say that the isolated individual, the voice crying in the wilderness, is entirely a straw man. On the contrary, that figure is troublingly powerful in American culture, and it continues to be seen as representing an admirable ethos. Like any other teacher of writing, I have several times had students who were reluctant to read because they believed that exposure to other authors might inhibit their own creativity. I once had a long argument with a friend about environmental protection during which she argued that property rights should be absolute. If she chose to put a smelting plant on her property, she insisted, no one had the right to stop her. If it harmed others through poisoning water, air, or soil, then, as equally autonomous individuals, they had the capacity to buy the property. That this was a capacity not open to the poor did not trouble her. Their poverty, she insisted, was their own fault; if they resented their lack of power, they could stop being poor. Parenting books such as T. Berry Brazelton's very popular book criticize certain practices (such as letting children sleep in one's bed) on the grounds that they may interfere with the development of autonomy. Some version of the myth of the autonomous male is central in such texts as Benjamin Franklin's *Autobiography,* Ralph Waldo Emerson's "Self-Reliance" and "American

Scholar," Horatio Alger Jr.'s stories for boys, Andrew Carnegie's "The True Gospel Concerning Wealth," and even current biographies of successful businessmen. Amy Lang argues that the notion of Antinomianism, essentially one version of the myth of the autonomous individual, is virtually a constant in American literature. As I have argued elsewhere, New England authorities took on the stance of Daniel in the lion's den or Isaiah crying in the wilderness even when they were engaging in behavior that was popular, and for which there was no genuine threat. Leslie Fiedler and Annette Kolodny have each criticized canonical American literature for its theme of the individual male striking out into (and against) the wilderness; his (often homoerotic) ties to other males and his use of the engendered and sexualized wilderness are obscured in the celebrated individualism of the hero. The idea of the "yeoman farmer" has had, as Henry Nash Smith has shown, extraordinary power on American culture, including the shaping of land use policies; much of Sandel's criticism of the Supreme Court's application of liberal theory amounts to his objection to their tendency to treat all obligations as external to identity, as though all individuals are equally free to make choices. All of these models of the self posit a centered and self-fashioned individual who can stand completely apart from tradition, dominant values, and authority.

However, the contrary notion—that individuals are strongly influenced by the dominant culture—is not especially new, despite the tendency that people have to attribute it to postmodernism. The whole point of the allegory of the cave is that it is possible for us to spend a lifetime with ideas that are given to us by our culture; as early as Aristotle's *Rhetoric,* handbooks on rhetoric assume a connection between one's membership in certain groups and one's thought; Bacon's idols of the crowd amounts to noting how powerful such group pressures can be. John Locke satirizes people who

> are apt to conclude that what is the common opinion cannot but be true; so many men's eye they think cannot but see right; so . . . [they] will not venture to look beyond the received notions of the place and age, nor have so presumptuous a thought as to be wiser than their neighbors. They are content to go with the crowd, and so go easily, which they think is going right, or at least serves them as well. (*Some Thoughts* 197; see also *Essay* 1:363)

For Kant (from whom the term autonomy is drawn), autonomy is a goal toward which one should strive precisely because it is so easy to defer to convention and tradition; Karl Popper takes some time to acknowledge that one's perceptions are shaped by one's culture (see especially *Open Society* 387). Dewey, in *Individualism Old and New,* offers a beautiful description of the contradictions implicit in American notions of individualism, such as "the irony of the gospel of 'individualism' in business conjoined with suppression of individuality in thought and speech" (45). Dewey argues that the older individualism was an economic, legal, and ethical theory, but that industrialization had reduced it to economic initiative alone (see "The Lost Individual" in *Individualism*); it has become little more than private profit. The whole premise of Elbow's "writing without teachers" or "closing one's eyes as one speaks" is that tradition, convention, and authority have tremendous power to shape our thinking. Thus, even (perhaps even especially) proponents of autonomy admit that our notions can be largely constructed for us.

In addition, the myth of the autonomous individual is powerful because it describes an experience we have had. We have, at times, felt ourselves in conflict with a group of whom we considered ourselves a member; we have all had dark moments of the soul when we had to decide whether to voice a strongly held position we knew to be unpopular. There are aspects of our tradition we reject, there are cultures we have chosen to leave. When I collected instances of individuals calling themselves voices crying in the wilderness, some were simply silly (such as George Bush invoking it when he wished to reduce aid to Israel), but some were moments when a person was taking a stance so unpopular that s/he might face serious punishment (such as the publisher of a pacifist newspaper during World War I). And surely we have all had moments when we felt that our conscience was in conflict with our culture. This is true even of critics of autonomy, who adopt the ethos of the individual knower in their critiques; James Berlin, for instance, does not write as a socially determined group, but as an individual who has seen certain problems in a dominant way of thinking about writing.[2]

It is also worth remembering that, as politically damaging as the myth of the autonomous individual might be, the equally extreme determinist model also has a long history of damage. Jerome Kagan discusses the inaccuracies and damages in notions of infant determinism, such as the idea that the first three years set the boundaries of future learning (83–150). Many of the darker horrors of eugenics were carried out in the

name of group determinism, the premise of forced sterilization and genocide. Historians of genocide, especially writers on the Nazi Final Solution, have often been horrified at the relative blandness of the people who
enacted the crime, people who claimed they were blameless because they
were powerless to resist cultural and political norms, even when the
punishment for doing so would not have been especially severe. In fact,
to some extent, liberal political theory, and especially the myth of the
autonomous individual, was intended to liberate people from the determinism implicit in many formulations of identity. In contrast to theories of human nature that equated class and intelligence, or that asserted
a necessary connection between one's place in the aristocracy and one's
capacity to think about politics, Enlightenment liberal political theorists
insisted that people from all sorts of different backgrounds could be
trusted to reason effectively about political issues.

But what exactly *is* autonomy? Gerald Dworkin points out that the
debate over autonomy tends to confuse very different notions. He lists
six different "characterizations of what it might mean for moral principles
to be one's own":

1. A person is morally autonomous if and only if he is the author of
   his moral principles, their originator.
2. A person is morally autonomous if and only if he chooses his moral
   principles.
3. A person is morally autonomous if and only if the ultimate authority or source of his moral principles is his will.
4. A person is morally autonomous if and only if he decides which
   moral principles to accept as binding upon him.
5. A person is morally autonomous if and only if he bears the responsibility for the moral theory he accepts and the principles he applies.
6. A person is morally autonomous if and only if he refuses to accept others as moral authorities, that is, he does not accept without independent consideration the judgment of others as to what
   is morally correct. (35)[3]

The first characterization is the kind paraphrased (and attacked) by
Giroux—the essentialized, unencumbered, and ahistoric individual. The
liberal model of the self criticized by Taylor, Sandel, Walzer, Etzioni, James
Berlin, Bartholomae, and others is some version of one of the first four—

a self who has the ability to stand apart from her or his own context, who can disentangle the culture's influence without unweaving her or his own identity. But those criticisms do not particularly apply to the fifth and sixth, as they do not rely on the notion of an unencumbered self.

For instance, Habermas carried the brief for liberal political theory for some time before shifting to deliberative democracy; in *Legitimation Crisis,* he gives a standard liberal theory history of thought. There are, he says, certain patterns one can see in the history of cultures:

- expansion of the secular domain *vis-à-vis* the sphere of the sacred;
- a tendency to develop from far-reaching heteronomy to increasing autonomy;
- the draining of cognitive contents from world-views (from cosmology to the pure system of morals);
- from tribal particularism to universalistic and at the same time individualistic orientations;
- increasing reflexivity of the mode of belief, which can be seen in the sequence: myth as immediately lived system of orientation; teachings; revealed religion; rational religion; ideology. (12)

This is, obviously, a secular teleology, and the criticisms of it are equally obvious (such as that, were it an accurate history, Christianity would have to be more rational than Judaism, and so on). The tenet that deserves particular attention is the assertion that orientation moves from tribal particularism to one that is simultaneously autonomous and universalist. Habermas does not say that a person moves from being a member of a particular tribe to an isolated individual, but, in a sense, from being a member of a particular polis to being a citizen of the world. In this view, as one separates from one's immediate group, one begins to identify with people as a whole. The ideal liberal citizen does not put his/her own needs first, but neither does s/he put the needs of his/her own immediate group first; instead, s/he feels the claims of the cosmopolis. Hence, in liberal theory, it is not necessarily a question of autonomous individual versus societally oriented person.

Critics argue that autonomy is impossible, and that describing individuals as autonomous is inaccurate, but it is not clear that this is a particularly important criticism of philosophical versions of the concept, as, for many philosophers, autonomy is not so much an empirical statement, describing how people behave, as it is a normative metaphor recommending a goal toward which one should strive. In Rousseau's state of nature, individuals are so autonomous that they do not even fight: "Men are not naturally enemies, for the simple reason that men living in their original state of independence do not have sufficiently constant relationships among themselves to bring about either a state of peace or a state of war" (145). The presocietal individuals of Locke and Hobbes are not as peaceable as Rousseau's, but they are similarly independent. More important, they are similarly hypothetical. Adam Smith's first edition of *Theory of Moral Sentiment* put so much faith in society's judgments that he was criticized for assuming that conscience and society could never be in conflict; in later editions he attempts to resolve that problem by positing an explicitly mythical spectator who will judge our actions (for more on this point, see Justman 88–91). As Bruce Ackerman says, the idea of a hypothetical observer is nearly a constant in liberal political theory (327). Among what Ackerman calls "contractarians" (such as Locke, Smith, or, more recently, Rawls) "the final judge is somebody who has the choice of entering society or remaining indefinitely in some prepolitical state" (327). Utilitarianism similarly posits a hypothetical observer whose goal is to maximize pleasure; more recently, utilitarians appeal to metaphors like "the invisible hand" or "the market." In *A Theory of Justice,* Rawls suggests we imagine a veil of ignorance behind which we stand while we define justice. Because we know nothing about the social roles we have in society, as they are blocked by the veil, we are unlikely to establish rules of justice that privilege one group over another. To object that any of these hypotheses is not literally true would be like objecting that Elbow's fiction of an autonomous writer is false; it means taking a metaphor literally.

Kant says that the "concept of freedom" (a term he uses synonymously with autonomy) "is a pure rational concept, which for this very reason is transcendent for theoretical philosophy, that is, it is a concept such that no instance corresponding to it can be given in any possible experience" (*Metaphysics of Morals* 14). He repeatedly insists that one cannot look for principles of right and freedom empirically, but that one must use metaphysics to define them. He elsewhere says, "Hence freedom is only an idea of reason, the objective reality of which is in itself doubtful" (*Groundwork* 60; see also 63), and he refers to the "capacity for freedom" as "wholly supersensible" (*Metaphysics of Morals* 32). While not quite as explicitly a metaphor (as it is in Smith or Rawls), then, this is still a concept it seems Kant does not want taken literally; he is not making claims about how people behave, but about how we can think about human cognition.

The idea of autonomy as a *goal* for how people should try to think has a long history. Dewey says that the notion has its origins in the personal soul of the middle ages. One might place the origin even earlier in Christianity, with Paul's rejection of corporate salvation; or one might place it in Socrates' insistence that his interlocutors think critically about tradition. The prototype of the politically autonomous individual, in short, is the individual conscience (for a good, brief explanation of this point, see "autonomy" in Caygill's *A Kant Dictionary*). To act autonomously means that one must be able to make decisions for one's self, but not necessarily by one's self. The argument of Locke's *Letter Concerning Toleration* rests on the premise that "true and saving religion consists in the inward persuasion of the mind, without which nothing can be acceptable to God" (20). It is not enough to behave well, and especially not enough to do things simply because one is told to do so, but one must take true religion to one's heart and mind:

> No way whatsoever that I shall walk in [to heaven] against the dictates of my conscience, will ever bring me to the mansions of the blessed. I may grow rich by an art that I take not delight in; I may be cured of some disease by remedies that I have not faith in; but I cannot be saved by a religion that I distrust, and by a worship that I abhor. (*Letter* 41)

This is not Dworkin's first kind of autonomy—Locke is not saying that individuals are the origins of their own ideas of morality—but the third. For Locke, one must will one's own behavior; behavior that is appropriate, but that comes merely from conformity, will not open the gates of heaven.

As liberal theory developed, it became increasingly skeptical of, and eventually deeply ambivalent about, tradition, but it kept the sense that autonomy is a normative statement about an epistemological act rather than a descriptive statement about identity formation. An individual is not autonomous, but a particular judgment of that individual should be. Dewey defines the individualism he wishes we could adopt:

> If we could inhibit the principles and standards that are merely traditional, if we could slough off the opinions that have no living relationship to the

> situations in which we live, the unavowed forces that now work upon us unconsciously but unremittingly would have a chance to build minds after their own pattern, and individuals might, in consequence, find themselves in possession of objects to which imagination and emotion would stably attach themselves. (*Individualism* 35)

Dewey's main argument in *Individualism* is that we have let technology and the economy make our decisions for us. We act autonomously when we make a decision, carefully and critically, about what we want to do with the things we have inherited. His argument is not that we are brains in vats, that we are capable of engaging in a kind of thinking uninfluenced by technology and economics, but simply that we should take the time to try to make conscious decisions about what to do with our technology and economy. In *Groundwork for the Metaphysics of Morals,* Kant provides his famous definition of autonomy:

> Autonomy of the will is the property of the will by which it is a law to itself (independently of any property of the objects of volition). The principle of autonomy is, therefore: to choose only in such a way that the maxims of your choice are also included as universal law in the same volition. (47)

This means, as he says elsewhere, that "I ought never to act except in such a way that I could also will that my maxim should become a universal law" (*Groundwork* 15). Thus, neither Dewey nor Kant is making an empirical claim about how people actually behave, but a normative claim about how people should make decisions.

It is not even clear that Kant thinks one either can or should engage in this kind of autonomy on all things; he mentions that a person who "*allows nothing to be morally indifferent* . . . and strews all his steps with duties, as with mantraps" would "turn the government of virtue into tyranny" (*Metaphysics of Morals* 167). In addition, he insists that virtue is "always in progress because, considered objectively, it is an ideal and unattainable" (*Metaphysics of Morals* 167). Nor is the autonomy isolating; in Sanford Lakoff's terms, "When Kantian actors enter into a social contract, they presumably legislate in accordance with the categorical imperative and experience an autonomy *which is at once individual and collective*" ("Autonomy" 390, emphasis added).

In *Metaphorical Theology,* Sallie McFague speaks eloquently of the power of metaphors as conceptual models. By saying that something is something else, we are reminded that it also is not that other thing: "By retaining the interaction of *two* thoughts active in the mind, one recalls, as one does not with a simile, that the two are dissimilar as well as similar" (38). A metaphor functions effectively because the statement both is and is not true at the same time, and, at least when new, it shocks us into a recognition of the "similarity and dissimilarity of both subjects" (39), the tenor and vehicle. If "autonomous individual" is a metaphor rather than a literal statement, the very incongruity of seeing a person as a city-state making laws reminds us that the statement is literally false. McFague says that the danger of metaphors is that they are easily taken literally, especially when they become conventional, that we forget that the equation is also, in important ways, not true (39–42). When a metaphor becomes a cliché, it either dies or becomes literalized; and then, "We are no longer like the Wizard of Oz who knew green glasses made Oz green, but, like all the other inhabitants of Oz, we believe that Oz *is* green" (41, emphasis in original). It seems to me that something along those lines has happened with the metaphor of autonomy; it has become a dead metaphor, so that it is taken literally (whether in an embrace or rejection).

The most striking examples in American life of taking the metaphor of autonomy literally are in law and, oddly enough, writing. Emerson's "Self-Reliance" and "The American Scholar," Thoreau's *Walden,* Whitman's preface to *Leaves of Grass,* Kerouac's *On the Road,* and Ginsberg's *Howl* all make fairly extreme statements about the ability of the individual to reject society and to construct one's self. Even so, these texts have different kinds of autonomy, with very different political consequences. It seems to me legitimate to criticize Kerouac and the Beats for rejecting society in a way that is ultimately politically reactionary (because of the ways it rejects responsibility for the community). The dharma bum philosophy can be seen as depending upon a social system rich enough for someone to live off the detritus; the bums reject a society whose checks they cash. But Thoreau's autonomy—equally rejecting of community—nourishes political activism. Hence, it is not entirely accurate to refer, as Bartholomae does, to *the* myth of the autonomous individual; the question is which myth?

The second area in which the myth of autonomy is literalized is law. The classic argument regarding pornography, as Andrea Dworkin says, is that it is not the business of the larger community as long as producers and consumers are all consenting adults. But to what extent did the women whose stories are told in *In Harm's Way* make unencumbered choices? Opponents of labor safety laws (whether those restricting child labor or those imposing safe practices) have always argued that the contracts between employer and employee are private transactions in which autonomous individuals freely engage and thus are no business of the government, but it is a dangerous illusion to pretend that the child is just as free to take another job as the employer is free to hire a different employee.

And yet.

Mill's *On Liberty* is genuinely troubling when he asserts that a community practice like polygamy is not a violation of his principle of liberty, even if members of the group are socially and legally coerced on the topic, because people can always leave the community. The assertion is troubling in that it ignores just how difficult it would have been for anyone to leave the Salt Lake City area at the time he was writing, and, more important, that such a "liberty" was not distributed equally—that men had more of it than did women. Although I cringe when reading Mill on the Mormons, I also cringe when he says that liberty is not to be accorded to people—and peoples—who are insufficiently mature. While Mill himself did not make that argument regarding women, most liberal theorists until the twentieth century did. It was the argument used not only for denying women the vote, but also for denying women autonomy concerning our labor, our income, our bodies, and even our children. It is important to remember that the most commonly invoked alternative to autonomy is paternalism. If women who make pornography are not to be seen as having made a free decision, then someone else has to make that decision for them. If one takes the metaphor of autonomy literally, then it seems to be an object one either does or does not have. If one has it, then one makes one's own decisions; if one does not have it, then someone else makes those decisions. Isaiah Berlin, after making the point that "not all choices are equally free, or free at all," goes on to enumerate some of the things to be considered in assessing the degree to which people are free:

> The extent of my freedom seems to depend on (a) how many possibilities are open to me . . . ; (b) how easy or difficult each of these possibilities is to actualize; (c) how important in my plan of life, given my character and circumstances, these possibilities are when compared with each other; (d) how far they are closed and opened by deliberate human acts; (e) what value not

merely the agent, but the general sentiment of the society in which he lives, puts on the various possibilities. ("Two Concepts" 130)

This, it seems to me, is a much richer way to think about liberty than a literalized version of autonomy. Since, by some definitions, no one has autonomy, and by other definitions, everyone has it—even people who are victims of long-term violence—autonomy as a category is not particularly useful. If we can keep in mind that the assertion of autonomy is not a statement of fact, but a normative metaphor about how people should make decisions, then we can think about the extent to which different people in different situations have autonomy and what might be done to increase it. To return to Andrea Dworkin's example: If women are forced to use pornography because their husbands beat them, then neither declaring those women autonomous individuals who have made free choices nor banning pornography increases their freedom.

While it is difficult to find major philosophers arguing for a brain in a vat, there is always a tension within the concept of autonomy. It can mean either a freedom from the intellectual encumbrances of tradition and culture, or it can mean a willingness to consider criticism of those encumbrances. The more that liberal political theory assumes or advocates the first kind of autonomy, and the more literally the metaphor is taken, the more aptly applied are the various criticisms in the previous chapter.[4] But when it does not make a claim about the ability of an individual to exist or think as an autonomous mobile floating in space, those criticisms are less powerful.

In liberal theory, to make a decision as an autonomous individual is to make it rationally. "Rationality" is another of those terms that make compositionists jump, but, as with autonomy, there is a complicated relation between what advocates of rationality mean by the term and the sense it has in more popular parlance. In popular terms, "rational" is synonymous with "objective," which is usually used to mean unemotional and free of personal prejudice. A different (but also very popular) definition of "objective" is "having actual existence" so that only material objects can be objective. A third is one used in ethics: an action is objectively right if the "agent's performing it (on that occasion) really *is* right, whether or not the agent, or anyone else, believes it" (Timmons 624). In other words, something cannot be objective unless it is true. In popular usage, these three different definitions are scrambled, so that there is a sense that an objective statement is true, unemotional, and descriptive of a material object—a person can (and should) be objective by unemotionally perceiving and announcing assertions, without prejudice, that truly correspond to the material world.

The flaws with this view are obvious. It is itself subjective, based on an arbitrary prejudice against emotions. It is false, in that one cannot perceive anything without at least some prejudice. It is also false insofar as emotional statements may be completely true and unemotional ones false. Because attacks on this notion of objectivity have been so effective (and justified), there is a tendency to assume that all conceptions of rationality and objectivity have been thoroughly discredited. Although these attacks are effective and appropriate for many more or less popular manifestations of the claim to objectivity, it is not clear to me that they are tremendously damaging to what many major philosophers mean by the term "objective."

In rhetoric and composition, discussions on this topic have tended to follow James Berlin, who set the pattern for dividing epistemologies into three categories: expressivist, social constructivist, and what amounts to positivist. Yet Popper, one of the most famous (or infamous) advocates of objectivity, does not promote the kind of epistemology Berlin and others, including its popular advocates, associate with positivism; Popper explicitly does not claim that it is possible for an individual to know anything objectively, to deny one's own subjectivity. He posits three distinct but mutually influential "sub-worlds":

> The first is the physical world or the world of physical states; the second is the mental world or the world of mental states; and the third is the world of intelligibles, or of *ideas in the objective sense;* it is the world of possible objects of thought: the world of theories in themselves, and their logical relations; of arguments in themselves; and of problem situations in themselves. (*Objective Knowledge* 154, emphasis in original)

One might call these the realms of ontology, epistemology, and discourse. And the first point one must notice is that Popper is not endorsing the popular view of objectivity as unemotional, material, and true. Popper defines the first and third worlds as objective, and the second world as subjective. Popper's complaint about much discourse on epistemology is that "there is so strong a temptation to interpret the third-world contents of thought as second-world thought processes" (*Objective Knowledge* 158). That temptation is exemplified in the argument that there is no such thing as an objective world because one cannot know it in an objective manner, which is, as John Searle pointed out, an attempt to prove an ontological claim through an epistemological claim.

In conventional usage, there is a conflation of epistemology and ontology—the material world is objective *and* a person can be objective when s/he correctly perceives that material world (which can only be done by freeing oneself from prejudice and emotion). Popper does not claim that one can be objective: By definition, subjects are subjects and cannot make themselves into objects. Nor does he claim that one should strive for objectivity. As Popper says, "The objective and 'value-free' scientist is not the ideal scientist" ("The Logic of the Social Sciences" 74). Instead, for Popper, knowledge is objective in the sense that when one speaks of "scientific knowledge," one is *not* speaking of the knowledge of any individual (thus he titles one of his chapters "Epistemology Without a Knowing Subject"). Scientific knowledge is objective precisely because there is no subject who possesses it:

> For scientific knowledge is not knowledge in the sense of the ordinary usage of the words 'I know'. While knowledge in the sense of 'I know' belongs to what I call the 'second world', the world of *subjects,* scientific knowledge belongs to the third world, to the world of objective theories, objective problems, and objective arguments. (*Objective Knowledge* 108, emphasis in original)

The third world is, he says, "autonomous" of the second world "in what may be called its ontological status" (*Objective Knowledge* 161; see also 159). This is not to say that it exists totally independent of human action; it is a human construct (159–60). It is objective in that it is open to testing by a variety of people, that it transcends the knowledge of any individual.

For Popper, objective statements are not necessarily true. Similarly, an "objective argument" is not an argument a subject makes in an objective way, nor is it an argument about which one can be certain, but an argument in the third world. Knowledge "is not the search for certainty. To err is human. All human knowledge is fallible and therefore uncertain" ("Knowledge and the Shaping of Reality" 4). Whether or not one agrees with Popper, one has to see that the conventional attacks on objectivity are fundamentally irrelevant to his argument.

This is not to say that such attacks are against a poststructuralist false construct. While Searle's complaint that many poststructuralist attacks on certainty function through a conflation of ontology and epistemology is accurate, it ignores the fact that many of the proponents of rationality make exactly the same conflation in order to assert the inverse argument, mixing up epistemological and ontological (and sometimes rhetorical) criteria. This scrambling is especially marked in composition textbooks' explanations of "facts," as when *The Bedford Guide for College Writers* defines a fact: "Facts are statements that can be verified by objective means, such as by observing or by reading a reliable account. . . . Facts are usually agreed upon by all parties in a dispute or by all reasonable people" (Kennedy 114). Ramage and Bean's definition is "A *fact* is a noncontroversial piece of data that is verifiable through observation or through appeal to communally accepted authorities" (135). The controversiality of a statement is a rhetorical criterion; to say that a statement can be verified is to make an ontological claim; to say that it can be verified through observation is to combine an epistemological and ontological claim.

In addition to muddling kinds of claims, definitions like the above are more positivist than those offered by most positivists. There is considerable debate among even the positivists whether any statement can be truly verified (for more on this point, see Ayer 13–21). The credo of the positivists, made most famous by Popper, is that a meaningful statement must be one that could, at least hypothetically, be falsified. A scientific experiment is supposed to specify the conditions under which a hypothesis might be falsified and then enact them; if the hypothesis has withstood numerous attempts to falsify it, then it is taken for a fact. This does not necessarily mean that it is true, but that it has not yet been proven false, and so can be taken as true. The distinction between verifying a statement and failing to falsify it is important; as Ayer says, one might fail to falsify the existence of inhabitants of Mars, but one should not therefore conclude that the hypothesis has been verified. Meanwhile, if one cannot articulate conditions under which the statement can be falsified (an issue to be raised later in regard to the interest-based model), then it is a credo, but not a scientific fact.

To suggest, as does *The Bedford Guide,* that there is something wrong with saying that facts are true statements right after having defined a fact as something that can be *verified* is ragingly incoherent, or implicitly an extremely unusual definition of "verify." There were some positivists who did say that one can (more or less) verify a statement, but they drew the logical conclusion that a verified fact is a true fact. Those who say that one cannot conclude that a fact is necessarily true are those, like Popper, who say that one cannot verify but only fail to falsify. The conventional postmodernist position is that a fact is not necessarily true. Thus, *The Bedford Guide* is postmodernist *and* positivist—positions that are usefully seen as mutually exclusive.

In addition, the above definition of "fact"assumes that facts are not controversial—a common assumption, but patently false. Many statements that can be tested through direct observation or that come from reliable authorities are tremendously controversial. I know from personal experience that it is very controversial to say that confederate states were motivated to secede in order to protect and preserve slavery. Yet that is a statement one can test through reading the declarations of secession, every one of which specifically mentions slavery (generally first). The controversy raised by the DNA results regarding Sally Heming's descendants, the Pentagon Papers, the videotape of the Rodney King beating, and innumerable other facts indicate that one of the most powerful things about truth is its ability to generate controversy (Arendt's point in "Truth and Politics").[5]

The blending of epistemological, rhetorical, and ontological criteria for objectivity has important political consequences. The assumption that "facts" are noncontroversial is a common one and often informs attacks on publicly funded media like PBS, CNN, and NPR. The argument is that such media should be objective, and that certain programs are, de facto, not objective because they are controversial. James Loewen has described the destructive effect this desire for noncontroversiality has had in the teaching of history, especially at the high school level (see especially chapter 11). This is essentially the critique presented by Edward Herman and Noam Chomsky regarding the illusion of objectivity—that something that confirms dominant prejudices is noncontroversial, so it *seems* objective. But, and this is the important point, the more that we assert that facts are noncontroversial, and that good public discourse is fact-based, the more we preclude the possibility of public argument that takes issue with dominant prejudices. We have abandoned the Enlightenment goal of a critical public sphere.

I am not arguing for relying on an ontologically based definition of fact, nor for abandoning the term entirely, but for recognizing the tendency on various sides of the realist versus social constructivist argument to commingle rhetorical, epistemological, and ontological criteria in definitions of terms like "fact," "objectivity," and "neutrality." Conservative attacks on the academy, for instance, often assert that there is such a thing as nonsubjective knowledge because there is an external reality (thereby making an epistemological claim and supporting it with an ontological one). Roger Kimball states his credo that "the human mind is capable of apprehending truths that exist apart from the perturbations of subjective fancy" (58). As with Kimball (or Bennett or Cheney), this assertion of the possibility of direct knowledge is almost always argumentatively connected to asserting (or assuming) that some specific belief exemplifies an instance of just such direct apprehension of truth (such as the fact of our being a nation of immigrants). There are two *different* conceptions of "fact" getting entangled here. One says that facts are statements that are universally accepted, and the other says that facts are statements that correspond to reality. By the first definition, facts are not necessarily universally accepted; by the second, they are not necessarily controversial. Either definition seems potentially useful to me, but to combine them is counterfactual.

The traditional definition of fact, and the one most attacked by postpositivist theory, is that a fact is a statement that corresponds with reality. This is generally known as the "correspondence theory of truth." Because advocates of the traditional-universal liberal tradition do assume that definition (e.g., the above quote from Kimball), postpositivist attacks on that theory of truth most clearly apply to traditional-universalist liberalism. It is not clear, however, that such criticisms are especially troubling for the deontological tradition, a point to be pursued later. At this point, I should try to clarify the distinction.

The deontological model distinguishes between the good and the right, and the more popular model (traditional-universal) does not.[6] Sandel captures the importance of this distinction for deontological liberalism in his summary of its "core thesis":

> society, being composed of a plurality of persons, each with his own aims, interests, and conceptions of the good, is best arranged when it is governed by principles that do not *themselves* presuppose any particular conception

of the good; what justifies these regulative principles above all is not that they maximize the social welfare or otherwise promote the good, but rather that they conform to the concept of *right,* a moral category given prior to the good and independent of it. (*Liberalism and the Limits of Justice* 1, emphasis in original)

Thus, society should be arranged such that Muslims and Lutherans—who might, for instance, have very different ideas as to whether the good life includes the consumption of alcohol—are both equally subject to laws that are not themselves derived from Muslim or Lutheran principles. Public discourse (i.e., discourse about governmental policies) should be "neutral" in regard to moral and religious questions in that it is neither derived from them, nor favoring one particular religion over another. So the question concerning whether or not to permit consumption of alcohol should not be debated on the basis of what religious texts say about it (questions of the good) but on the basis of the universal and reciprocally binding rights (questions of justice and fairness).

Rawls has made this argument in two very different ways. In *A Theory of Justice,* he argues on the basis of a hypothetical and prepolitical moment. Were we to imagine that we stood behind a veil of ignorance regarding our corporeal lives—our gender, economic status, nationality, religion, ethnicity, and so on unknown to us—there would be, Rawls posits, certain principles upon which we would all agree, especially ones that favor fairness and equality. Rawls's argument is that the points of agreement represent universal foundations for justice. Ackerman summarizes the major objection to Rawls's theory; it requires

us to suppress our own identities as social beings—whose identities and objectives are defined through interaction with other concrete individuals—so that we may catch a fleeting glimpse of some transcendent individual who may sit as higher judge of our social conflicts. (331)

Ackerman remarks,

it is impossible to choose *any* principle of justice until [the hypothetical person] is endowed by his creator with *some* set of preferences to guide his judgment . . . Thus, a good deal of *A Theory of Justice* is devoted to explaining just what sorts of information that Rawls will allow to pierce the veil. (339)

Rawls (or anyone else) can get a certain outcome by what kind of information is allowed through. The paradox is that with no information we can make no decisions, so a truly unencumbered individual can never be a truly reasonable one, but, as soon as s/he has information, s/he is no longer unencumbered.

After *A Theory of Justice,* Rawls moved away from discussion of this hypothetical moment, toward a discussion of what sort of public discourse could maintain liberal theory's coexistent privileging of rational discourse and reluctance to make "the good" an object of argument or policy. Granting that the principles he articulated in *A Theory of Justice* were not universal, but were influenced by his own political tradition, Rawls began looking instead for a secure foundation for the kinds of arguments that are themselves foundations in political discourse: issues of constitutionality. With such a move, Rawls did thereby avoid many of the problems in traditional-universal liberal theory, but he did so by distributing off most political argument.

As a consequence, the deontological model requires minimum agreement among parties to function effectively, but it necessarily limits "public" argument to a small number of topics. The more popular model (traditional-universal) has a more expanded definition of "public" issues but ends up requiring much more agreement. So, for example, questions about general welfare are relevant in the latter kind of discourse, so much so that the traditional-universalist liberal model often becomes utilitarianism, but are essentially nonexistent for a deontological liberal like Rawls: "Each person possesses an inviolability founded on justice that even the welfare of society as a whole cannot override" (*Theory of Justice* 3; for more on that point, see Sandel, *Liberalism and the Limits of Justice* 16–17). Simone Chambers emphasizes the importance of this rejection of utilitarian analyses of rights; she says that deontological liberals maintain "that we have duties toward each other which trump the particular or collective ends we might wish to pursue" (21).

The metaphor of individual rights "trumping" all other concerns, even the general good, is important for Rawls (and Ronald Dworkin, discussed below). Unlike utilitarians, deontological liberals assume that the general good can never justify the abrogation of even a single individual's rights. This assumption necessitates a minimal number of rights. That is, one cannot assert equally inviolable rights to free speech and to not being offended, to drive and to be protected from unsafe drivers, and so on. The longer the list of "rights," the more likely a conflict between at least two of them. Thus, the traditional-universal version of liberal political theory asserts an apparently endless list of rights (letters to the editor and other popular forms of public discourse assert a right not to be offended, a right to free speech under any circumstances, a right to privacy; proponents of school prayer assert a right to worship; death penalty advocates cite a right to vengeance, even a right to watch the execution) but talks openly about the need to balance them.

Rawls is explicit that his notion of public reason does not apply to many questions of policy; after explaining that the "limits" of public reason only apply to "questions of basic justice," he says,

> Many if not most political questions do not concern those fundamentals, for example, much tax legislation and many laws regulating property; statutes protecting the environment and controlling pollution; establishing national parks and preserving wilderness areas and animal and plant species; and laying aside funds for museums and the arts. ("Idea of Public Reason" 94)

One can see from his list of issues that are not "questions of basic justice" that the distinction is far from neutral—for many environmentalists, preserving species *is* a question of basic justice; the same could be said of libertarians and property rights, members of posse comitatus and tax legislation, advocates of the arts and public funding.

The passage implies a severe restriction of topics discussed this way, implying that other topics can be discussed in other ways, but it is not entirely clear that Rawls is consistent on that point. Later in the same essay, Rawls says that "the ideal of public reason does hold for citizens when they engage in political advocacy in the public forum, and thus for members of political parties and for candidates in their campaigns and for other groups who support them" ("Idea" 95). While we may think about certain kinds of issues ("personal deliberations and reflections about political questions" ["Idea" 95]) in ways not limited by the constraints of public reason, it must control how people ultimately vote: "Otherwise, public discourse runs the risk of being hypocritical: citizens talk before one another one way and vote another" ("Idea" 95). Yet the objection Rawls raises regarding discourse and voting remains regarding personal and public deliberations—either we think about a topic in a way that is different from how we talk about it, or we talk about it in ways that Rawls seems to reject (exactly the problem with personal experience and argumentation courses that emphasize traditional-universal notions of rationality).

One can see the difference in terms of argument between deontological and traditional-universalist liberal models in two exchanges over the same issue, specifically the arguments raised by MacKinnon and Dworkin's project to enable civil prosecution of pornographers. In *In Harm's Way,* Catherine MacKinnon and Andrea Dworkin describe their efforts toward laws that would enable victims of rape to sue pornographers (on much the same grounds as some municipalities are suing gun manufacturers and several states sued cigarette manufacturers). This book was critically reviewed by John Irving in the *New York Times Book Review* and by Ronald Dworkin in the *New York Review of Books.* Andrea Dworkin replied to Irving's review, and MacKinnon to Dworkin's. While the initial subject is the same(the book), the different exchanges focus on different topoi, as a result of the kind of liberalism assumed by each of the reviewers. John Irving (a traditional-universalist) argues that the harm to freedom of speech of the proposed law is greater than the harm to women from pornography. Andrea Dworkin's response focuses on that question of degree of harm. Ronald Dworkin (a deontological liberal) argues that MacKinnon's argument for the laws does not demonstrate that pornography constitutes a violation of women's rights. Ronald Dworkin does not raise the question of the number of women whose rights might be violated, but simply whether any woman's rights are violated. One can see in the different topoi of these arguments the different emphases of traditional-universalist versus deontological: The former tends to describe political conflict as a question of weighing competing rights, while the latter suggests the possibility of the rights of even one woman trumping everything else.

Deontological liberals are not, as Chambers says, entirely deaf to issues of consequence:

> Today, most deontological proceduralists acknowledge that in constructing a procedure to test moral principles, one cannot be blind to the concrete interests and needs of individuals or to the consequences that would follow if the principles were in fact implemented in a real social world. (22)

The idea is that putting more emphasis on the sacrality of certain rights is necessary for remaining neutral on metaphysical assumptions. Yet, Sandel has suggested this striving for neutrally has led, ironically and unintentionally, to an infringement of the rights of those whose lives are deeply embedded in seeking the good; in his discussion of various Supreme Court decisions on separation of church and state, he posits that these decisions have put undue burdens on religious people, in effect, discriminating against them (I will suggest something similar happens in classroom instantiations of liberal practice). Sandel's analysis suggests that the very attempt to distinguish between the right and the good undermines the goal of that distinction: protecting certain practices from governmental incursion.

Rawls's discussion implies some kind of topical distinction between public and nonpublic reason; it may instead be rhetorical. Rawls says that public reason

> is public in three ways: as the reason of citizens as such, it is the reason of the public; its subject is the good of the public and matters of fundamental justice; and its nature and content is public, being given by the ideas and principles expressed by society's conception of political justice, and conducted open to view on that basis. ("Idea" 93)

That is, as for Kant, we must present reasons we believe all reasonable people would accept. It is not enough that people believe that their reasons are true, but that "we should sincerely think that our view of the matter is based on political values everyone can reasonably be expected to endorse" ("Idea" 115). We should not make arguments that are grounded in "private" reasons—personal preferences or values we know are not (and would not be) shared. This conclusion is the natural outcome of assuming that conceptions of the "good" are both private (and therefore nonpublic) *and* that they are not subject to reason.

There are several consequences of requiring that our reasons be ones we think universally accepted. The most obvious is that it prohibits a certain kind of Machiavellian bargaining, such as arguing that one can ignore the needs of the poor since they rarely vote. Less obvious is that it prohibits arguing to what Chaim Perelman calls the "particular" audience. The requirement is partially a sincerity requirement—that the speaker sincerely believe that people should assent to the reasons—and also similar to Perelman's description of the "Universal Audience," a hypothetical audience consisting of what reasonable and educated people *would* think.

In practice, then, the liberal distinction between private and public amounts to how one makes one's argument, the reasons one gives. If one can argue in terms of general good, it seems to be a "public" issue; if one refers to personal experiences, morals, issues of spirituality or religious dicta, or minority cultural mores, then it seems to be "nonpublic." It is clear that this is a question of rhetoric and not topic if one notices that the same topic—whether or not to dam and flood a valley in Yosemite National Park, for example—could be discussed in these two different ways. One person might argue that the number of people who will benefit from the cheap water source is more important than National Park policy, while another might argue that damming such a beautiful valley is a kind of desecration. The first argument would likely make quantitative arguments and cost comparisons, while the second would narrate a personal experience of transcendence. The Hetch Hetchy controversy is a helpful example, as it highlights the point that this way of distinguishing the public from the personal entitles some positions to greater consideration. John Muir, whose very position regarding the controversy was the result of personal experience and a belief in the significance of spiritually transcending experiences, could not make his argument in a way that would look public—at least in Rawls's terms—without seeming to endorse the very values he had spent much of his life arguing against. A strong critic of utilitarian attitudes toward nature, he could hardly be enthusiastic about making utilitarian arguments for preserving it. In short, this division between public and nonpublic ways of making arguments is not a neutral basis, but one that advantages some positions at the expense of others.

Communities trying to restrict policy argument to Rawls's public reason are left with limited options. Either one must bracket out of communal discussion those topics most prone to "nonpublic" argument (a common strategy for teachers of argument), or communities must be relatively homogeneous (as implied in Rawls's comments regarding "the plain truths now widely accepted, or available, to citizens generally" ["Idea" 103] and "comprehensive doctrines reasonable people affirm" [97]), or one must encourage people to make arguments based on reasons other than the ones they most sincerely hold.

There are two different ways that one might follow this last approach: One might use arguments that, while one genuinely holds them, are not one's major reasons for one's position but are the ones most likely to persuade one's particular audience (e.g., a Christian who does not cite

Scripture when trying to persuade an atheist); or one might use arguments with which one actively disagrees, but that will be compelling for one's particular audience (e.g., an atheist citing Scripture when trying to persuade a Christian). The difference is substantial. As will be discussed later, Habermas builds much of his theory regarding communicative action on the assumption—supported by speech act theory—that sincerity is always assumed to be a speaker's obligation. While one could argue that the first example—someone presenting his/her second or third most personally compelling reasons—is still sincere, that is a more difficult claim in regard to the second—someone who fundamentally disagrees with the reasons s/he is presenting.

There is a deeper problem, especially as far as proponents of the liberal public sphere are concerned (and, to a large degree, many proponents of deliberative democracy as well). The above examples concern a rhetor who is shaping the discourse for the particular intended audience, rather than presenting reasons directed at a more general audience. The rhetor is perceiving the reasons as particularly valid—valid for this audience—but not implicitly or explicitly claiming that the reasons are universally valid. Many theorists of public discourse reject this particularizing of reason, insisting that assertoric discourse always involves people making assertions that they think are universally valid, "for any kind of restrictions with regard to the circle of those over against whom the claim to validity is raised would amount to restrictions of the claim to validity and would contradict the meaning of an assertion as an argumentative act" (Böhler 116). By this definition, to engage in persuasion is to make assertions of universal validity—assertions that one believes must be granted by oneself and one's intended audience and all other potential audiences. Dietrich Böhler says,

> An assertion's claim to validity implies that what is asserted is not solely recognized as valid by the fortuitous listeners who are present, indeed not even solely by an expert contemporary public but that it is so constituted that it could also be recognized by an ideal community of argumentation. (115)

One problem with this argument is that it is definitional and circular; it is not a claim about what really happens in discourse—that people make universally valid claims—but about what happens in people's minds in a certain kind of discourse and that kind of discourse is defined by what happens in people's minds.[7] And what they have in mind is, as Gerald Gaus summarizes it:

> If (1) I am committed to giving good reasons for my political proposals and (2) I am also committed to the idea that these reasons must (in some sense) be seen as good reasons by every member of my public, I seem committed to the further claim that (3) my proposal *P* is justified only if, supposing all members of the public were rational, all would accept it. (209)

Gaus's objection to this hypothetical public is eloquent:

> What would be done by fully rational and informed people with unlimited ability to process information does not seem an appropriate benchmark for *our* practice. That demigods would agree hardly seems a reason for us to aspire to actual political consensus. Ours is a condition of scarcity of cognitive resources and information, in which the pursuit of minimal rationality is challenging enough, without seeking to model our practices on what we would do if we had such semidivine status. (210)

Gaus's objection is to the ideal normative agreement implicit in Böhler's (and others') asserting that we always assume a hypothetical perfectly rational public. My objection is more mundane: It is a surprisingly complicated process to ensure that hypothetical (and essentially counterfactual) suppositions regarding audience are helpful for a public sphere of inquiry in the midst of difference, as the process is likely to devolve into condescension and wishful thinking.

These complications are particularly evident and important for teachers of composition, as we often ask our students to do exactly what Böhler and Rawls advocate—we ask that students write to a "general" audience, which is a hypothetical construct, and we often ask that students revise papers on the basis of what they imagine this hypothetical audience would imagine the relevant counterarguments to be (for more on this point, see Susan Wells). This is appealing to Perelman's "Universal Audience." On the other hand, textbooks and teachers also sometimes simultaneously ask that students write to an opposition audience, or imagine how an opposition audience would react, and most pedagogies involve peer review. This is Perelman's "Particular Audience." My first point, then, about this approach to the opposition is that it is, quite often, asking that students do two very different writing tasks at the same time.

But, it seems to me, liberal theory similarly asks citizens to engage in contradictory tasks. The theory requires sincerity on the part of interlocutors and universality on the part of their arguments. Rawls and others grant that we have transcendent backing for our views, but we should not make our public arguments on the basis of those backings, *and* we must be sincere. Yet if we are presenting reasons other than the ones we sincerely hold—as required by this notion of universality—we are not sincere; if we present the reasons that we sincerely hold, we are not making universally valid arguments. Behind this apparently contradictory advice—in composition pedagogy and liberal political theory—is indecision regarding whether or not people really disagree. For Rousseau and Locke, for instance, disagreement is the result of misunderstanding; could we get our language and perception down right, then disagreement would evaporate, so sincerity and universality are compatible. If, however, we do really disagree, then sincerity and universality are in conflict.

My second point is more complicated, and it has to do with the advice that students imagine how an opposition would react to their argument. Thomas Nagel answers the question "What is it like to be a bat?" by talking about the process of imagining being a bat:

> Our own experience provides the basic material for our imagination, whose range is therefore limited. It will not help to try to imagine that one has webbing on one's arms, which enables one to fly around at dusk and dawn catching insects in one's mouth; that one has very poor vision, and perceives the surrounding world by a system of reflected high-frequency sound signals; and that one spends the day hanging upside down by one's feet in the attic. In so far as I can imagine this (which is not very far), it tells me only what it would be like for me to behave as a bat behaves. But that is not the question. I want to know what it is like for a *bat* to be a bat. (439, emphasis in original)

That is the first problem with asking that students imagine how an opposition audience would respond: The best answer we are likely to get will include reasons why that student would hold an opposition position, but not the real reasons that real people have for really disagreeing.

When we imagine the reasons that other people have for positions with which we disagree, we are likely to assume that the reasons are necessarily stupid. As political theorists like Gerald Gaus and Joshua Cohen have noted, whatever people "believe to be false they also believe to be unreasonable" (Gaus 215). There is a kind of straw man fallacy that is very difficult to avoid. Obviously, people who disagree with me are stupid, so I will attribute stupid arguments to them. It is extraordinarily difficult for people to imagine that people who disagree with them might have good reasons for doing so.

After all, we live in a culture where conflict with other people is evaded. It is considered bad form to talk about politics or religion; a conversation that turns into a disagreement is assumed to be a disaster; parents have made the argument to school boards that children even as old as their teens should not be asked to read things that might contradict what their parents have said; best-selling books tend either to describe argument as conflict to be avoided (e.g., Tannen's *The Argument Culture*) or battles to be won through any means available (Nicholas Capaldi's *How to Win Every Argument*). These characterizations are, of course, self-fulfilling—being certain that disagreement must be unproductive virtually ensures that people engage in exactly those practices that make it so. But this self-fulfilling prophecy about argument also means that we have little experience of difference. Opponents of abortion may never have talked at length with someone who is prochoice—how, then, could they possibly know what such a person would be like?

If people often have very little experience talking productively with others who disagree with them, then it becomes difficult to distinguish between imagining the reasons that someone might disagree with us and engaging in wishful thinking. Students' imagined oppositions are likely to be simple in several senses of the word: simple-minded, simple to summarize, and simple to refute. Asking students to imagine an opposition really is asking them to imagine what it would be like to be a bat. Democracy of difference requires a public sphere where people who disagree can argue with, rather than at, one another. There are several things that prevent such a sphere; one of them is people thinking that they need not listen to one another. By telling students that they can imagine opposition arguments, we are reinforcing the notion that one need not listen terribly carefully to other people, as one can oneself accurately predict their arguments. I should note that this problem is not resolved by presenting students with "both" sides of an argument if one is presenting a balance of arguments that are themselves fairly predictable, fairly shallow, or examples of enclave-based discourse (that is, things not written to an informed and intelligent opposition audience).

It may seem that the current emphasis on group work contradicts my characterization of practice, but group work can ensure that students hear opposition arguments only if one of two conditions exist. First, students must be writing on the same topics, or topics on which their peers are knowledgeable, *and* groups must have students who disagree with one another. That is, there must be informed discursive conflict within the classroom, a situation with which, as Jarratt remarks, many teachers and students are deeply uncomfortable. Second, if the peers are not people who genuinely disagree with one another, then they must be able to imagine being the opposition. In this latter case, the problem of condescending audience construction is not solved but simply displaced.

The reason we are especially likely to imagine what it is like to be a bat in terms of what it would be like for us to be a bat is that the bat cannot tell us if we have it right or wrong. What distinguishes the liberal public sphere from a democracy of difference is that the latter requires that we gain assent from the people with whom we are disagreeing, if not on our central argument, at least on our own description of *their* argument. Young explains the distinction:

> It is necessary to distinguish between taking the perspective of others into account in making moral judgments, on the one hand, and reversing positions with them, on the other. Dialogue participants are able to take account of the perspective of others because they have heard those perspectives expressed. ("Asymmetrical Reciprocity" 59)

There is an extraordinarily important difference between a person summarizing an argument one imagines someone might make and being able to point to an argument someone really has made. And that is a distinction that we lose when we encourage students to deal with hypothetical audiences. Obviously, there is a moment when we must imagine another person's point of view, but it is the next step that matters—we must confirm that our imaginings are fair. Such a requirement means that we participate in a public sphere of conflict; if people are to disagree with one another, then there must be a public sphere where people do more than simply say their piece and then retreat to the enclave. There must be a continued interaction of people who are disagreeing with one another; an area of expression is not enough.

I keep asserting that a better understanding of political theory can usefully inform debates within rhetoric and composition, but the connections between liberal political theory and composition scholarship may seem somewhat obscure. The connections, however, are numerous, especially when it comes to issues of freedom and autonomy. There are two slightly different visions of the value of the individual in the liberal model. The first is that the individual is the ultimate good, so that a community is good to the extent that it promotes autonomy in individuals. The second is that the individual is the source of political action, so that an individual is good to the extent that s/he promotes the good of the community. These are essentially what Isaiah Berlin famously called the two concepts of liberty.

Isaiah Berlin calls the first sense of liberty "negative liberty." He summarizes Mill's argument on that point (while noting that it dates back at least as far as Erasmus):

> To threaten a man with persecution unless he submits to a life in which he exercises no choices of his goals; to block before him every door but one, *no matter how noble the prospect upon which it opens,* or how benevolent the motives of those who arrange this, is to sin against the truth that he is a man, a being with a life of his own to live. ("Two Concepts" 127, emphasis added)

That is, a society that crushed individualism, no matter what it achieved by doing so, would have made a bad bargain. James Berlin identified this as a central tenet of expressivist pedagogy:

> This focus on the individual does not mean that no community is to be encouraged. . . . The community's right to exist, however, stands only insofar as it serves all of its members as individuals. It is, after all, only the individual, acting alone and apart from others, who can determine the existent, the good, and the possible. ("Rhetoric and Ideology" 689–90)

Isaiah Berlin has shown that this negative conception of liberty tends to emphasize freedom *from* external sources of coercion. Hence it is often referred to by political theorists as *freedom from;* liberals with this view tend to worry most about what the government or institutions might do to restrict the liberties of individuals. One might make the same point about Elbow and other liberal compositionists; they worry most about the coercion imposed by externals—especially teachers—or the ways that those externals may have been internalized by writers. Their recommendations involve students freeing themselves *from* those external constraints. By worrying so much about the external coercion of the immediately present institution (teacher, grades) they may miss other, more systemic coercions: to avoid conflict, to get along well with others, to conform with dominant values. As Arendt has said in regard to teaching, there are ways the tyranny of fellow students can be even harder to resist than the tyranny of the teacher ("The Crisis in Education").

The second concept of liberty is the wish, as Isaiah Berlin puts it, "to be conscious of myself as a thinking, willing, active being, bearing responsibility for my choices and able to explain them by references to my own ideas and purposes" (Two Concepts" 131). This is the sort of freedom assumed by advocates of the civic-republican and agonistic public spheres. It is the *freedom to* do things, to change the conditions of one's own life, to have political power. Isaiah Berlin points out that philosophers like Mill often assume that the two conceptions are necessarily connected, but they are not. Indeed, as indicated by the argument between Bartholomae and Elbow, they can be mutually opposed. To achieve freedom to improve my work situation, I might have to join a union, an act that would restrict my negative liberty, as the union might impose various obligations on me.

Isaiah Berlin argues that positive liberty ("freedom to") easily slides into a tendency to declare some aspect of the individual to be the true individual, and everything else to be the result of blindness, cupidity, corruption, or ignorance. That, paradoxically, can then result in exactly the sort of coercion and conformity the privileging of the individual was intended to prevent. In political terms, this can mean that the person who claims to know what people really want is "in a position to ignore the actual wishes of men or societies, to bully, oppress, torture them in the name, and on behalf, of their 'real' selves" ("Two Concepts" 133). Berlin is speaking of the Leninist politics that engaged in coercive practice and liberal rhetoric. But one can make the same observation about certain kinds of teaching practices, such as ones that assert a "universal" response of readers that is clearly not universal (such as that advocated by Roger Kimball, Allan Bloom, or Lynne Cheney). One can ignore the actual response of real readers in order to force them to have a response that one believes they should have had. Just as Leninists could attribute a view to "the people" that had nothing to do with what real flesh and blood people thought, so Kimball can attribute a view to "all readers" that has nothing to do with what real readers believe.

This ability to ignore the people in front of us in favor of some idea of what such people should think can also manifest itself when teachers only count a certain kind of subject as an authentic one. When I was directing a program in which instructors were encouraged to have students write about an experience that changed them, I became aware that instructors have strong prejudices about what sorts of experiences (especially what sorts of conversion experiences) count as profound. This is exactly the process described by Lester Faigley, who has noted our current preferences for a conflicted (and essentially postmodern) self in personal narratives. It is also essentially the concern raised by Hairston, who worries that some composition instructors only identify certain political viewpoints as legitimate. In the course of freeing students, we free them to think just like us.

The problem with emphasizing the first sort of freedom, the autonomy of the individual, is that it can involve a disturbing fiction of isolation, in which people reject the world by engaging in "some process of deliberate self-transformation that enables them to care no longer for any of [the world's] values, to remain, isolated and independent, on its edges, no longer vulnerable to its weapons" (I. Berlin, "Two Concepts" 135–36). This view leads one to the conclusion that one should reject all forms of "tampering with human beings, getting at them, shaping them against their will to your own pattern" (138). This is, I would suggest, the central assumption behind Elbow's deep ambivalence about grades, and often implicit in defenses of contract grading—an unwillingness to impose one's own notions of the good upon other individuals. It is also, quite obviously, an unintended paraphrase of exactly the argument that Jeff Smith makes in favor of letting students' goals determine teacher behavior.

In short, the argument between Elbow and Bartholomae results from different conceptions of liberty: Elbow assumes what Isaiah Berlin calls the negative view of liberty, whereas James Berlin and Bartholomae assume the positive. Elbow is most concerned with freeing students *from* the coercion of too much advice about writing, too many grades, and too much teacher authority; J. Berlin and Bartholomae are most concerned with freeing students *to* engage in political action. Smith, Flower, Hairston, and others who make similar arguments assume and exemplify the liberal model's assumptions about government. Just as the liberal model tends to worry about the power of the state (and is therefore criticized for worrying too little about the coercive power of forces outside the government, such as industry), so Smith, Flower, and others worry about the coercive power of the teacher (and thereby ignore the coercive power of other forces, such as industry). Teachers, for instance, perceive an assignment as "open" and the students "free" to choose the topic, simply because the teacher did not specify it, thereby ignoring the constraints on students' freedom—particularly regarding topics for argument—created by forces outside of (and previous to) the immediate classroom. Just as the liberal model makes government instrumental, ostensibly leaving the issue of ends to individuals while actually rewarding some ends above others, so such teachers make their own teaching instrumental, ostensibly leaving the question of ends to their students but within a larger system that actually privileges some ends above others. And just as critics of the liberal model argue that this places important questions outside of the realm of public argument, so critics of certain pedagogies argue that this instrumentalizing of teaching leaves students as instruments of forces that remain outside the realm of argument and critique.

Yet this criticism can sometimes just slightly miss the point of liberal political theory. Ohmann attacks what he calls "pseudo-argument" because it is "divorced from power, money, social conflict, class, and consciousness" (158). He summarizes his objections to this approach to argument:

> The study of abstractly rational persuasion (a) plays down materially rooted conflict of interest, (b) supports the ideology of the open society with decisions democratically and rationally made by citizens all of whose arguments have an equal chance of success, and (c) trains students to be skillful at putting into a standard and "objective" form arguments in which they have no great personal stake—arguments, in fact, that someone else may have required them to construct. (159)

My contention is that Ohmann is right, at least insofar as he is talking about approaches to argumentation that come out of the liberal model of the public sphere. But, from the perspective of that model, Ohmann's objections are irrelevant. Liberal theorists never argue that public discourse actually *is* divorced from power, money, and so on, but that it *should* be. A liberal pedagogy will teach students what Stephen Holmes called liberal rhetoric and, ideally, teach them the criteria to use in order to identify injustice. Perhaps wrongly but perhaps rightly, liberal pedagogues assume that requiring students to behave as though they were in the utopian public sphere will make the actual more like that utopian one.

Like the ideal citizen in the liberal public sphere, the ideal student in the liberal classroom is an autonomous individual who has the right to engage in rational discourse on matters of public policy. The classroom discourse (in terms of class discussion and papers) is rational in that it appeals to universal principles (e.g., logic) and experiences (thus, it avoids personal experience) and is oriented toward the common good. Private experiences are inappropriate, either as paper topics or methods of proof. An individual, while autonomous, transcends the particularities of his/her identity and experiences in order to evaluate policy proposals from a neutral perspective to which all reasonable people can assent.

Liberal pedagogy can manifest this goal in two very different ways. The first, the one most often attacked by liberatory pedagogy but not advocated in composition theory in quite some time, grows from within the traditional-universalist liberal model. That model tends toward the most extreme statements regarding need for conformity, the transience of difference, and the accessibility of truths. It is the one summarized and advocated by Roger Kimball and others who see the purpose of liberal education as introducing students to a fairly stable set of texts whose meaning is clear to the instructor and whose inherent value must remain unquestioned. This is education as inculcation or acculturation: "Liberal education is education in culture or toward culture" (Strauss, "What Is Liberal Education" 3); it consists "in studying with the proper care the great books which the greatest minds have left behind" (3). This model is unabashedly elitist and, as demonstrated in Allan Bloom's tirade against rock music, deeply hostile to mass culture. It is intended to "free" people from mass society; Leo Strauss says that "liberal education is the ladder by which we try to ascend from mass democracy to democracy as originally meant" (5). Such advocates sometimes grant the paradox at the center, an inclusive but elite culture; Strauss defines democracy as

> a regime in which all or most adults are men of virtue, and since virtue seems to require wisdom, a regime in which all or most adults are virtuous and wise, or the society in which all or most adults have developed their reason to a high degree, or *the* rational society. Democracy, in a word, is meant to be an aristocracy which has broadened into a universal aristocracy. ("What Is Liberal Education" 4, emphasis in original)

In this view, a liberal education is mass education only in the sense that it is provided to everyone, and not in the sense that everyone will actually partake of it: "We must not expect that liberal education can ever become universal education. It must always remain the obligation and the privilege of a minority" (Strauss, "Liberal Education and Responsibility" 24). There is no longer even the pretense of a democracy, but the hope for meritocracy (a kind indistinguishable from plutocracy).

The instructor knows the things that the students must learn, and those things (texts, interpretations, and so on) are simultaneously culturally enriching and culturally neutral; they are apolitical because they provide the basis for politics, but they cannot themselves be the object of political argument. With such a model of politics and education, the teacher's politics (especially as enacted in forms like policies, grading standards, methods of leading class discussion, estimation of the texts) are never up for debate but are simply assumed to be objective or neutral. In addition, because knowledge of things and skills is the apolitical basis of politics, one can assess the effectiveness of education by assessing the extent to which students have inculcated those culturally neutral/enriching things and skills. Hence, this view of education is closely tied to the endorsement of standardized testing.

While this approach is not advocated in composition journals, it is certainly present in composition classrooms. Lindemann associates it with the "product-centered" approach to teaching composition:

> The teacher in this course assumes the role of an expert, a literary critic imparting knowledge about texts, ways of reading them, and principles governing their form and style. She uses primarily lecture and discussion to convey these subjects. She may give tests and pop quizzes (other products) to insure that students have learned the material. ("Three Views of English 101" 7)

Paolo Freire famously called this approach "the banking method," describing the teacher as someone who knows things that are deposited into the students brains during the course in the form of lecture and readings and then withdrawn at the end in the form of exams and papers. Generally called "objectivist" or "presentational," this approach to the teaching of writing is an easy opponent to set up and knock down because there is a substantial body of research indicating that it does not actually improve student writing (Hillocks, *Research* 113–28, 223–24; see also *Ways of Thinking*). Hillocks has argued that this approach to teaching writing comes from assumptions about students' abilities (or lack thereof) and is persistent because it is self-fulfilling *(Ways of Thinking);* when lecturing does not work especially well, the instructors who are drawn to it dumb down their material and lecture even more. Rather than consider that the objectivist and presentational approach might be the culprit, such instructors blame the students and engage in even more objectivist and presentational pedagogies.

I would suggest that it is so pervasive because it effectively enacts the assumptions about self and knowledge implicit in the traditional-universalist model of the liberal public sphere—that engaging in public discourse means adopting the ethos of an autonomous, impartial, and enculturated person who can present his thesis clearly and support it rationally. One can easily imagine how this approach to teaching could be associated with the assignment that I earlier described as typifying one of the more common ways of teaching argument.[8] As Wells, Lindemann, Ohmann, Hillocks, and other critics of this approach to writing have argued, the "topic" of the paper can be unspecified because the content ultimately does not much matter. In addition, as argued above, an unspecified topic is likely to look more "free" to someone who shares the liberal tendency to worry more about Isaiah Berlin's "freedom from" rather than his "freedom to." Nor does it much matter which opposition argument the student selects or what relation the topic of the paper has to anything that has been discussed in class. What matters is the form in which the student presents the topic, such as the correctness (in format and usage), the extent to which the student effectively adopts the traditional-universalist ethos, and the degree to which the implied audience is one the teacher considers universal. While not an expressivist model of writing (in fact, it is generally quite hostile to the personal voice central to expressivism), it does imply an expressivist model of the public sphere; the point of the paper assignments is to permit all students to express (or display) their own arguments in a "correct" form.

The other way of enacting the liberal public sphere is better represented in composition theory, but it can (ironically enough) end up producing the same assignment. Closer to the deontological version of the liberal public sphere, this approach is essentially what Dewey described, and what has recently been advocated by Stephen Fishman and Lucille McCarthy. They describe Fishman's teaching philosophy, explicitly connecting it to Dewey:

> Like Dewey, Fishman's ideology is liberal. In other words, at the core of Fishman's teaching is a respect for the integrity of each student and a commitment to defend that student's right to think for him or herself. In the classroom this means he wants to grant each student as much liberty as is commensurate with granting similar liberties to every one of that student's classmates. He aims to be tolerant about pupils' deeply held beliefs and to profess a neutrality which encourages the critical and constructive skills which he and Dewey hold dear. As a consequence, Fishman tries to intercede in student debate only when he believes someone's liberties and opportunities to make up his or her own mind are being transgressed. ("Teaching for Student Change" 347)

In this version of liberal teaching, teachers take on the role proceduralist or deontological liberalism assigns the government. We are not to make judgments about the beliefs of students (the good), and we certainly do not dictate such issues to them; on all such issues we remain neutral. Instead, we are to concern ourselves with issues of justice (the right), ensuring that all students have equal rights in and equal access to the classroom discourse. The teacher aspires to respect the students as autonomous individuals and to act as an umpire, intervening in the discussion only when one student interferes with the autonomy of another student—the position classically assigned to government in liberal political theory.

Having had teachers who aspired to this kind of role, I can attest to its extraordinary power; in many ways and in many circumstances it is liberating. I still very clearly remember a high school teacher who let us argue about the issues raised by *The Scarlet Letter*—whether Hester should have accepted the punishment given her, whether she should have exposed the minister, and various other questions that were very pressing to students who were contemplating our own moral transgressions, betrayals, and cowardices. I certainly gained much more from that class than I would have had she chosen instead to lecture to us about Hawthorne's use of light and dark imagery, or his relation to Calvinism, or the history of the American novel. I also gained a respect for myself and my own ideas because the teacher was so obviously interested in listening to us, and in letting us think through the questions on our own. Yet, as much as I can appreciate the virtues of this approach, I would not say that such an approach to teaching is exempt from the criticisms of liberal public theory, specifically that the claim of neutrality screens the ways that the authorities actually favor certain positions.

For instance, Fishman and McCarthy describe an Introduction to Philosophy course in which students discuss the issue of free will. The article identifies some answers on the question of free will as more self-reflective, more "sophisticated," "richer, less narrowly grooved" (360), and simply better than others. According to the article, Fishman is "pleased" with one student's change in position (360)—hardly a neutral stance. Fishman's pedagogy favors the fragmented and self-reflective self that Faigley has said typifies the essays in *What Makes Writing Good* (120–30). Thus, Fishman's students are in the situation described by Faigley, in which the apparent freedom of the course "hides the fact that these same students will be judged by the teachers' unstated assumptions about subjectivity and that every act of writing they perform occurs within complex relations of power" (128).

That Fishman has a privileged subject position is not inherently wrong; but it does belie his claims of neutrality, and that means that his claim to respect his students' autonomy is suspect. Fishman and McCarthy clearly perceive moving away from absolutist positions as a good thing, especially absolutism regarding individual free will—they are not neutral on that issue. In fact, they express condescension (if not contempt) for some of the "deeply held beliefs" of the students (as when they refer to one's student's beliefs being "built around the Horatio Alger narrative"). A certain kind of soft determinism is assumed to be a more "sophisticated" position than individualism; in consequence, religious students operate at a disadvantage in the class discourse and are pressured to accept Fishman's views.

There are two ways to read Fishman's narrative of student change. One—not noted in the article, but a definite possibility—is that the students did not change their opinions at all but correctly inferred the instructor's agenda and began to perform in the ways that would gain them the instructor's approval. The second possibility is that the students really were persuaded by the discourse to move away from the positions for which Fishman has contempt, but there is something odd about seeing that change as necessarily an increase in students' abilities to think critically, or as a move toward positions necessarily more sophisticated. If they adopted Fishman's preferred positions simply out of respect for his authority, for instance, it would seem to be a reduction in autonomy rather than an increase.[9]

That Fishman is far from neutral is not in and of itself a problem, but it does strike me as a problem that Fishman appears not to see the contradiction between the claims of equal respect for all positions and the actual favoring of certain kinds of stances. This is exactly the criticism made of deontological liberalism—that its apparent neutrality on questions of the good in fact privileges certain philosophies, and that deeply held spiritual beliefs are disadvantaged in liberal public discourse. Yet, due to the claims of neutrality, the very issue of disadvantage is distributed out of public discourse itself, and one position is inappropriately generalized to stand for Reason altogether.

I want to emphasize that such criticisms of liberal political theory apply to specific practices—whether philosophical, political, or pedagogical—to varying degrees. While Rousseau and Rawls are both in the liberal tradition, for instance, their theories are not identical. The more that the metaphor of autonomy is literalized, the larger the number of beliefs designated self-evident, the narrower the notion of logic, the more that reason is assumed to be scientific-materialist-empiricist, the more that the notion of "universal" is a prescriptive or proscriptive hiding as a descriptive, the more that the underlying epistemology posits an objective knower, then the less capable the model is of theorizing a public sphere where people with genuinely different points of view can argue with one another. One can make the same point about pedagogies that enact the liberal theory of the public sphere; the more that they engage in the practices above, and especially the more that they do so unselfconsciously, the more problematic they are as preparation for a world where difference is a fact.

3

CLOSING MY EYES AS YOU SPEAK

> This privateness and primary concern with money-making
> had developed a set of behavior patterns which are expressed
> in all those proverbs—"nothing succeeds like success,"
> "might is right," "right is expediency," etc.—that necessarily
> spring from the experience of a society of competitors.
> —Hannah Arendt, *The Origins of Totalitarianism*

One dilemma in liberal political theory is that the government is to remain neutral in regard to values (the good), yet any particular policy necessarily represents the triumph of some set of values. The Hetch Hetchy Valley is preserved in a wilderness state (a preservationist value) or dammed and flooded (an instrumentalist value); policies cannot be neutral. Two common responses to this paradox are to look for a mechanism that is itself neutral (such as a hypothetical prepolitical moment, cost-benefit analysis, and so on) or to abandon the goal of neutrality. The interest-based model of the public sphere represents the hope that government can simply duck the dilemma by letting people fight it out among themselves.

By interest-based model, I mean the model that assumes that individuals can and should pursue their own self-interest; the public sphere is the marketplace of ideas, where proponents of ideas compete with one another for consumers just as producers of commodities compete for consumers (see Young, "Communication and the Other"). Just as commodity producers are assumed to be motivated by self-interest (hoping to profit by selling a product), which they may mask through essentially disingenuous claims (by, for instance, claiming the consumers will benefit by the product), so policy producers are assumed to be genuinely motivated by self-interest (for instance, hoping to increase or solidify their own power), which they may disguise in claims of altruistic motives or appeals to community benefit. As a seatmate on an airplane once told me, everyone is selling something, but some people are more honest about it than others (a conversation that marks the last time I made eye contact on an airplane).

This neo-Hobbesian view assumes that self-interest is not only inevitable, but potentially beneficial, in that the policies that result will necessarily represent the interest of the majority. That is, just as the fact that a particular model of mousetrap has succeeded in economic competition is taken as proof that it is a better mousetrap *and* that it is the one most people want (the second being, essentially, the definition of the former), so the successful competition of a particular interest group, political party, or political ideology is taken to mean that this group best represents the preferences of the people. The implicit theory of rhetoric is what Thomas Conley defines as "motivistic" (45). The assumption is that rhetoric is a battle, principle is a lie, all discourse is enclave-based, persuasion is fundamentally irrational (essentially a kind of stimulus and response), and the function of the public sphere is to provide a place where people can express their interests—the interests then fight it out. Rhetoric is always asymmetric manipulation of the audience.

The interest-based model is tremendously common in popular culture, as indicated by the prevalence of the war metaphor for argument, the popularity of books like *How to Win Every Argument,* and my own difficulty getting some students to imagine that a scorched-earth policy might not be the most effective rhetorical strategy. In rhetoric and composition, one does not see much in the way of books or journal articles arguing for it (except, arguably, Stanley Fish's "Change," "Critical Self-Consciousness," and "No Bias, No Merit" in *Doing What Comes Naturally*), but it is certainly common in practice. One sees this assumption in pedagogies that describe the major responsibility of a rhetor as making his/her policies the most attractive, and using rhetoric that is conciliatory and pleasing. Lisa Ede and Andrea Lunsford long ago pointed out that this pandering approach to discourse tends to result from focusing on the real audience, and, indeed, there is a connection between it and the rhetorical advice that writers should imagine their audiences (or analyze a piece of discourse) primarily in terms of the audience's socioeconomic interests—the implication being that such interests are the cause of political ideas. At first glance, this theory of public discourse seems to make rhetoric tremendously powerful—as in *Encomium on Helen,* in which it is likened to rape or an irresistible drug—but I will suggest that it is actually a distinctly odd view for teachers of persuasion to espouse. It is also a fundamentally circular model in two significant ways. First, it asserts that all claims of motives other than self-interest are false; thus, one cannot try to disprove the model itself by showing that people have other motives. Second, it is self-fulfilling, in that it assumes that people cannot be persuaded at the same time that it promotes a model of discourse that cannot persuade an intelligent and informed opposition. The failure of this kind of rhetoric is not taken to indicate something might be wrong with the rhetoric, but as evidence of the fundamental futility of discourse.

The central assumption behind the interest-based model of democracy (also sometimes called the pluralist or adversary model)[1] is that the political process is most accurately seen as "a struggle for power among competing interests rather than as a search for the common good" (Bohman and Rehg xi). It assumes that political action is best explained as a case of "rival sovereignties fighting it out" (Dahl, *Who Governs* 184; see also 188). Similarly, Anthony Downs asserts that members of a political party

> are motivated by their personal desire for the income, prestige, and power which come from holding office. Thus, carrying out their social function is to them a means of achieving their private ambitions. . . . Since none of the appurtenances of office can be obtained without being elected, the main goal of every party is the winning of elections. Thus all its actions are aimed at maximizing votes, and it treats policies merely as means towards this end. (34–35)

An identical argument is made by Joseph Schumpeter, who similarly asserts that principles occur *after* and *because* a group has decided to gain power:

> For all parties will of course, at any given time, provide themselves with a stock of principles or planks and these principles or planks may be as characteristic of the party that adopts them and as important for its success as the brands of goods a department store sells are characteristic of it and important for its success. But the department store cannot be defined in terms of its brands and a party cannot be defined in terms of its principles. A party is a group whose members propose to act in concert in the competitive struggle for political power. (283)

All assert that the particular policies that people (or some group of people) advocate are not sincerely held on principled grounds but are the result of some deeper psychological, pathological, or economic motive. What people say in public—the principles they claim to have—are shaped after and because of those motives. The logical consequence of this view of the futility of discourse is that the public sphere is not and cannot be a realm of argument but is one of bargaining.

While the model no longer has many strong proponents among political theorists, it remains in the popular imagination and parlance as the public sphere being "the marketplace of ideas," a metaphor literalized in congressional changes to FCC doctrine, FCC practice (especially regarding the "fairness doctrine"), and Supreme Court rulings on freedom of speech (for more on this point, see Mansbridge, "A Deliberative Theory"). The notion is that people listen to different policies in the same way that they listen to different ads, and they select among them as they select among products; voters are consumers of political agenda. This model seems liberal (and is occasionally assumed to be the liberal model of democracy, as in Francis Fukuyama's famous essay) because it seems to keep the government neutral in regard to ends. As Young says, "In this model, citizens never need to leave their own private and parochial pursuits and recognize their fellows in a public setting to address one another about their collective, as distinct from individual, needs and goals" ("Communication and the Other" 121). The hope is that self-interest has democratic consequences—people who desire to win elections compete for the voters by paying attention to what interests they express; voters will vote for the person whose own expressions of interest match theirs; these public officials will create policies they believe to be in the self-interest of people like them; the resulting policies will match the interests of most people. If politicians do not create policies that match what they promised in order to get elected, they will not get reelected. As with the liberal theory, the government's role is umpire, simply ensuring that the competition is fair. The difference between this and the liberal model (which also tends to valorize the market and insist upon governmental neutrality) is that the interest-based model makes no assumption of rational discourse appealing to universal principles.

Describing the philosophical foundation of the interest-based model is considerably more difficult than describing the foundations of other models. Throughout the history of political theory, there have been theorists who, at least in some places or at some times, can be read as advocating some aspect of the interest-based model (Callicles, several speakers in Thucydides, Machiavelli, Hobbes, Bentham, James Mill, Adam Smith, James Madison, Schumpeter, Dahl), but none consistently articulates a philosophy that bears much resemblance to the adversarial motivism one sees in texts and practices that exemplify interest-based rhetoric. For instance, the theorists who say that self-interest is an appropriate basis for public discourse and policy such as Adam Smith or Jeremy Bentham treat "self-interest" as essentially synonymous with "public interest"— assuming no fundamental conflict between the two. When Bentham asserts that "ethics . . . , in as far as it is the art of directing a man's actions in this respect, may be termed the art of discharging one's duty to one's self" (312), he does not imply any conflict between that and discharging one's duty to one's neighbor. A man will necessarily consider the happiness of his neighbors because "there are no occasions in which a man has not some motives for consulting the happiness of other men" (313). Adam Smith's "enlightened self-interest" is similar: A sensibility grounded in empathy would keep a reasonable man (as Bentham and Smith were talking exclusively about men) from doing anything that would cause serious harm to his neighbors or his community. For such thinkers, public interest *is* self-interest (for more on the changing meaning of "self-interest" see Holmes's "The Secret History of Self-Interest" in *Passions and Constraints*).

Other theorists advocate self-interest as an appropriate basis only under some circumstances. In *Federalist* 10, Madison makes some comments suggesting that people always vote out of self-interest, as when he argues that the causes of faction cannot be removed because

> No man is allowed to be a judge in his own cause, because his interest would certainly bias his judgment, and, not improbably, corrupt his integrity. With equal, nay with greater reason, a body of men are unfit to be both judges and parties at the same time; yet what are many of the most important acts of legislation but so many judicial determinations, not indeed concerning the rights of single persons, but concerning the rights of large bodies of citizens? And what are the different classes of legislators but advocates and parties to the causes which they determine? (79)

Yet elsewhere, even in the same paper, he refers to "enlightened statesmen" who would "be able to adjust these clashing interests and render them all subservient to the common good" (80). Madison's very definition of the term "faction" assumes that there is such a thing as "the permanent and aggregate interests of the community" and that these interests are different from the interests of the members of the faction, even when the faction is a majority. Hence, at least as argued in *Federalist* 10, the interests of the majority and the "permanent and aggregate interests of the community" can be in conflict:

> By a faction I understand a number of citizens, whether amounting to a majority or minority of the whole, who are united and actuated by some common impulse of passion, or of interest, adverse to the rights of other citizens, or to the permanent and aggregate interests of the community. (43)

Indirect election of the Senate and president, lifelong terms for Supreme Court justices, and many other aspects of the Constitution (and Madison's defense of it) rest upon a view of human nature similar to Mill's and Smith's: that certain men have a refined sensibility that enables them to perceive the public interest. In my introduction, I cited Clifford as exemplifying the interest-based model, but this is only partially true. Marxists (like Marx) often equate political interests and class identity, but the very notion of ideology assumes that there is a true common good that some people can recognize (but which ideology distorts). Neither Marx nor Marxism assumes that it is impossible to see beyond false ideology; the prevalence of narrow self-interest is a sign of distorted communication.

This is not to say that the interest-based model is unheard-of in the history of political traditions. It may well be that it does not have a single origin, but the notion that looking out for one's own self (regardless of the cost for one's community) reappears at different moments inspired by popular movements outside of political theory. While there is no evidence that Callicles is based on a real person, one might infer that his point of view was common enough for Plato to take it seriously. Social Darwinism (a tradition one still sees in business magazines and books from time to time) is very likely to justify if not advocate a rapacious attitude toward the common good; that attitude was troubling enough that Dewey pauses at moments in his writings to refute it. And, of course, there are writers who have never been taken seriously within philosophy or political theory who advocate a form of interest-based politics, but who do have followings of nonexperts (such as Ayn Rand or Stanley Fish). The consequence of this slip between practice and theory is that one can find examples of authors who behave as though "the public area exists solely as a form in which self-interest is either won or lost" (Nie et al. 15), but it is difficult to find a well-considered theoretical explication and defense of that view.

The closest is Dahl, with his argument for polyarchy in *A Preface to Democratic Theory.*[2] As Held says, Dahl's "version has had a pervasive influence, although relatively few political and social scientists would accept it in unmodified form today (though many politicians, journalists, and others in the mass media still appear to do so)" (202). Held's parenthetical comment is important: While political theorists have moved away from, significantly modified, or, in some cases at least, never accepted the argument Dahl makes in *Preface,* it is still a culturally powerful model. Held summarizes this view:

> Political outcomes are the result of government and, ultimately, the executive trying to mediate and adjudicate between the competing demands of groups. In this process, the political system or state becomes almost indistinguishable from the ebb and flow of bargaining, the competitive pressure of interests. . . . . Thus, the making of democratic governmental decisions involves the steady trade-off between, and appeasement of, the demands of relatively small groups, although by no means all interests are likely to be satisfied fully. (203)

The main attraction of this theory is that it appears to be scientific, because it is grounded in the science of economics, and realistic, because it is not utopian.

These attractions are, however, problematic. To take the second one first—there is, despite claims to the contrary, a normative agenda:

> The ideals and methods of democracy become, by default, the ideals and methods of the existing democratic systems. Since the critical criterion for adjudicating between theories of democracy is their degree of 'realism,' models which depart from, or are in tension with, current democratic practice can be dismissed as empirically inaccurate, "unreal", and undesirable. (Held 209)

It is no less normative than the liberal tradition, then, but, oddly enough, the normative project is not one that enables people to decry injustice.

The hidden normative ideal is plutocracy. Mansbridge has argued that the interest-based model is democratic only if there is a common interest. That is, if everyone has the same interest, then it makes no difference that some people have more power than others. Her example is two people in a car who both want to go to the same city; because they have the same interest, the fact that the driver has more power than the passenger is irrelevant. If, however, "there is no public interest, it is not easy to make a normative case for interest groups within the framework of a democracy that legitimates decisions by weighing each citizen's preference equally" ("A Deliberative Theory" 34). If the driver and passenger disagree on their destination, then the difference in relative power is a threat to the situation's being democratic. In short, unless one makes some extremely unrealistic assumptions about human nature and behavior (a serious problem for a theory whose major merit is supposed to be its realism) then this is not a model of democracy at all, but of plutocracy.

Certainly, as the work of the pluralists shows, no single interest group is able to enact its agenda unilaterally; conflict and compromise among interest groups affect the final policy outcomes. But there is no reason to think that this conflict and compromise among interest groups genuinely reflect what would happen were the general public more involved, unless one makes two theoretical assumptions. First, one has to abandon the notion of one person/one vote and move toward a model of democracy that assumes that people with stronger preferences should have more votes; second, one has to define "stronger preferences" in a way that makes the whole argument circular (as effect on outcome). Thus, one has to assume that people with stronger interests are people who get involved in interest groups. One thereby begs the question (interest groups represent people with the strongest interests because people with the strongest interests would get involved in interest groups).

It's important to emphasize that this circularity precludes the possibility that the interest-based model is genuinely scientific. After all, a basic criterion for an experimental hypothesis is that it is falsifiable; the circular definitions involved in this model, however, mean that it is not possible to falsify the model itself. It is what logicians call a closed system. My major criticism of this model is that it is neither democratic nor empirical; it is a circular argument for plutocracy.

In *Modern Dogma and the Rhetoric of Assent*, Wayne Booth describes this as "motivism," a view that paralyzes discourse because it assumes that people do not actually have reasons, but motives, for what they do: "conscious thought, deliberation, open talk about why we should or should not seek this or that value is either ignored or reduced to other deeper or truer causes" (29). Booth argues that the tendency toward motivism prevents people who genuinely disagree from finding discursive solutions to their conflicts because, while it greatly simplifies complicated problems, it makes persuasion impossible. This naturally leads to discourse in which people do not listen to one another, and it helps to explain the approach to "debate" that Berubé condemns. Linda Brodkey, for instance, has a powerful description of her own extremely frustrating and mostly unintentional excursion into national politics when her revision of the University of Texas's first-year composition program was taken up by people like George Will as exemplifying all that was wrong with political correctness. To an informed person like Brodkey—someone who would notice Will's confusion between a textbook and a reader, for example—articles like Will's about the University of Texas program were affected by a misunderstanding of what was going on. As Brodkey points out, all indications are that Will never bothered to try to find out what arguments there might have been for the changes; he never tried to listen to his opposition. Nor did he try to persuade them. An informed and intelligent opposition would simply be irritated (or possibly enraged) by Will's articles on the topic, but, of course, Will was not trying to reach such an audience.[3]

The result is enclave politics with a vengeance. There is no real point in having a public sphere of argument if people are simply going to vote with and for their pocketbooks; all that is necessary is a sphere of display, where the different products are clearly placed before the consumers. There is also no real reason to distinguish between discursive and other methods of expressing preferences—voting or speaking in favor of a particular candidate or policy is just an expression of preference in exactly the same way that purchasing a particular product is, then giving money to a political candidate is identical to speech. This is the argument made in *Buckley v. Valeo,* in which the Supreme Court rules against restricting campaign contributions. For the majority of the Court, it is not so much that giving money is a kind of speech as it is that speech is a kind of giving money (see also the Reagan administration arguments for vetoing the "Fairness Doctrine" and George Will on limitations on campaign donations.)

This approach amounts to enclave-based discourse, and it permits (perhaps even encourages) sloppy argument. In *Telling the Truth,* Lynne

Cheney complains about some very shabby treatment she feels she received at the hands of academics. She describes a conference at North Carolina where academics like Stanley Fish demonized her "to shouts and jeers and other noises of encouragement from the audience" (14). Yet what is her own book, but a demonizing of virtually all current movements in academia? Her proposal is, to use her own metaphor, to "take back" academia from academics, and her argument is based on misunderstanding and misrepresenting many of those movements and academics. Her discussion of topics like the problem of universal themes, Martha Nussbaum's arguments concerning patriotism, the use of readings in composition programs, and the "politicization" of literature makes clear that she has not read (or has not understood) the arguments she is attacking.

For instance, Cheney's central claim is that scholars have abandoned the search for and promulgation of truth, something she attributes to "the postmodern approach." She says she wants to "look at the origins of the radical skepticism of our time; examine its claims to legitimacy; and, finally, suggest what we can do to blunt its force and restore truth and reason to a central place in our lives" (21). Yet, in the course of this examination, she employs examples and quotes from people who are not radical skeptics, who—like Martha Nussbaum or Donald Lazere—explicitly and repeatedly condemn radical skepticism in favor of a search for and promulgation of the truth. Their actual stance, as opposed to the views she attributes to them, considerably complicates her claim to be telling the truth.

The situation becomes even more striking when one considers the history of the book. Cheney initially presented the argument in the form of a pamphlet published by the NEH (when she was head of that organization). This pamphlet version included an attack on Donald Lazere that took a quote completely out of context, so that he seemed to be making the opposite argument from what he was really saying. Outraged, the editor of *College English* (where Lazere's article had been published) demanded a retraction. Although Cheney never formally retracted her pamphlet, she did not include that passage in the book version. Yet, in the book, she did the same thing to Nussbaum.

Cheney quotes from Nussbaum's criticism of patriotism, yet she does not mention the larger context for that quote. Nussbaum's argument in *For Love of Country* is that one's loyalty to one's country and any other groups should be subsumed to pursuit of the truth ("Patriotism and Cosmopolitanism"). Nussbaum is a counterexample to Cheney's assertions about what is happening in universities—thus, to include Nussbaum among the postmoderns, let alone to say she is a person who does not care about the truth, is not to tell the truth. One could make similar arguments about the political radicals whom Cheney also abhors; whatever the faults of such movements, they are not grounded in radical skepticism. Either Cheney completely misunderstood their arguments, or she assumed that her readers were so ignorant of Nussbaum and Lazere's actual arguments that they would not recognize her own evasion of truth and reason.

Whether Cheney did not read Nussbaum's essay or was intentionally misrepresenting it, it is very clear that she never perceived herself as writing to Nussbaum—doing so would have necessitated acknowledging the context for the passages she quotes. One might opt for the charitable interpretation that Cheney was unaware of the problems with her version, but that is hardly a defense. Were that true, it would mean that, at best, Cheney engaged in sloppy research, not reading the books she was quoting, not engaging in fact-checking, and not trying to find out the other side of any question. Even that rather limping defense cannot apply to the book because the book version does not have the attack on Lazere or the two stories for which he criticized her pamphlet. Yet, in what is perhaps one of the most breathtakingly disingenuous passages of the whole book, she says,

> The name-calling and invective that my forays brought down on my head struck me as curious. Why didn't my opponents offer counterarguments to what I had to say? Why didn't they try to show where weak evidence had led me to false conclusions or where a lack of knowledge had kept me from seeing the truth? (15)

They did. The book does not acknowledge the pamphlet's inaccuracies, nor that, in contrast to what Cheney is saying, at least some of her opponents did point out weak evidence and ignorance, but neither did pointing out those inaccuracies cause Cheney to change the strategy of misrepresenting academics (for a more detailed analysis, see Lazere "Ground Rules").

At the very least, given her having been publicly exposed as having engaged in very shoddy scholarship, one would expect her to be careful about characterizing leftists as inaccurate. Yet, in a book whose argument depends upon misrepresenting the opposition, she includes passages like, "So little did these assertions have to do with the facts that they seemed an apt illustration of how debased argument can become when one discounts, as so many academic activists do, traditional standards of accuracy and evidence" (61). Either Cheney did not read the people whom she quotes, or she left the contexts out because it would show her argument to be wrong. Either way, she has abandoned traditional standards of accuracy and evidence.

But she could because she had no reason to think that her audience would have read Nussbaum or Lazere, or that they would read any reviews written by people who had. She was remaining within an enclave, speaking to like-minded people, and shaking demonized versions of academics for the purposes of encouraging people to jeer and shout. I am not doubting that Fish did shake her pamphlet and misrepresent her argument, and that his audience shouted and jeered; I am saying that I see no difference between his behavior and hers, and that both are standard behavior in any form of a degraded liberal public sphere, but especially interest-based politics. And that standard behavior does not depend upon or encourage intelligent discussion of differences of opinion.

I am fairly sure I will be misunderstood on this point, and that it will seem to many that my criticism of Cheney is itself guilty of the same faults of which I am accusing her, but such a misunderstanding results from the common tendency to assume that there is agreement or there is disagreement, and that all disagreement is shouting and jeering. Tannen's many legitimate criticisms of "the argument culture," for instance, fail to acknowledge that some hostile arguments may be productive. When she gets to the affirmative part of her argument, however, she points to people who evade conflictual disagreement. Tannen's criticisms of our culture's obsession with adversarial argument are apt and are echoed in other places as well (in composition studies, see the works of Gage Lynch et al.; or Jarratt; in communication studies see Cappella and Jamieson). But Tannen ignores the possible existence, let alone value, of criticism or conflict—even impassioned conflict—that is not a battle in verbal form.

Thus, as Lazere so elegantly argues in "Ground Rules," impassioned argument is not all the same; it can be more or less fair. The distinction is not how nice one is (a point William Rice seems to miss in his reply to Lazere's article), but whether one is ultimately fair to the material one is quoting—does the person make the arguments one claims they make? In the case of Cheney, the answer is no. I am not criticizing Cheney for condemning many modern movements in the academy—even movements with which I am sympathetic—but for doing so in ways that depend upon actively misrepresenting her opposition.

One of the recurrent criticisms of argument (made by colleagues as well as students) is that it is ultimately ineffectual, that one cannot really persuade a committed opposition. I have my doubts as to whether or not that is true, but I am certain that it is true if one engages in enclave-based discourse, exemplified by Cheney's book. Certainly, an informed reader would not be persuaded by Cheney's book, but that is hardly an indictment of rhetoric. One thing that strikes me as fascinating about the American Puritan approach to discourse is that they set out an approach to persuasion that was almost certain to fail. When it did fail, that failure did not cause them to reconsider their model of rhetoric, but to conclude that something was wrong with the audience. I would suggest that teachers of argument can easily make the same self-fulfilling prophecy. The more we teach our students to engage in enclave-based discourse, the more we ensure that they will fail to persuade informed and intelligent people. Unless they learn skills of argument from someone other than us, then, we will have a large group of citizens who cannot argue with people who disagree with them; the fault, then, will not be in our stars.

The argument for interest-based politics assumes that the accumulated best interest of the majority of individuals is the same thing as the best interest for the community. So, for instance, Bentham says, "The community is a fictitious *body,* composed of the individual persons who are considered as constituting as it were its *members.* The interest of the community that is what?—the sum of the interests of the several members who compose it" (3, emphasis in original). But, as critics of this model have pointed out, there are several thought experiments that demonstrate that this is not the case, such as the "tragedy of the commons."[4]

Even the best world of interest-based democracy is not very good. If this model worked perfectly, it would result in a tyranny of the majority—if voters vote for people who seem like them, and those people vote

for policies that benefit their interests, then the best one could hope for
would be a set of policies in the relatively narrow self-interest of the
majority of the people. In such a world, difference is a political and rhetorical liability, and it is difficult to imagine the place that concern for
minority rights and interests might hold in public discourse. In fact, it
is difficult to see the place of any abstract questions or issues of principle.
As Elster puts it,

> If people affected each other only by tripping over each other's feet, or by
> dumping their garbage into one another's backyards, a social choice mecha-
> nism might cope. But the task of politics is not only to eliminate inefficiency,
> but also to create justice—a goal to which the aggregation of prepolitical
> preferences is a quite incongruous means. (Introduction 10–11)

The challenge of politics is to find ways to balance the rights and needs
of people whose interests are different; interest-based democracy cannot
do so.

This model also has troubling consequences in regard to public discourse, as it makes identification the main rhetorical strategy—showing that one is just like the people to whom one is speaking. It is unclear, for example, what place the arguments of political minorities would
have—their only effective rhetorical strategy would be to deemphasize
their minority and disadvantaged status and to emphasize ways they are
like the advantaged majority. While there are important documents in
political history that use identification powerfully (such as "Letter from
Birmingham Jail," in which King emphasizes that his concerns are just
like the clergymen's), there are other arguments for which the strategy
of identification is ineffective. As eloquent as it may seem to us today,
Sojourner Truth's "Ain't I a Woman" did not persuade white men to give
the vote to African American women; they could not identify with her,
nor accept her identification of herself as a woman.

The result of insisting upon identification as the central rhetorical
strategy, as in the interest-based model, is that public discourse tends to
bounce between pandering and voices crying in the wilderness. It is not
simply the disempowered who must conciliate the audience; as Jamieson
has argued in *Eloquence in an Electronic Age,* even the apparently powerful engage in pandering and avoiding conflict at all cost. Under these
circumstances, a community can not have principled argument. That is,
arguments asserting that one should follow a particular policy because

it is right are marginalized while arguments that a particular policy will benefit the already advantaged majority become central. Thus, one gets white suffragists arguing that they should be given the vote to counteract the consequences of the Fourteenth Amendment, or liberals arguing that welfare and Social Security are necessary to preserve social order, or people concerned with foreign policy arguing that Americans need to pay more attention to it in order to reduce anti-American terrorism, or John Muir arguing that the Mokelumne River is a cheaper source of water.

As Held, Mansbridge ("The Rise and Fall"), and Elster ("The Market and the Forum") say, one of the attractions of this model was that it seemed more "hard-nosed" and thus more realistic, so it is ironic that empirical research suggests that it is not in fact an accurate description of how people behave. Mansbridge's "The Rise and Fall of Self-Interest in the Explanation of Political Life" summarizes the research that, by the 1980s, caused researchers in the study of social movements to conclude that "the evidence for the importance of non-self-interested motivation had become incontrovertible" (14). Mansbridge notes that,

> In departments of psychology, management, and economics, hundreds of recent experiments with prisoners' dilemma and other games that reward self-interested behavior at the expense of the group indicate a stubborn refusal on the part of a significant fraction (usually 25 percent to 35 percent) to take rational self-interested action, even under conditions of complete anonymity with no possibility of group punishment. ("Rise and Fall" 17)

This is not to say that self-interest is irrelevant in political decisions, but that it is only one of many possible motivations, and that it is sometimes one of the least important. Studies indicate that people are also motivated by a desire to make good public policy (William Muir), self-definition, such as thinking of themselves as liberal (Sears and Funk), a sense of what is in the best interest of the general public (Jamieson, *Everything*). Cappella and Jamieson cite the considerable research that contradicts the cynical readings of politicians' behavior once elected and instead indicates that politicians are strongly motivated by a desire to fulfill campaign promises. Benjamin I. Page and Robert Y. Shapiro's meta-analysis of fifty years of public opinion polls concludes that

> public opinion as a *collective* phenomenon is nonetheless stable (though not immovable), meaningful, and indeed rational in a higher, if somewhat looser sense: it is able to make distinctions; it is organized in coherent patterns; it

is reasonable, based on the best available information; and it is adaptive to new information or changed circumstances, responding in similar ways to similar stimuli. (14, emphasis in original)[5]

Not only is the interest-based model circular (and hence not empirical) and inaccurate, it is harmful. In *Spiral of Cynicism,* Cappella and Jamieson argue that media coverage of political events is dominated by a "strategy" frame: Everything that politicians do is narrated as part of a series of strategic maneuvers on the part of cynical politicians who are simply trying to get themselves elected. Such coverage replaces discussing politics in terms of policies, governance, or issues. For instance, their research on major media coverage of the health care reform debate indicates that "67 percent of newspaper articles were primarily strategic while 25 percent were basically issue oriented or factual; 67 percent of broadcast segments were strategic, and 20 percent issue based" (34). As is suggested by the title of their book, Cappella and Jamieson see this kind of coverage as part of a spiral wherein cynical coverage leads to a cynical public who will not pay attention to questions of governance and policy; thus, public figures will not pay attention to such questions, so the media does not. Cappella and Jamieson conclude: "As our studies suggest, the price for these reinforcing beliefs is ultimately paid in public disengagement both from the political process and from the press" (239). Adopting the cynical point of view about politics and politicians fills the public sphere with speculations about motive, thereby pushing to the fringes any discussion of the merits of particular policies. As Jamieson argues in *Everything You Think You Know about Politics,* the question of governance—what kinds of policies the candidate will pursue, and whether s/he will be able to enact them—drops away while we spend our time and energy wondering about whether or not someone can get elected.

Interest-based argument is what Diego Gambetta calls the culture of "Claro!" or discursive machismo. Gambetta uses Albert Hirschmann's description of the attitude that values "having *strong opinions* on virtually *everything* from the *outset,* and on *winning an argument* rather than on listening and finding that something can occasionally be learnt from others" (qtd. 20, emphasis in original). Strong expressions of belief do not necessarily preclude good discussion; they do in a "Claro!"

culture because the opinion "is packaged in such a way as to silence the audience rather than to invite further argument" (29). Also, opinions are strong in the sense that they are presented as definitive—expression of doubt is a kind of weakness, as is any hesitation. That is, pausing to consider one's answer is not a sign of thoughtfulness, but of an emasculating uncertainty; hence, the kind of skepticism or "intellectual diffidence" central to agonistic rhetoric is precluded. Gambetta suggests that the "Claro!" attitude results from what he calls an "indexical" theory of knowledge—in which "knowledge is assumed to be *holistic:* knowledge or ignorance about x is taken as a sign of knowledge or ignorance of the whole. It reveals more than a local failure; it stands for lack of *Kultur*" (25, emphasis in original). For instance, in a culture that assumes that the correct answers on philosophical or moral questions are obvious to anyone of moderate intelligence who has given the issue any thought, then one cannot admit to error without admitting that one is stupid or thoughtless. Discursive machismo forbids the possibility of informed error; if correct answers are obvious and two people disagree, then not only must one of them be wrong, but *obviously* wrong.

Gambetta outlines four possible responses interlocutors have in a "Claro!" dialogue after someone has made a strong assertion. First, a person can agree. But doing so not only amounts to declaring the other person the winner of that game, it means admitting "a more general kind of inferiority not limited to the issues in question" (30); one has declared oneself not simply ignorant on this matter, but an ignorant sort of person. Second, one can agree, but simultaneously trivialize the assertion in such a way that one has not admitted ignorance. This option is the origin of Gambetta's use of the term "Claro!" as it is Spanish for "Obvious!" or "I knew it all along!" This response is not an admission of ignorance or loss because, as Gambetta says, "if anything, the 'Claro!' response gives a slight edge to the counterclaimant, for not only did he know it all along, but he also did not waste other people's time voicing such triviality" (31). The third option is to make an equally strong counterassertion. This option means that the discussion will consist of strongly (and probably loudly) asserted claims and counterclaims until the exchange is broken off or escalates into violence. A fourth option is to be silent: "By keeping silent, one avoids creating an opportunity for a dispute that one may end up losing" (29).

Gambetta's account is extremely useful because it emphasizes that discursive machismo results from and reinforces the sense that one's very self is on the line in a disagreement. Admitting a mistake, being persuaded, asking for clarification, taking time to think, qualifying one's claims, or agreeing with someone else are all ways of admitting to being a bad person. In addition, disagreeing with someone is necessarily an insult, as one is accusing that person of being stupid or immoral or both. In such discourse, all interactions are hopelessly and unproductively personalized.

Experts in conflict resolution always insist that the first step in discursive resolution is to depersonalize the conflict—to disagree with and discuss the ideas of the person, to separate the person from the ideas, and to hear disagreement or criticism not as an attack on one's self (there is a distinction to be pursued later between depersonalized discourse and impersonal discourse). Fisher and Fisher's *Getting to Yes,* one of the fundamental books in productive negotiation strategies, insists that people must work with another's ideas and not one another's identities (see especially 17–39). According to Fisher and Fisher, if people equate ideas and identities, they then spend their time attacking and defending people—a formula for fights rather than discussions: "Each side tends to become defensive and reactive and to ignore the other side's legitimate interests altogether" (37). In such a fight, any criticism is an attack that must be rebuffed rather than a point to be considered.[6] Obviously, discursive machismo makes just such a distinction impossible; for that reason, it precludes the possibility of discursive conflict resolution. There are pedagogical consequences of any model of discourse that equates self and arguments that are important: The extent to which we encourage students to perceive their very self on the line (that is, to see criticisms as always necessarily personal attacks) is the extent to which we teach them attitudes that will preclude their being able to resolve conflict discursively.

Distinguishing between self and argument is particularly important when dealing with women students, or students from cultures in which argument is discouraged. In "Feminist Responses to Rogerian Argument," Phyllis Lassner speaks of the difficulty that some of her women students had with the Rogerian approach. Asked to identify with and understand the opposition's point of view, her students felt that they were thereby denying the reality of their own experiences. The most difficult hindrance, according to Lassner, is the recommendation that dialogic discourse involves recognizing the feelings of others and potentially changing one's own; for several of Lassner's students, this turned into the fairly threatening prescription that "they must change their way of thinking in order to be part of the majority culture" and that such a method "would simply mean that women will repress their authentic feeling and comply with values and expectations of what others wish them to be, not with what they feel themselves to be" (227). They felt, she says, that they were being put back into precisely the situation they had spent a lot of time escaping—having to pass as members of the dominant culture. That is, they felt that their identity was the object of persuasion. Someone who cannot agree *with* an atheist or a Christian might be able to agree *that* personal freedom is precious. Finding common ground is no longer a question of conceding points or changing oneself, but of determining particular arguments on which the author and opposition audience can agree.

Kenneth Bruffee has remarked on the essentially adversarial model of the reader-writer relationship in the American tradition of writing instruction: "The tradition sees the writer as an individual who prepares a product designed to have a specific effect on another individual. That person in turn is obliged to read defensively, with conscious awareness of the writer's design" ("Writing and Reading" 566). Bruffee has famously argued that this model is false, that all knowledge is collaborative knowledge. Group work, by causing students to learn (and to see themselves learn) through talking with other people appropriately highlights the fundamentally social nature of coming to an interpretation. By making groups irenic, however, we inhibit the possibility that they might achieve Bruffee's goal. But making groups potential sites of conflict makes many instructors nervous. Almost anyone who has taught argumentation can describe class discussions that quickly degenerated into fights, or classes in which students simply refused to articulate their places of disagreement because they were afraid of a fight developing, classes that, in effect, degenerated into the yelling or silence described by Gambetta. The problem is that getting the kinds of insights into one's opposition that effective persuasion necessitates requires that students argue with each other; and encouraging students to argue with each other can lead to classes that are unpleasant for everyone. But classroom fights are not the inevitable result of disagreement, not even when the points of disagreement are on emotional topics. It may seem that fights result from student disagreements, but the difficulty with getting classroom conflict to be productive results from problems with our dominant models of audience, not with anything inherent to argument. If our students cannot experience disagreement as anything other than interpersonal and discursive coercion, it may be because that is what we tell them it must be. In general, the more that we encourage students to think of identity, interest, and argument as interchangeable, the more we reinforce the interest-based model of the public sphere, and the less we make the public sphere (or our own classroom discourse) a place of argument, and the less we enable our students to resolve conflict discursively with people with whom they deeply disagree.

If we really accept the notion that all politics is interest-based, then we have to accept the interest-based politics assumption that genuine persuasion is impossible, and that's an odd assumption for teachers of writing to make. If opinions are the result of identity, then one cannot really set out to change someone else's opinions; persuasion is outside of discourse. There are only two things that one can do discursively: First, one might be able to make minor changes in perception, such as correcting false identifications of self-interest; second, one could change the audience's perception of one's self. That is, I cannot persuade you to think that urban wilderness habitat is valuable—your belief on that matter will be a result of your identity—but I can persuade you that I think it is valuable, that you and I share that identity. In Aristotelian terms, ethos becomes the central mode of persuasion, so that concerns regarding presentation and style become paramount.

We then have what amounts to a kind of expressivist argumentation, in which the purpose of engaging in argument is to express one's opinions in ways that seem authentic representations of one's self. Our classrooms and writing situations are exclusively enclaves, preparing students to engage in an expressivist public sphere. If research were involved, it would be research to support one's own position, and perhaps even to refine it, but never to reconsider it completely. The result, thus, is most likely to be an assignment that would tell students to pick a political topic, take a stand, summarize and reject an opposition argument, and possibly even cite sources. The interest-based model of the public sphere, like the liberal model, leads one to precisely the kind of writing assignment that is extremely common in first-year writing courses, and which is also one many instructors loathe.

But this is really only an incoherently partial adoption of the interest-based model, and this partial adoption leads to an internal contradiction in regard to instructors' evaluating student work. Textbooks may make the assumption that identity and beliefs are necessarily connected when it comes to teaching audience, but instructors do not make that assumption when it comes to grading. If one is going to grade on how effective the argument is, then one would have to be part of the audience—one would have to have the same viewpoints as the audience the student is trying to reach. Or one would have to grade entirely on formal considerations, such as the number of sources, use of transitional sentences, and so on. One might try to grade on the extent to which the argument looks like other arguments people have found effective—how colorful the language is, for instance, or how vivid the examples. But there is an odd self-consumption of the whole argument going on once one raises the question of grading—any of these grading standards is a kind of muddled acceptance of some of the premises of interest-based democracy.

It's muddled because if, in fact, people's opinions are the result of their identity, especially the result of their profession, then instructors' opinions are themselves the results of being teachers of English. If we are really going to teach students to thrive in interest-based democratic discourse, then we can best do so by teaching them how to smoke out the opinions of the teacher and kow-tow to them without appearing to do so. In essence, we should encourage students to take an extremely cynical stance toward their instructors, and we should explicitly grade them on the extent to which the students defer to us. I think most of us would rather shovel roadkill.

While one rarely sees a composition pedagogy that is a fully blown interest-based public sphere, one does see moments of it in regard to arrangement, tone, and topic. Many instructors (and textbooks) encourage approaches admittedly unpersuasive to an intelligent and informed opposition—a troubling number of textbooks actively discourage students from even trying to include such an audience in their thinking. Instead, one is supposed to appeal to some kind of hypothetical (and, I might add, generally nonexistent) neutral audience.

Students are often encouraged to consider the opposition at a later stage in the writing process. One invents one's argument through collaborative (not conflictual) group work, or one does research with the intention of supporting one's own views, or the very assignment asks that students begin with a topic about which they already feel settled. Then a consideration of the opposition becomes a kind of ornament, prolepsis as a figure of speech rather than figure of thought.

A more subtle intrusion of interest-based democracy involves the tendency textbooks have to recommend that students imagine their audience in socio-economic terms rather than in terms of beliefs—thus implying that beliefs are reducible to economic interest. Even advice concerning how to evaluate sources can reflect an unconscious and unconsidered adoption of the interest-based model. Kathleen McCormick, for example, in her otherwise breathtakingly intelligent suggestions for teaching research papers, says that we should have students evaluate the credibility of sources by asking "such questions as Who holds this position? Who benefits from it?" (49). The second question assumes some connection between the source's credibility and interest—an assumption that may seem commonsensical but is surprisingly problematic.

In addition to the fact that some people may be deeply interested and still putting forward strong arguments (a point made by Bentham long ago), this critique tends to assume that beliefs result from interest. So when Clifford lists the interests that keep people from being persuaded by cool reason, he includes Jesse Helms's stand on abortion and a professor's stand on tenure. While I am certainly no fan of Jesse Helms, it's quite clear to me that he is sincere, and that his interests (which one might loosely define as taking the policy stand on various topics that will preserve his situation as a conservative senator) are not the cause of his political policies, but the result of them.

Instructors also often reward writing strategies that would alienate an intelligent opposition—praising students for adopting an aggressive voice, requiring that introductions have a strong statement of thesis (rather than partition), advising that the paper structure be a list of reasons. And the pieces of writing students are presented as forms to emulate are themselves often instances of aggressive alienation of an opposition.

There is a more complicated way that a very common pedagogical practice reinforces the interest-based model. The interest-based model assumes that the truth or accuracy of statements is not particularly important, only the extent to which an argument is effective—the degree to which the audience will think the assertions are true. So, for instance,

Cheney did not imagine herself writing to Nussbaum or to anyone else informed enough to have caught her errors, but to an audience who would believe the inaccurate characterizations of various authors because they were like other assertions being made at the same time about "political correctness" and university campuses. So those assertions would look reasonable to a "general" audience. Similarly, instructors often put themselves in the position of being a reader who does not know enough about the topic at hand to catch errors—we take the role of the "general" audience who can only evaluate an argument on the degree to which it fits other assertions we may have heard—the extent to which it seems reasonable to an uninformed person. We thereby (almost certainly unintentionally) reinforce the interest-based model's description of public discourse as a means of sophistry and coercion.

We have an essentially expressivist approach to argumentation, although it may or may not have any emphasis on authenticity. Just as the interest-based public sphere is not a place of inquiry, but a place where people stand up and speak their piece (a piece that may or may not be related to what anyone else has said), so an interest-based public sphere classroom would have students' papers speaking their pieces on topics that may or may not be related to one another's—a teacher might have one paper on gun control, and another on sexual harassment, and another on hate speech codes, and so on. One has Arendt's situation of students trapped in the singularity of their own experiences.

The paradox is that this view of rhetoric seems to make it powerful but in fact makes it as ephemeral as a passing intoxication. Discourse might be useful for getting people to vote for one, or to support one's policies, but it cannot really change them. It is simply an expression of economic interest, an assertion of power, and neither more nor less effective than other assertions of power. As I said earlier, this semideterminist view of discourse does not even have the virtue of accuracy, except insofar as it is a self-fulfilling prophecy. Certainly, if we teach our students that discourse is force, and that the public sphere is an arena for smash and grab tactics, then we will have a public sphere dominated by discursive violence.

In *The Structural Transformation of the Public Sphere,* Habermas narrates the degradation from the liberal model to the interest-based model.

While this view is often accepted, there is something tremendously wrong with it; it ignores the actual condition of the Enlightenment "public:"

> The state did not deal in abstractions such as social justice, equality, or fraternity, though it was to protect positive legal rights. Indeed, the central offices of government were themselves cockpits of factional private interests. (Porter 269–70)

As Porter says, "The Georgian state was thus personal, venal, and nepotistic in its administration" (134). *Structural Transformation* has been criticized for an implicitly hegemonic conception of "public," and the notion of "counterpublics" posited as a correction (for more on that topic, see Asen and Brouwer). Yet the "public" Habermas describes—the discursive world of salons, coffeehouses, and journals—was itself a counterpublic, a reaction against the naked self-interest of eighteenth-century politics. The interest-based model is not a degradation of the liberal model; the liberal model was theorized as a corrective to the prevalence of the interest-based model.

Following C. B. MacPherson, many critics have argued that the interest-based model is simply the natural extension of the possessive individualism inherent in liberal theory. But that history also fails to explain how the same theory—as argued by Callicles or Cleon, for instance—could predate the eighteenth century. Another possibility, however, is that the interest-based model is connected to the agonistic tradition in rhetoric, a rich and currently neglected strain that I cannot discuss adequately here. This genealogy would explain how that approach could predate and coexist with liberalism.

It also helps explain a certain hostility to passionate argument. Because the rhetoric of this venal, nepotistic, and self-serving politics was passionate, there is a tendency (evident in many liberal theorists) to assume that a less self-serving political system would generate a less passionate rhetoric, and vice versa. And because the interest-based model of politics ensures that people trying to call attention to injustices are marginalized if not silenced, and the attendant rhetoric is confrontational and aggressive, there is a tendency to assume that confrontational and aggressive rhetoric operates against the oppressed. Thus, when people throw out the baby of argument, it may be the bathwater of the interest-based public sphere they are trying to empty. Advocates of agonism, Arendt in particular, insist that a confrontational method of public discourse may be the best way to prevent tyranny and totalitarianism, to ensure that injustices are discussed.

Arendt is probably most famous for her analysis of totalitarianism (*The Origins of Totalitarianism, Eichmann in Jerusalem*), but political theorists have recently begun to pay attention to her criticism of mass culture (*The Human Condition*). Arendt's main criticism of the current human condition is that the common world of deliberate and joint action is fragmented into solipsistic and unreflective behavior. In an especially lovely passage, she says that in mass society people

> are all imprisoned in the subjectivity of their own singular experience, which does not cease to be singular if the same experience is multiplied innumerable times. The end of the common world has come when it is seen only under one aspect and is permitted to present itself in only one perspective. (*Human Condition* 53)

Isolation and individualism are not synonymous insofar as individuality depends upon a collective against (or with) whom one argues in order to direct collective agency. Isolation means refusing to participate in or direct that common world and thus often means that one refuses to take responsibility for it. Self-obsession, even (especially?) when coupled with isolation from one's community is far from apolitical—it has political consequences; perhaps a better way to put it is that it is political precisely because it aspires to be apolitical. This fragmented world where many people live simultaneously and even similarly but not exactly together is what Arendt calls the "social"; it is the realm of interest-based behavior.

Arendt argues that the classical world was divided into private (family) and public (one's participation in the polis). With the rise of bureaucracy came the rise of the social, which was not private (it is visible to others), but neither is it public. The public world is the realm of the *vita activa,* a place of play, competition, argument, and responsibility. The last concept is most difficult but is best expressed in Gerald Dworkin's fifth kind of autonomy: "A person is morally autonomous if and only if he bears the responsibility for the moral theory he accepts and the principles he applies" (35). In the social, on the contrary, one is freed from taking responsibility for anything one does. This ability to evade responsibility is, Arendt argues, both banal and evil at the same time. It enables perfectly banal people, with no especially vicious intentions, to engage in genocide. Arendt said that this was brought home to her when she observed the trial of Adolf Eichmann. Having been taught that evil results from arrogance, envy, hatred, or covetousness, she expected to see some monster who would exemplify such vices.

> However, what I was confronted with was utterly different and still undeniably factual. I was struck by a manifest shallowness in the doer that made it impossible to trace the uncontestable evil of his deeds to any deeper level of roots or motives. The deeds were monstrous, but the doer—at least the very effective one now on trial—was quite ordinary, commonplace, and neither demonic nor monstrous. There was no sign in him of firm ideological convictions or of specific evil motives, and the only notable characteristic one could detect in his past behavior as well as in his behavior during the trial and throughout the pre-trial police examination was something entirely negative: it was not stupidity but *thoughtlessness*. (*Life of the Mind* 4, emphasis in the original)

He was able to engage in mass murder because (1) he was able not to think about it, especially not from the perspective of the victims, and (2) he was able to exempt himself from personal responsibility by telling himself (and anyone else who would listen) that he was just following orders. It was the bureaucratic system that enabled him to do both. He was not exactly passive; he was, on the contrary, very aggressive in trying to do his duty. He behaved with the "ruthless, competitive exploitation" and "inauthentic, self-disparaging conformism" that characterizes those who people totalitarian systems (Pitkin 87).

Arendt grants that there are people who willed the Holocaust but insists that totalitarian systems result not so much from the Hitlers or Stalins as from the bureaucrats who may or may not agree with the established ideology, but who enforce the rules for no stronger motive than a desire to avoid trouble with their superiors (see especially *Eichmann in Jerusalem* and *Life of the Mind*). They do not think about what they do. One might prevent such occurrences, or, at least, resist the modern tendency toward totalitarianism, by thought: "critical thought is in principle anti-authoritarian" (*Lectures on Kant's Philosophy* 38).

By "thought," Arendt does not mean eremitic contemplation; in fact, she had great contempt for what she called "professional thinkers," refusing to become a philosopher or call her work philosophy. Young-Bruehl, Benhabib, and Pitkin have each said that Heidegger represented just such a professional thinker for Arendt, and his embrace of Nazism epitomized the genuine dangers such "thinking" can pose (see "Heidegger the Fox"). "Thinking" is not typified by the isolated contemplation of philosophers; it requires the arguments of others *and* a close attention to the truth. It is easy to overstate either part of that harmony. One must consider carefully the arguments and viewpoints of others:

> Political thought is representative. I form an opinion by considering a given issue from different viewpoints, by making present to my mind the standpoint of those who are absent; that is, I represent them. This process of representation does not blindly adopt the actual views of those who stand somewhere else, and hence look upon the world from a different perspective; this is a question neither of empathy, as though I tried to be or to feel like somebody else, nor of counting noses and joining a majority but of being and thinking in my own identity where actually I am not. The more people's standpoints I have present in my mind while I am pondering a given issue, and the better I can imagine how I would think and feel if I were in their place, the stronger will be my capacity for representative thinking and the more valid my final conclusions, my opinion. ("Truth and Politics" 241)

[handwritten marginalia: believing against imaginative play]

There are three points to emphasize in this wonderful passage. First, one does not get these standpoints in one's mind through imagining them, but through listening to them; thus, good thinking requires that one *hear* the arguments of other people. "Hence," as Arendt says, "critical thinking, while still a solitary business, does not cut itself off from 'all others'" (*Lectures on Kant's Philosophy* 43). Thinking is, in this view, necessarily public discourse; "critical thinking is possible only where the standpoint of all others are open to inspection" (*Lectures on Kant's Philosophy* 43). It is rhetoric, and rhetoric is potentially an antitotalitarian force.

Second, agonism presumes that speech *matters*. It is not asymmetric manipulation of others, nor merely an economic exchange, but must be a world one enters and by which one might be changed. For that reason, to engage in argument, she says, is risky. That is significantly different from motivism, which assumes that neither people nor their ideas can really change through argument.

Third, passages like the above make some readers think that Arendt puts too much faith in discourse and too little in truth (see Habermas's critique in *Philosophical-Political Profiles*). But Arendt is no crude relativist; she believes in truth, and she believes that there are facts that can be more or less distorted. She does not believe that reality is constructed by discourse, or that truth is indistinguishable from falsehood. She insists that the truth has a different pull on us, and, consequently, a difficult place in the world of the political, so truth matters. Facts are different from falsehood because, while they can be distorted or denied, especially when they are inconvenient for the powerful, they also have a certain positive force, which falsehood lacks:

> Truth, though powerless and always defeated in a head-on clash with the powers that be, possesses a strength of its own: whatever those in power may contrive, they are unable to discover or invent a viable substitute for it. Persuasion and violence can destroy truth, but they cannot replace it. ("Truth and Politics" 259)

Facts have a strangely resilient quality partially because a lie "tears, as it were, a hole in the fabric of factuality. As every historian knows, one can spot a lie by noticing incongruities, holes, or the junctures of patched-up places" ("Truth and Politics" 253). While she is sometimes discouraging about our ability to see the tears in the fabric, citing the capacity of totalitarian governments to create the whole cloth (see "Truth and Politics" 252–54), she is also sometimes optimistic. In *Eichmann in Jerusalem,* she repeats the story of Anton Schmidt—a man who saved the lives of Jews—and concludes that such stories cannot be silenced (230–32). But for facts to exert power in the common world, these stories must be told. Rational truth (such as principles of mathematics) might be perceptible and demonstrable through individual contemplation, but

> factual truth, on the contrary, is always related to other people: it concerns events and circumstances in which many are involved; it is established by witnesses and depends upon testimony; it exists only to the extent that it is spoken about, even if it occurs in the domain of privacy. It is political by nature. ("Truth and Politics" 238)

Arendt is neither a positivist who posits an autonomous individual who can correctly perceive truth, nor a relativist who positively asserts the inherent relativism of all perception. Her description of how truth functions does not fall anywhere in the three-part expeditio so prevalent in both rhetoric and philosophy—it is not expressivist, positivist, *or* social constructivist. Good thinking depends upon good public argument, and good public argument depends upon access to facts: "freedom of opinion is a farce unless factual information is guaranteed" ("Truth and Politics" 238).

The sort of thinking that Arendt propounds takes the form of action only when it is public argument, and as such, it is particularly precious: "For if no other test but the experience of being active, no other measure but the extent of sheer activity were to be applied to the various activities within the *vita activa,* it might well be that thinking as such would surpass them all" (*Human Condition* 325). Arendt insists that it is "the same general rule—Do not contradict yourself (not your self but your thinking ego)—that determines both thinking and acting" (*Lectures on Kant's Philosophy* 37). In place of the mildly resentful conformism that fuels totalitarianism, Arendt proposes "a tough-minded, open-eyed readiness to perceive and judge reality for oneself, in terms of concrete experience and independent, critical theorizing" (Pitkin 274). The paradoxical nature of agonism (that it must involve both individuality and commonality) makes it difficult to maintain, as the temptation is great either to think one's own thoughts without reference to anyone else or to let others do one's thinking.

For agonists, rhetoric must be agonal because thinking itself is fundamentally so. Ong, who considers agonism an instance of what he calls "adverservativeness," says it "has provided a paradigm for understanding our own existence: in order to know myself, I must know that something else is not me and is (in some measure) set against me, psychologically as well as physically" (15–16). Like Arendt, agonal rhetors emphasize the importance of being able to shift perspectives, and not simply as a way to consider arrangement, but as inherent to thinking. As James Kastely says, "one can gain perspective on a position only if he or she is allowed to play that position off another position" (216). The importance rhetoric accords agonistic thinking is, as Kastely notes, evident as early as Aristotle's treatise on rhetoric, a book that makes the ability to consider both sides of an argument more than a clever way to predict possible arguments (see especially 10). Like Arendt, Kastely says that the centrality of refutation in rhetoric prevents the "enstonement" of a single political judgment into sacred ideology:

> What rhetoric transforms is the present operation of past persuasions (that we call ideology) into a receptive tentativeness that can allow us to explore the shape or form of our positionedness and to reform those positions to better deal with the injustice that is uncovered. (254)

While rhetoric cannot prevent the formation of ideologies, it can make any single ideology temporary through forcing it to engage with whatever voices, perspectives, or persons the ideology excludes. Through this recursive process, agonistic rhetoric breaks up enclaves.

In a different sense from how the saying is usually used, people engaged in agonistic rhetoric must agree to disagree. That is, rather than agree not to try to persuade each other (which is what people usually mean by the saying), rhetors must agree to engage one another in what Kastely calls "the play of difference" (240) or "the play of disagreement" (233). As he says, "The vitality of rhetoric involves a continual achieving and risking of agreement, and this means that rhetoric in order to continue must paradoxically seek difference" (233–34). As he points out, rhetoric stops once perfect agreement is reached, and it only exists as long as there is enough difference between the participants to make persuasion necessary. Sloane notes that "Without a firm and *continuing* sense of the opposition there can be no debate, no controversy" (*Donne, Milton* 245, emphasis added). Paradoxically, then, successful persuasion is the end of rhetoric in both senses; hence agonistic rhetors like Arendt tend toward an intentionally provocative stance.

Consensus is not, therefore, necessarily the goal of discourse, and this assumption is something that distinguishes agonists from liberal political theorists, and potentially even from many theorists of deliberative democracy. Democracy necessitates compliance, but it makes a tremendous difference what one sees as the reason for one's compliance, or what one theorizes is the kind of consensus and conflict for which a polis (whether classroom or political entity) should strive. At least since Habermas's *Legitimation Crisis,* political theorists have distinguished among various reasons people might have for complying with a law:

1. There is no choice in the matter (following orders or coercion).
2. Little or no thought has ever been given to existing political circumstances and we do as we have always done (tradition).
3. We cannot be bothered one way or another (apathy).
4. Although we do not like a situation (it is not satisfactory and far from ideal), we cannot imagine things being really different and so we accept what seems like fate (pragmatic acquiescence).

5. We are dissatisfied with things as they are but nevertheless go along with them in order to secure another end; we acquiesce because it is in the long run to our advantage (instrumental acceptance or conditional agreement).

6. In the circumstances before us, and with the information available to us at the moment, we conclude it is 'right,' 'correct,' 'proper' for each of us as an individual or member of a collectivity: it is what we genuinely *ought to* or *should* do (normative agreement).

7. It is what ideal circumstances—with, for instance, all the knowledge we would like, all the opportunity to discover the circumstances and requirements of others—we would have agreed to (ideal normative agreement). (Held 194, emphasis in original)

Reasons 1–4 exemplify Arendt's social, whereas 5–6 typify action. The ideal for Enlightenment theorists (and those who remain in that tradition, even if they advocate deliberative democracy) is normative or ideal normative agreement. The ideal world that results from Kant's imperative, for instance, is one where people behave lawfully because they believe the laws are right, rather than because they wish to follow tradition, avoid punishment, are too apathetic to do otherwise, or cannot imagine the laws to be different. In this ideal world, laws (and society) are consensus-based, rather than coercion-based. The "laws" of this society (that is, how people actually behave) are ones to which people have consciously assented as just and reasonable. For this kind of thinking to result in a just society, people must imagine themselves as part of a fictional universal. It does not work if I think to myself, "I am glad that everyone else must teach from a textbook, but I don't have to." I must imagine myself as Universal Citizen to whom the law applies equally.

Such notions of universality and imagination may seem quaint and premodern, but teachers often invoke them. When we tell students to write the kind of peer review they would like to get from their peer reviewers, or that they should treat other students in class discussion the way that they would like to be treated, or even when we ask that they treat us as they would like us to treat them, we ask that students—imaginatively, at least—step outside of their own individualities and imagine themselves as part of something larger. In liberal political theory, this larger entity is the universal; in Arendt, it is the common. Similarly, while there are critiques of consensus in the classroom (critiques which, as this book makes clear, I largely endorse), there are some kinds of consensus we do want. Most of us consider ourselves successful if students engage in the coursework—writing the assignments, doing the readings, reviewing one another's papers, engaging in class discussion, contributing thoughtfully to a class mailing list, coming to individual or group conferences—because they think that work will improve their writing, whereas we feel frustrated and unsuccessful if students do that same work simply in order to avoid punishment, please us, or get a better grade. We want students to have consented to certain principles of the class; in that way, we want a class that is based in consensus rather than coercion.

The consensus may be hypothetical. We may recognize that our students—especially at the beginning of the semester—engage in the coursework because they want to avoid punishment or they want to reap rewards. The students have not really agreed to the policies (except insofar as they have chosen to remain in the class after the policies were explained—a defense of policies that is not too far off of Etzioni's claim that people can avoid excessive community pressure through moving or changing jobs), but we probably hypothesize that they would agree to the policies if they knew what we know about the teaching of writing. Our policies are reasonable not simply in the sense that we find them helpful to keep order, but in the sense that we believe knowledgeable people would also recognize them as appropriately contributing to the educational goals of the class. We assume a community of knowledgeable people who *would* assent to our policies; it is often our hope that our students will become real members of that community long before the semester ends. We hope the ideal normative agreement will become real normative agreement.

Such a way of thinking about one's policies, like Kant's categorical imperative, makes present the possibility of deliberate disobedience. By placing the work of the course policies in the realm of helping students write, we also place it where students can argue with us about whether or not it really is helping them. We have moved our own policies into the realm of rhetoric. We have also raised the possibility of people doing more than the law requires. If we are successful, not simply at teaching writing, but at getting our students' consent to our methods of teaching writing, then at least some of our students are likely to do more peer reviews than required, to do more research than required, to write additional drafts, contribute more often to the mailing list than required, and so on. Even those who do not do so will recognize that they could have, that such an option was available.

For agonists, however, the ideal normative agreement is not ideal, as it necessitates an erasure (or, more accurately, transcendence) of difference. Agonists emphasize the instrumental acceptance or normative agreement as ideal, often describing instrumental as exactly the kind of contingent agreement that is possible and desirable. The strengths of this position became vivid to me when I was involved in trying to direct a composition program collaboratively. Decisions regarding policy were made by the Composition Committee, a large and ad hoc group consisting of whoever chose to show up to the meetings. Change was slow, and decisions often went against my preferences. Thus, I was left enacting (as I taught in the program) and enforcing practices that I never thought were bad, but that I sometimes thought were not ideal. Using Held's terms, one could characterize my acquiescence either as instrumental (I went along with policies with which I disagreed because I wanted to secure the end of a collaborative and reasonably coherent composition program), or as normative (I thought everyone should do what the Composition Committee decided). My acquiescence to the decisions of the Composition Committee was not ideal normative agreement, largely because I do not claim to have any idea what people who have complete knowledge would do. The very idea of having all the knowledge I would like is so alien to me that I cannot guess what differences it would make in my decisions. But one thing is clear—interlocutors with perfect knowledge are interlocutors who have nothing to learn from argument;[7] agonism presumes that no such goal is possible or even desirable. For agonism, it is conflict all the way down.

As such, it differs from the liberal model, which aspires to ideal normative agreement. Motivism, because it denies the possibility of thought, and thereby frees people from responsibility for their own ideas, pushes toward the first four kinds of compliance (coercion, tradition, apathy, pragmatic acquiescence); and it means that the very nature of those agreements will be decided by whoever has the ability to advertise the best and most. If agonism is to be anything other than a synonym for interest-based discourse, it must be oriented toward something other than the first four kinds of compliance. It must, as it does in Arendt or Burke, make *thought* central.

As mentioned above, agonism does have its advocates within rhetoric—Burke, Ong, Sloane, Gage, Jarratt, for instance—but, while each of these proposes a form of conflictual argument, they are still less adversarial than Arendt. Agonism can emphasize persuasion, as does John Gage's textbook *The Shape of Reason* or William Brandt et al.'s *The Craft of Writing*. That is, the goal of the argument is to identify the disagreement and then construct a text that gains the assent of the audience. This is not the same as what Gage calls "asymmetrical rhetoric": theories that "presuppose an active speaker and a passive audience, a speaker whose rhetorical task is therefore to do something *to* that audience" ("The Reasoned Thesis" 6)—asymmetric rhetoric is not and cannot be agonistic. Persuasive agonism still values conflict, disagreement, and equality among interlocutors, but it has the goal of reaching agreement, as when Gage says that the process of argument should enable one's reasons "to be understood and *believed* by others" (*Shape of Reason* 5, emphasis added).

Arendt's version is what one might call polemical agonism, which puts less emphasis on gaining assent, and which is exemplified both in Arendt's own writing and Donald Lazere's "Ground Rules" and "Teaching the Political Conflicts." Both forms require substantive debate at two points in a long and recursive process. First, one engages in debate in order to invent one's argument; even silent thinking is a "dialogue of myself with myself" (Arendt, *Lectures on Kant's Philosophy* 40). The difference between the two approaches to agonism is clearest when one presents a product to an audience assumed to be an opposition. In persuasive agonism, one plays down conflict and moves through reasons to try to persuade one's audience. In polemical agonism, however, one's intention is not necessarily to prove one's case, but to make public one's thought in order to test it.

For Arendt, public argument serves the same function in philosophy that replicability serves in the sciences; it is how one tests the validity of one's thought. In persuasive agonism, success is achieved through persuasion; in polemical agonism, success may be marked through the quality of subsequent controversy.

Arendt quotes from a letter Kant wrote on this point:

> You know that I do not approach reasonable objections with the intention merely of refuting them, but that in thinking them over I always weave them into my judgments, and afford them the opportunity of overturning all my

most cherished beliefs. I entertain the hope that by thus viewing my judgment impartially from the standpoint of others some third view that will
improve upon my previous insight may be obtainable. (qtd. in *Lectures on
Kant's Philosophy* 42)

Kant's use of "impartial" is here interesting, as he is not describing a stance
free of all perspective; it is impartial only in the sense that it is not his
own view. This is the same way Arendt uses the term; she does not advocate any kind of positivistic rationality, but instead a "universal interdependence" ("Truth and Politics" 242). She does not place the origin
of the "disinterested pursuit of truth" in science, but at "the moment
when Homer chose to sing the deeds of the Trojans no less than those
of the Achaeans, and to praise the glory of Hector, the foe and defeated
man, no less than the glory of Achilles, the hero of his kinfolk" ("Truth
and Politics" 262–63). It is useful to note that Arendt tends not to use
the term "universal," opting more often for "common," by which she
means both what is shared and what is ordinary, a usage that evades many
of the problems associated with universalism while preserving its virtues
(for a brief but provocative application of Arendt's notion of common,
see Hauser 100–103).

   In polemical agonism, there is a sense that one's main goal is *not* to
persuade one's readers—persuading one's readers, if this means that they
fail to see errors and flaws in one's argument, might actually be a sort of
failure. It means that one wishes to put forward an argument that makes
clear what one's stance is and why one holds it, but with the intention
of provoking critique and counterargument. Arendt describes Kant's
"hope" for his writings not that the number of people who agree with
him would increase but "that the circle of his examiners would gradu-
ally be enlarged" (*Lectures on Kant's Philosophy* 39); he wanted interlocutors, not acolytes.

   Another way to put this is that agonistic rhetors are suspicious of closure. Among some recent compositionists, it seems a given that an aversion to closure means that one must avoid closure in one's own prose.
Thus, the editors of *Composition and Resistance* say that they decided,
"rather than making a settlement within the field of composition, we
resist ending events and settling differences. . . . Even as we are now revising this beginning, we are talking one another out of trying to tie all
the loose ends together" (Hurlbert and Blitz 1). As one can tell from

Arendt's own style, agonism does not mean that one's public presentations are presented as tentative, partial, and preliminary. There is, in fact, a startling arrogance in the notion that one might achieve closure on a debate simply by writing with closure; I have no illusions that I might cause my colleagues to consider an argument settled by how confidently I assert my points or how elegantly I tie up loose ends in my argument.

This is not consensus-based argument, nor what is sometimes call consociational argument, nor is this argument as mediation or conflict resolution. Arendt (and her commentators) use the term "fight," and they mean it. When Arendt describes the values that are necessary in our world, she says, "They are a sense of honor, desire for fame and glory, the spirit of fighting without hatred and 'without the spirit of revenge,' and indifference to material advantages" ("Crisis" 167). Pitkin summarizes Arendt's argument: "Free citizenship presupposes the ability to fight—openly, seriously, with commitment, and about things that really matter—without fanaticism, without seeking to exterminate one's opponents" (266). My point here is two-fold: First, there is not a simple binary between persuasive discourse and eristic discourse, conflictual versus collaborative, or argument as opposed to debate. Second, while polemical agonism requires diversity among interlocutors, and thus seems an extraordinarily appropriate notion, and while it may be a useful corrective to too much emphasis on persuasion, it seems to me that polemical agonism could easily slide into the kind of wrangling that is simply frustrating; Arendt does not describe just how one is to keep the conflict useful. Although she rejects the notion that politics is "no more than a battlefield of partial, conflicting interests, where nothing count[s] but pleasure and profit, partisanship, and the lust for dominion" ("Truth and Politics" 263), she does not say exactly how we are to know when we are engaging in the existential leap of argument and when we are lusting for dominion.

On that first point, agonistic rhetors do not describe conflict and collaboration (or conflict and community) as opposed. This is yet another way that proponents of agonistic rhetoric (like Arendt) seem very different from the civic-republicans or communitarians like Sandel, MacIntor, or Taylor, who tend to worry about the ability of diverse communities to argue productively. Kastely reiterates Young's critique of some concepts of community, those that "reduce heterogeneity and multiplicity to unity" (Kastely 234). Such an ideal is most likely either to purchase unity through exclusion or suppression of those whose needs are irreconcilable:

> If one acknowledges the possibility that all needs and interests cannot be reconciled, then community leads inevitably to hierarchy and to normative transvaluing of difference. Such transvaluing inevitably follows the paths of power, and this means that the unity of community is procured at the sacrifice of the interests, values, and identities of those with less power. However well intentioned, assimilation cannot help being imperialistic. (234–35)

For a notion of community that requires identity, difference will lead to exclusion, and a past exclusion can never be remedied. Rhetoric, on the contrary, is a partial solution to this problem in that it both acknowledges and requires that individuals have different views, different needs, and different identities. This is the sense in which rhetoric is necessarily confrontational. But rhetors must share a considerable amount as well; rhetoric must be collaborative as much as conflictual. As Kastely argues, participating in rhetoric is risky, so one must have some degree of trust in the other participants: "For the genuine risks that such discussion requires one must have a confidence in the others involved that allows one to risk an understanding of a current identity in an open-ended play of difference" (240–41). Kastely uses the example of Meno as someone not engaged enough in the process of speech for a dialogue to effect genuine change in his thinking—he does not share with Socrates the project of reconsidering convenient notions. Philoctetes cannot be persuaded because he does not trust the Greeks. Hecuba exemplifies someone who cannot persuade her interlocutors because they cannot see themselves as sharing anything with a powerless slave. In all these cases, rhetoric fails because the rhetors cannot agree enough—they do not share enough—to disagree productively. And this is one especially important difference between agonistic rhetoric as it is theorized and what popular culture experiences as public conflict—the latter is conflict without collaboration.

Like other proponents of agonism, Arendt argues that rhetoric does not lead individuals or communities to ultimate Truth, but to decisions that will necessarily have to be reconsidered. Even Arendt, who tends to indicate a greater faith than many agonists (such as Burke, Sloane, or Kastely) in the ability of individuals to perceive truth, insists that self-deception is always a danger, so public discourse is necessary as a form of testing (see especially *Lectures on Kant's Political Philosophy* and "Truth and Politics"). She remarks that it is difficult to think beyond one's self-interest and that "nothing, indeed, is more common, even among highly sophisticated people, than the blind obstinacy that becomes manifest in lack of imagination and failure to judge" ("Truth and Politics" 242). Sloane says that a rhetor "must explore each case, like a case at law, anew, proving or disproving charges and reaching a decision based both intrinsically on the merits of the case and extrinsically on whatever prior agreement, such as law, is applicable to the matter" (*Donne, Milton* 89). Kastely, similarly, praises both Burke and Socrates for describing "an ongoing need for refutation, for a rhetoric that undoes past rhetorical acts" (228).

Agonism demands that one simultaneously trust and doubt one's own perceptions, rely on one's own judgment and consider the judgments of others, think for oneself and imagine how others think. The question remains whether this is a kind of thought in which everyone can engage—is the agonistic public sphere (whether political, academic, or scientific) only available to the few? Benhabib puts this criticism in the form of a question:

> That is, is the "recovery of the public space" under conditions of modernity necessarily an elitist and antidemocratic project that can hardly be reconciled with the demand for universal political emancipation and the universal extension of citizenship rights that have accompanied modernity since the American and French Revolutions? ("Models of Public Space" 75)

This is an especially troubling question not only because Arendt's examples of agonal rhetoric are from elitist cultures, but also because of comments she makes, such as "As a living experience, thought has always been assumed, perhaps wrongly, to be known only to the few. It may not be presumptuous to believe that these few have not become fewer in our time" (*Human Condition* 324).

Ancient Athens was homosocial, slave-based, and, as indicated in its treatment of Socrates, much more conformist than Arendt's discussion of agonal rhetoric might suggest. Republican Rome was elitist, with a system of privilege and patronage that can hardly be considered democratic and with conflicts more "centered upon the men who were to make or execute policy rather than upon the policy itself" (Gruen 6). It went from a system of patronage to outright corruption, intrigue, and violence.

Collin Wells describes the last years of the Republic; he says that from 133 BC

> Violence was endemic in Republican politics, and to the destruction wrought by violence must be added the horrors of proscriptions and confiscations, whereby whole communities might suffer. Poverty, hardship, and unrest were widespread. Men raised private armies. . . . Senators travelled between their numerous estates guarded by a strong retinue. Even in Rome, they might need an armed escort to go down to the Senate. Their houses might be attacked and virtually besieged. (14–15)

Early America moved from a system close to the Roman system of privilege and patronage (one that Gordon Wood calls aristocratic) through a brief period of civic-republicanism (lasting, according to Wood, less than a generation) to a form of democracy based on self-interest (something of which he is not critical). None of these eras is one to which I would want to return, nor does any seem, to me at least, to exemplify a particularly admirable form of public discourse. If one ignores the sexism, elitism, and racism of the American moment of civic-republicanism, then one might have an admirable form, but an admittedly fragile one. One must wonder, then, whether, at least as formulated by Arendt, agonistic rhetoric is not excessively utopian.

I have emphasized the sense of play and competition that the agonistic model can bring, but that very sense can be profoundly dismaying. Lynch et al. have described the ways that students' approach to argument as a competition with winners and losers can be a lively glimpse of hell:

> Students have learned to argue vigorously and even angrily, but not think about alternatives, or listen to each other, or determine how their position may affect others, or see complexities, or reconsider the position they began with, or even to make new connections across a range of possible disagreements. (61)

This is how the agonistic model goes wrong—in a strange sense, the students have not really left the enclaves of their own thinking; they remain within them while throwing reasons like rocks at people in other enclaves.

Ramistic (or perhaps post-Ramistic would be more accurate) rhetoric removes debate from the thinking process but keeps one form appropriate to polemical agonism: a clearly stated thesis with supporting reasons and a prolepsis in which one briefly considers and rejects an opposing argument. In agonism, those moments of debate result from seeing all positions as momentary and contingent; one advocates this position because it has the best reasons at this time, but that might change. In Ramistic rhetoric, one discovers the truth and presents it to an audience who will then go out and promulgate this same truth. And that is what we see in the kind of agonism bemoaned by writing teachers and cultural critics. We do not see a debate intended to enable people to invent arguments or test one's thinking; we do not see debates in which listening is as important as speaking. Benhabib summarizes one of the most significant insights in Arendt's celebrating of the agonistic public sphere:

> What is important here is not so much what public discourse is about as the way in which this discourse takes place: force and violence destroy the specificity of public discourse by introducing the dumb language of physical superiority and constraint and by silencing the voice of persuasion and conviction. Only power is generated by public discourse and is sustained by it. (Benhabib, "Models of Public Space" 80–81)

What distinguishes genuine agonistic rhetoric from verbal professional wrestling is whether one is inventing or discovering arguments—whether changing one's argument is perceived as changing teams and thereby betraying one's loyalties or as an intelligent reconsideration and reinvention, whether listening to one's opposition is done in order to change one's own mind or theirs. Thus, while agonists are not positivist or foundationalist in their epistemologies, and they assume that it is not possible to hold the truth like an object in one's hand, they do describe it as a call that one must hear, a standard to which one should strive. If one respects facts—the facts of other's experiences, the facts of our own observations, the facts of our stories—then one is in a place where one would change one's own argument for a better one, then one listens to one's oppositions because they might be right.

The interest-based model attempts to be morally neutral but ends up facilitating plutocracy rather than democracy; there is a moral (or, one might say, immoral) agenda. Arendt's advocacy of the agonistic sphere helps to explain how the system could undermine injustice. It is not an overstatement to say that a central theme in Arendt's work is the evil of conformity—the fact that the modern bureaucratic state makes possible extraordinary evil carried out by people who do not even have any ill-will toward their victims. It does so by "imposing innumerable and various rules, all of which tend to 'normalize' its members to make them behave, to exclude spontaneous action or outstanding achievement" (*Human Condition* 40). It keeps people from thinking, and it keeps them behaving. The agonistic model's celebration of achievement and verbal skill undermines the political force of conformity, so it is a force against the bureaucratizing of evil. If people think for themselves, they will resist dogma; if people think of themselves as one of many, they will empathize; if people can do both, they will resist totalitarianism. And if they talk about what they see, tell their stories, argue about their perceptions, and listen to one another—that is, engage in rhetoric—then they are engaging in antitotalitarian action.

To be antitotalitarian, however, is not to be anti-authority. I have found Arendt's argument is easily misunderstood, possibly because she is right that the modern world is tremendously confused on the subject of authority. The commonsensical view of authority is to equate it with coercion—to view an authority as necessarily authoritarian—perhaps because the common view of power is essentially Hobbesian (see, for instance, *Origins* 139). As Arendt says in "What Is Authority," there is a tendency to view power as something that necessarily flows downward in a hierarchy, to assume that the people have only as much power as the person at the top grants them. And each grant of power is a diminution of the Leviathan's power—thus, several years ago when the theme of a 4Cs was "empowering students," innumerable papers asserted that this task would require the instructors' giving up power. As far as Arendt is concerned, this view of power is only partially right (but still only partially wrong).

Arendt says that power has three possible sources: coercion, authority, persuasion. The assumption prevalent at 4Cs—that power has limited quantity, so that sharing reduces the power of the previously more powerful—is true of coercion, but not of power resulting from authority or rhetoric. A political system based in coercion is a tyranny, in which "the tyrant rules in accordance with his own will and interest" ("What Is Authority" 97). I have found this an extraordinarily useful way to think about power in a classroom situation as well (or, for that matter, in an administrative structure). The more that the rules of the classroom are created for the ease of the teacher, rather than the educational benefits of the students, the more coercive the situation. Teachers who hold students to higher standards than they hold themselves—having stringent late paper policies while regularly returning student work late, holding students to tardy policies while themselves showing up whenever convenient—are engaged in tyranny.

In my experiences supervising teachers (and in my own teaching), tyranny is a problem, but not as much a problem as totalitarianism. Totalitarianism, it should be remembered, is a situation in which the objects of policies have no opportunity to argue with the people who created them. The policies seem hegemonic and irresistible because the people enforcing them do so while disavowing their own agency. Linda McNeil studied what might usefully be seen as totalitarian teaching in high school social science classes, showing the close connection between a controlling administration and what she calls "defensive" teaching. McNeil defines teaching defensively as "choosing methods of presentation and evaluation that they hope will make their workload more efficient and create as little student resistance as possible" (158), a good definition of Arendt's "social." Pedagogical decisions are based on the extent to which they will increase teacher control rather than student knowledge. Administrations who focussed on student behavior (dress codes, truancy) over issues of education ended up similarly subverting educational goals in favor of behavioral controls, both directly and indirectly. They did so directly by, for instance, forcing teachers to spend class preparation time monitoring halls, and indirectly by encouraging teachers to choose teaching practices that were easy, efficient, and conflict-reducing over ones that might have served educational purposes better. The more that the administrators emphasized control, the more the teachers did. McNeil says, "In accommodating to institutional priorities for order and efficiency, the teachers demonstrated the very technocratic values that they did not respect in administrators and on which they placed much of the blame for the need for efficiency" (185). If the administration placed the need for order above educational values, then so did the teachers, the whole time blaming the administration. The teachers were, then, in Arendt's social; engaging in behaviors that they did not choose and for which they would not accept responsibility.[8]

Arendt is clear that coercion is an utterly inappropriate source of power for the teacher, and that a coercive educational system is a failure of responsibility. A system grounded in authority does not depend on power taken from people (or even given to them, an incipiently authoritarian view of an apparently egalitarian classroom); people choose to give the power to someone they deem an authority. Authority is power given to someone due to that person's knowledge and competence. This is, I have found, regularly misunderstood, and every time I teach Arendt, at least one student rages against the reading, citing Freire as an opposition. In fact, Freire's argument seems to me quite consistent with Arendt; both assert that education is liberatory when it involves sharing knowledge, and both are concerned with enabling people to resist oppressive institutions through argument. Arendt's argument is confusing because of her attempt to revivify a dead notion of "authority"; it might be clearer had she instead used the term "credibility" or "legitimacy." The more legitimacy a political system has, or the more that students believe teacher knows what s/he is doing (is giving well-informed advice, is assessing work in meaningful ways, is helping them), the less the system or teacher will have to rely on bribes, threats, bargains, and tricks. Thus, an authority-based system does not reduce the freedom of the people: "Authority implies an obedience in which men retain their freedom" ("What Is Authority" 106). Authority is highly contingent in that the people can change their minds at any moment and refuse obedience. In a classroom, this means that the teacher should be "the person who, turn it whatever way one will, still knows more and can do more than oneself" ("Crisis" 182). That is, students choose to do what the teacher says because they think s/he knows what s/he is doing, rather than because they fear his/her punishments. What confuses readers about Arendt's argument is that it is easy to ignore her insistence that authoritarian teachers have no authority, and authoritarian teaching is the opposite of authority-based teaching.

Coercion-based teaching is threatened by an increase in student power; hence, as McNeil shows, teachers obsessed with controlling students will do so through controlling the students' access to knowledge. They might do it through mystifying, over-simplifying, or even simply evading subjects altogether. Or they might do it through ensuring that students do not ask questions. McNeil describes one teacher who graded students down if they asked or made comments during class (195–96). Another teacher who aspired to be an administrator taught a world studies course that remained on an extremely superficial level (196). McNeil points out that such teachers end up in a bargaining relationship with their students: "the teacher gets [students] to cooperate without resisting by promising that, in fact, the study of this topic will require no commitment of effort, and little time, on their part" (175, see also 190–93, 209).

There are, as McNeil says, political consequences of this kind of teaching:

> The message of the social studies content in the most controlling of these classes is that the system can be trusted, it does not need to be questioned, it does not need our active involvement. The classroom rewards for passive student roles have confirmed the value of acquiescence. (208)

Perhaps the most troubling, and likely most damaging, aspect of this kind of teaching situation is the modeling that the teachers do. Pitkin summarizes Arendt's argument: "Characterologically, then, Arendt suggests, free citizenship is hampered by parvenu conformism, resentment, and revenge and facilitated by courage, responsibility, and the capacity for being (in the) present, for realistic initiative" (268). Teachers who engage in defensive teaching (and, it should be emphasized, not all teachers in McNeil's study did) do not simply require acquiescence, they model it, and they model exactly the kind of resentment and revenge that Arendt condemns. They enact policies in which they do not believe, but which they are not acting to change. Just as they make mildly resentful clients of their students, so they are mildly resentful but ultimately conformist clients of their administrations.

There is another way that one might look at McNeil's research in light of Arendt's theories. Arendt says that the political is the realm of action, and that the social is the realm of behavior. It is striking that both the controlling administrations and controlling teachers focus on behavior—tardiness, dress codes, graduation requirements—not on action. In fact, the controlling teachers told McNeil that they had felt threatened by student action, and they consciously shaped their teaching to ensure that students would not be able to act in concert on political issues (190; see also teachers' comments regarding Vietnam, Watergate, and student protests). Agonistic argument is action; it is not behavior. But not all argument is agonistic—it is certainly possible to teach argument in such a way that it becomes a set of behaviors rather than a kind of action. And that, essentially, is what the interest-based model of the public sphere—and its instantiation in the classroom—does. It reduces action to behavior, and argument to coercion.

4

WHAT ANGELS OF OUR NATURE?
COMMUNITARIANISM, SOCIAL CONSTRUCTIVISM,
AND COMMUNITIES OF DISCOURSE

> Moral voices achieve their effect mainly through education
> and persuasion, rather than through coercion. Originating in
> communities, and sometimes embodied in law, they exhort,
> admonish, and appeal to what Lincoln called the better
> angels of our nature.
> —Amitai Etzioni, *The Essential Communitarian Reader*

I distinguished the liberal model of the public sphere from the inter-est-based model on the grounds that the former tries to balance self-interest and public good while the latter ignores public good altogether. Communitarians argue that the distinction is essentially false—the liberal model necessarily ends up in the interest-based model due to its un-willingness to impose a particular set of morals on its citizens. They argue that it is impossible for a democratic government to remain neutral because it requires a democratic culture. There is empirical support for this claim. Dahl and others have articulated the conditions historically connected to democratic practice, some of which are institutional (e.g., civilian control of the military, a distinction between the military and the police forces, multiple sources of power) but many of which are cultural. The ethos must be one that values honesty, promotes concern for the public good, urges tolerance, reveres long-term over short-term planning, demands quality universal education, encourages people to work within political systems to effect political change (Nie et al. 16–24; see also Dahl, *Democracy and Its Critics* 244–51, *On Democracy* 145–59). As Sandel says, the communitarian premise is that to be free is to share in governing a political community that controls its own fate. Self-government in this sense requires political communities that control their destinies, and citizens who identify sufficiently with those communities to think and act with a view to the common good. (*Democracy's Discontent* 274)

Because it undercuts the development of such an ethos, the liberal model's neutrality toward morals is both misleading and damaging.

It is misleading because the liberal model does have a moral agenda (autonomy is assumed to be an inherent good), and damaging because it encourages people to think of morality as a private issue (thereby enabling people to ignore their responsibilities toward their communities). Beiner's reductio ad absurdum typifies this criticism:

> The liberal state ought to be uncompromisingly neutral [toward] a conception of the good life geared toward the attainment of chemical euphoria at every opportunity and a conception of the good life focused on ideas of social responsibility. . . . It should not require a very sophisticated moral reflection to see that this provides a recipe not for principled liberal statesmanship but for the moral self-destruction of the liberal state. To the extent that the state comes to understand itself in these terms, it brings down upon itself just this kind of self-vitiating calamity. (67)

Communitarians argue that liberalism's attempt to preserve individual autonomy at all costs has killed the spirit of community engagement. And the main critical project of communitarianism is to revivify that spirit.

Political theorists usually use the terms "civic-republican" and "communitarian" interchangeably (Benhabib, "Models of Public Space"; Habermas; Bohman and Rehg; Sandel), so that Arendt, Aristotle, Sandel, and Taylor are all in the same category. But Arendt seems to me to be in a very different category from Beiner, Etzioni, Sandel, or Walzer. First, Arendt does not endorse a social constructivist model of discourse (I am not convinced all communitarians do either, though). Second, for agonists, the value of rhetoric comes from its ability to disrupt communities, to flummox consensus, and thereby hamper hegemony, but community and consensus seem closely connected for communitarians. Finally, agonism is heavily conflictual, and that is not clearly the case with communitarians. Thus, heterogeneity is a necessary condition for agonists, while homogeneity is the necessary condition for communitarians.

Communitarians argue that there should be more argument about morals, that public discourse should not avoid such topics, at the same time that they call for more community. But, depending on their model for discourse, this is potentially either contradictory, or a hidden call for the government to enforce more conformity. The potential problem, in other words, is that communitarianism may be even less able to handle difference than liberal political theory.

Earlier, I described a matrix in which there were four kinds of public discourse—irenic/expressive; irenic/deliberative; agonistic/expressive; agonistic/deliberative. In an irenic and expressive public sphere, difference is troublesome, but only if someone notices. Since, in an expressivist public sphere, one always has the option of speaking without listening, participants may be able to deny the presence of deep disagreement. Thus, if communitarians imagine an expressive public, then having more argument about morals and more community is not a contradiction, and it would not necessitate more conformity. If that is their argument, however, I fail to see any absence of such discourse; it seems to me that we already have a public sphere with plenty of moralistic sermonizing in which people do not listen to one another.

Difference is devastating, however, if one wants an irenic and deliberative public sphere. To deliberate together, people must listen, so they would be well aware of the disagreement. The mere fact of disagreement means that something is wrong with the community, so there is a push to exclude or re-educate some side in the disagreement. If, as I infer, communitarians imagine an irenic and deliberative public sphere, they must necessarily imagine an extremely homogeneous community, and/or one in which major disagreements are evaded. This is a vision in which calling for more argument and more community is contradictory, unless one also imagines a situation in which considerable conformity is enforced.

Hence my organization of this chapter. The questions I want to pursue are two. First, how do communitarians theorize discourse? Second, how do they define community?

focus of chapter

Communitarians take issue with liberal political theory on two counts: first, whether the moral conditions necessary for democracy are socio-historical constructs; second, whether liberal political theory's goal of autonomy means that there is too much emphasis on individual rights and too little on the public good. In regard to the first, Habermas offers a succinct quote on the distinction between liberal and communitarian political theories (using the term "republican" for the latter):

> For republicans, rights ultimately are nothing but determinations of prevailing political will, while for liberals, some rights are always grounded in a "higher law" of transpolitical reason or revelation. . . . In a republican view, a community's objective, common good substantially consists in the success of its political endeavors to define, establish, effectuate, and sustain the *mores* of that community. Whereas in a contrasting liberal view, the higher-law rights provide the transactional structures and the curbs on power required so that pluralistic pursuit of diverse and conflicting interests may proceed as satisfactorily as possible. (F. I. Michelman, qtd. in "Three Normative Models" 242)

Some communitarians (e.g., Etzioni) position themselves between people who want the government to enforce moral behavior and those who argue that morality is always a private issue that is no one else's business. This middle ground has more discourse about morality, but not (at least in theory) more laws requiring moral behavior; it is therefore not Big Government. The "Responsive Communitarian Platform" says:

> Moral voices achieve their effect mainly through education and persuasion, rather than through coercion. Originating in communities, and sometimes embodied in law, they exhort, admonish, and appeal to what Lincoln called the better angels of our nature. (xxvi)

Criticizing liberalism's distinction between the right and the good (or arguments about fairness and arguments about morality), communitarians argue that legislation always does and always must have a moral basis, and that a society must be grounded in some kind of moral consensus. But "while we search for moral consensus, the ideas underpinning a moral consensus are mutual dialogue and persuasion, not imposition" (Etzioni xix).

Communitarianism tends to be a very pragmatic discourse, with little in the way of theorizing in the way that, for example, Rawls or Habermas ponder ontological issues. If there is some kind of philosophical basis, it tends to be Alasdair MacIntyre's work (especially *After Virtue*), in which he argues that "the Aristotelian tradition can be restated in a way that restores intelligibility and rationality to our moral and social attitudes and commitments" (259). MacIntyre calls for rejecting the Enlightenment search for universal bases of moral discourse, suggesting that we should instead simply acknowledge and accept that our moral systems are particular. Accepting that they are not universal, we can also acknowledge that they need preservation and regeneration, that the duty of philosophy is and should be to encourage a specific set of ethics.

Sandel applies MacIntyre's argument to government and civic discourse. In his view, liberal political theory has become increasingly proceduralist, an approach he summarizes as depending upon "the priority of individual rights, the ideal of neutrality, and the conceptions of persons as freely choosing, unencumbered selves" (*Democracy's Discontent* 28). Sandel emphasizes the last part, the autonomous self. Sandel's criticism of this myth of the autonomous self is twofold. First, it does not truly lead to governmental neutrality, as it fails to acknowledge the different degrees of obligation that people feel (in this argument he assumes that practitioners of institutionalized religion always feel a stronger obligation than agnostics or atheists, an assumption I think unfounded); it thereby gives an advantage to people who aren't terribly bothered by conflicting obligations. To make this argument, he takes issue with the Supreme Court decision that assumes that an individual is free to choose between attending church and going fishing; he maintains that the two are not equally freely chosen (a somewhat dubious assertion regarding any religion that promotes the notion of free will, an even more dubious assertion when applied to some fly-fishers I've known). Second, "More than a legal condition, citizenship requires certain habits and dispositions, a concern for the whole, an orientation to the common good. But these qualities cannot be taken as given. They require constant cultivation" (*Democracy's Discontent* 117). That is, democracy does not simply happen but depends upon the conscious enculturation into democratic values, like altruism, civic-mindedness, mutual respect.

The relation of this argument to MacIntyre's (and the related assumption that communitarianism is inherently antifoundational) is problematic. Did Sandel really subscribe to the notion that values are social constructs, then his criticism of procedural liberalism would itself be contradictory, as it depends upon the assumption that institutionally dictated obligations necessarily have deeper foundations than others.[1] This raises the possibility that communitarianism is no less foundational than liberalism and is simply liberalism without the claim to neutrality (a liberalism that openly enforces certain values—an issue to be pursued below).

Some communitarians criticize Enlightenment theory for positing foundations, arguing that what looks like universal principles are in fact the consequence of cultural development. Taylor has suggested that the very model of the self upon which democracy depends is just such a cultural construct and not a foundational (or transcendent) premise (*Philosophy and the Human Sciences* 309; see also Alasdair MacIntyre on the autonomous individual, 34). There are, however, several problems with this argument. In addition to the one mentioned above—that there are foundations, but they are hidden—there is the question of dissent. If rights are nothing but determinations of prevailing political will, then the tyranny of the majority looms large. Without appealing to principles of some sort that undergird or transcend particular sociohistorical preferences, it becomes difficult to determine when, if ever, individuals should reject the community mores. As a result, it is difficult to imagine the communitarian argument for preserving minority rights. The Civil Rights movement was a very anticommunitarian movement in that it violated numerous preferences of segregated communities; the whole argument depended upon rhetors like King being able to say that some laws were transitory and prejudiced (e.g., ones segregating public parks) while other laws were foundational (e.g., *Brown v. Board of Education*). If one abandons the quest for transpolitical foundation, then how does one criticize *any* community?

And, perhaps most important, what happens to dissenters? One possible answer, and one explicitly given by some communitarians, is that people who are unhappy with the ethos dominant in any given community have the ability to form their own communities (for example, Etzioni xiv). Beiner describes the logical problems in this solution, saying:

> The withdrawal into particularistic communities merely confirms what defines the problem in the first place. Here the communitarian is landed in a quandary that exactly matches that of the liberal. If what is required is a truly national community, the communitarian promise would seem to be a hopeless one, for clearly no modern industrial state can sustain this sort of community without stoking up the very hazardous fires of nationalism. On the other hand, if what is sought is the autonomy of local communities as such, there is no assurance that this will not give further momentum to the relativization of tastes and morals that mandated liberal neutralism in the first place. So the appeal to community, far from resolving the quandaries of liberalism, merely confirms them in another guise. (31)

As discussed previously, the liberal value of autonomy is criticized (by communitarians, among others) as insidious because people are not really independent of one another (no man is an island, so to speak), and because the value encourages us to ignore our very real interdependence. But the very notion that someone who dislikes the mores of one community could simply join another merely shifts the still problematic concept of autonomy from individuals to communities. There is no reason to think that the inaccuracy and damage of autonomy suddenly dissipates by shifting the concept to autonomous communities rather than autonomous individuals; no community is an island, and lifeboat ethics is no ethics at all. In other words, communitarianism simply shifts, but does not resolve, the problem of autonomy.

There is another communitarian criticism of liberalism that applies equally well to communitarianism, and it comes from the ostensible antifoundationalism of communitarianism—a tendency to mistake their own preferences for values with a foundational basis. In "The Responsive Communitarian Platform," for instance, one can see instances when the authors have mistaken their own prejudices for validated premises. The platform's ringing endorsement of the two-parent family assumes that such families are necessarily heterosexual—an assumption that is not justified in the already problematic social science research the authors cite as support. And it is striking that this is the only plank based on social science research.[2] The communitarian platform has no coherent underlying principle that informs when social science should determine public policy and when it should not.

One can make the same observation about communitarianism in general. While its pragmatic quality is very attractive, especially to rhetoricians, it gives the movement a kind of ad hoc quality that makes consistent applications of principles unlikely. Even though the central goal of communitarianism is that people should rely on persuasion more than on governmental intervention, the various authors in the *Essential Communitarian Reader* argue for governmental intervention for such diverse purposes as to preserve affirmative action (Selznick 64); repeal no-fault divorce laws (Selznick 45; "Responsive Platform"); actively engage in public health campaigns to promote marriage; attain full employment (Selznick 68); ban the sale of tobacco or turn it into a prescription drug (121); use "taxation and regulation to reduce the incidence of cigarette smoking" (224 Kleiman); make drinking alcohol a privilege that requires a license (224); engage in reinstitutionalization of the mentally ill (Siegel 194); institute antibegging ordinances (Siegel 195); ban guns ("Responsive Platform"); and engage in random drug testing of people who have been previously convicted of drug possession (Kleiman 225).

I do not list these because I think they are all absurd, but because the length of the list belies communitarians' claims that this philosophy is different from Big Government. The length and randomness of the list of policy proposals suggests that "communitarianism" can be invoked to defend whatever happens to be the pet irritation of the particular author. If theorists engage in this kind of behavior, it is hard to imagine that communities would not do so as well; thus, despite theorists' claims that communitarianism would not result in simple imposition of majority religious, social, and economic prejudices on minorities, the theorists' own writings suggest that this is exactly what would happen.

Communitarian theorists are not always clear just when speech is action, and when it may even inhibit action, so that it sometimes seems as though the goal is a vibrant and active public sphere of discourse, with little thought as to the real consequences or costs of that speech. For instance, "The "Responsive Communitarian Platform" says that people should be encouraged to voice their disapproval of one another and to "express our moral concerns to others when it comes to issues we care deeply about" (xxxi). The platform comments that people probably should not chastise one another about not keeping lawns green, but that is exactly what would happen—community associations are notorious for trying to intervene in the deepest corners of personal lives, and often on very shaky bases.[3] But, more important, what this vision of speech fails to keep clear is the issue of difference—that speech has different costs for different people—and that mere speech is not enough.

This last point is best explained through a consideration of William Chafe's history of the Civil Rights movement in Greensboro, North Carolina. Chafe describes the "mystique of progressivism," which, he argues, unintentionally—but very seriously—inhibited progress on racial justice. The "mystique of progressivism" has several qualities, one of which is a tendency to confuse speech and action. Chafe says that southern white liberals often mistook willingness to listen to unorthodox ideas as a kind of action: "After all, even the delicate issue of racial change could be discussed, and discussion, in turn, could be seen as a step toward action" (8). Chafe suggests that this sense that talking was action meant that they felt no need to do anything more than talk. Therefore, white liberals thought that changes were happening in regard to racial issues because there was talk of changes, but, because there were no discernible policy consequences of these discussions, African Americans did not see the situation as similarly productive. Chafe suggests that this "courtesy toward new ideas" in effect obstructed social action—the confusion between open discourse (among a small and elite group of people) and action contributed to complacency among white liberals. By the standards of the white progressives Chafe discusses—who simply wanted agonistic and expressive speech—their speech was perfectly good. By the standards of people who wanted political change—who wanted deliberative speech—it was not.

In addition to a fundamental vagueness regarding what kind of discourse is supposed to be conducted in communities, communitarians maintain a vague, if not contradictory, use of the term "community." Joseph Harris points to the two uses of the term "community of discourse" in composition studies. Sometimes it means "specific physical groupings of people . . . an actual group of speakers living in a particular place and time" (*A Teaching Subject* 101). At other times it means something more abstract: "individuals who share certain habits of mind" (101) or "a free and voluntary gathering of individuals with shared goals and interests—of persons who have not so much been forced together as have chosen to associate with one another" (102).

One of the important theoretical bases for communitarianism is the notion—argued perhaps most forcibly by MacIntyre—that effective discourse requires consensus on a large number of points. If people do not agree on basic principles, they cannot even agree enough to have an argument. Communitarians extend this argument to the polis, concluding that a competent polity necessitates "a commonality of shared self-understanding" (Sandel, *Liberalism* 181). This is obviously Harris's second use of the term—communities constructed by shared mental habits.

Yet this analysis of what is wrong with current argument (and what makes medieval practice so much better) seems odd to me. In addition to the fact that I have trouble seeing the age that MacIntyre admires as so much better—the consequences for people in the Middle Ages who argued themselves onto the wrong side of a declaration of heresy certainly keep me from seeing that era as especially golden—I see no reason to assume that shared definitions and better arguments go hand in hand. Agreeing on numerous things does not ensure that interlocutors will reach agreement on whatever they initially disagreed about. The Federalists and Anti-Federalists are a case in point—Brutus and Publius have more in common than not, but the one thing they do not have in common (a desire that the United States become a great commercial power versus a desire that it remain in a pastoral middle landscape peopled by petty bourgeois and yeoman farmers) was enough to preclude agreement on the need for the Constitution. The Bartholomae-Elbow debate (discussed earlier) is another example. To anyone outside of composition studies, they would seem to share a tremendous amount, but they did not reach agreement. The question is not simply how much people agree, but on what they agree.

Communitarians like Sandel do not explicitly call for a univocal moral discourse, and the most attractive (I think) aspect of their argument is the idea that we should not be so afraid of moral arguments in the public sphere. Sandel cites as an instance of such fear Joycelyn Elders's reaction when then-President Clinton said that having children out of wedlock is wrong. Elders, Sandel says, "continued to display the nonjudgmental reflex characteristic of contemporary liberalism . . . stating, 'Everyone has different moral standards. You can't impose your standards on someone else'" (*Democracy's Discontent* 328). Sandel's example is perfect, but for pretty nearly the opposite of his point: The appalling hypocrisy of Clinton (or Gingrich, who was making the same point at the time) condemning the sexual behavior of others is precisely what makes people want major political figures to remain silent on moral issues.

In addition, the examples that Sandel cites as indicating a revivifying of moral argument are not instances of people arguing *about* morals; they exemplify people asserting, but not being willing to argue about, a specific moral code (and usually for purposes of political posturing). If the goal is to have a public sphere where people argue with one another, then arguments *from* "self-evident" morals are debilitating. The problem with arguing from morals is that it ensures that people perceive an opposing argument as an immoral person. Why talk with someone who is immoral? Why listen?

Arguing *from* a specific (and unarguable) moral code means seeing one (and only one) side as the moral one; hence such arguments are so full of hate. And that too is something communitarians fail to acknowledge—that a tremendous amount of "moral" discourse is hateful. Even the arguments from MacIntyre's golden era (the high Middle Ages) are filled with accusations of heresy. The liberal answer is to avoid moral discourse altogether, and I agree that such evasion is disturbing. But the solution is not to invite more argument from morals unless one wants a kind of hate-filled expressivism, or moral hegemony. The agonistic (and deliberative) answer is that one must be willing to argue *about* the morals. The communitarian answer seems to be that discourse can only be productive among people who share moral systems. Communitarians simply assume, but never show, that an irenic public sphere is both necessary and good.

This assumption of the necessity and desirability of an irenic public sphere, especially if connected to a definition of "community" as one with "shared moral visions," is subject to a fairly straightforward criticism: Under such a formulation, dissent is dangerous. The moment that one fundamentally disagrees with the group, the community—by that definition—no longer exists. A person who disagrees has made clear that s/he does not share the community's goals and interests, and that s/he has different "habits of mind," so there can never be significant dissent from within a community. Fundamental conflict and community are mutually exclusive.

Chafe describes the way that this presumption of the need for communities to be in agreement—another part of "the mystique of progressivism"—also prevented progress on racial issues:

> The underlying assumption is that conflict over any issue, whether it be labor unions, race relations, or political ideology, will permanently rend the fragile fabric of internal harmony. Hence, progress can occur only when everyone is able to agree—voluntarily—on an appropriate course of action. (Chafe 7)

As Chafe says, this assumption tends to benefit the status quo—because an intransigent conservative can keep any change from happening—while it tends to demonize dissenters—because it makes them the ones who seem to have disrupted the consensus and destroyed the happy community. When they criticize the status quo, it appears that everyone was happy until the malcontents started stirring things up. This was exactly the argument used in the antebellum era for assassinating abolitionists and censoring their publications; it was repeated ad nauseam in defenses of the gag rule (that prohibited discussion of antislavery petitions in Congress); it has continued in histories of that era that say abolitionism caused the war. It was also the argument made by the "Eight Alabama Clergymen" who so famously called Martin Luther King Jr.'s actions in Birmingham "unwise and untimely" (42). They "point out that such actions as incite to hatred and violence, however technically peaceful those actions may be, have not contributed to the resolution of our local problems" (42).

And in making this argument, critics of the dissenters appeal to communitarian principles. Sandel argues that Stephen Douglas's proposal that slave states be left alone was a liberal argument because it deferred to the autonomy of the slave states. On the contrary, it was a communitarian argument in that it deferred to the autonomy of communities, not individuals (a liberal argument would assert that the autonomy of slaves is a foundational value that no community can legitimately violate). John Calhoun describes slavery as integral to the community: "The relation which now exists between the two races in the slave-holding States has existed for two centuries. It has grown with our growth, and strengthened with our strength" (2:488). Because slave holding constitutes the community ethos, any attack on it is an attack on the identity of the South itself. Calhoun argues that Congress's even permitting the antislavery petitions to be received for consideration would necessitate secession: "There would be to us but one alternative—to triumph or perish as a people" (2:489). The recurrent argument was that the South had its "peculiar institution," about which there was community agreement; any criticism of slavery (*not* slavery itself) would lead to conflict, conflict that would be blamed on the critics of slavery.

The immediate consequence of this sense that conflict threatens community is that injustices—such as the injustice of segregation—never enter the realm of public discourse or are treated as local and temporary aberrations best resolved through observing "the principles of law and order and common sense" (Carpenter 43). When civility prevails, no one wants to bring up such a divisive topic; when the topic is finally brought up, the issue becomes the behavior of those who violated the code of civility rather than their concerns regarding the injustice. Thus, attempting to have a public sphere without conflict means that one loses the ability to argue about central issues. This is what Chafe refers to as "the chilling power of consensus to crush efforts to raise issues of racial justice" (8). Prizing civility means that people who become confrontational or argumentative have violated a basic principle of social discourse, and they should be shunned and condemned. Evading conflict contributes to social harmony and can even facilitate an effective public sphere as long as the disagreements are relatively minor, but it cannot accommodate people who are deeply unhappy with the system itself.

To the extent that one can say there is a community, it is a community committed to injustice. Anthropologists have suggested that community identity is often formed by identifying some group as hated; the shared mental habits that define a community are not necessarily as benevolent as communitarians might hope. Even Sandel grants this possibility: "To accord the political community a stake in the character of its citizens is to concede the possibility that bad communities may form bad characters" (*Democracy's Discontent* 321). Etzioni responds to this kind of criticism—that communities may be committed to injustice—by saying that people are members of many different communities: "they can, and do, use these multi-memberships (as well as a limited, but not trivial, ability to choose one's work and residential communities) to protect themselves from excessive pressure by any one community" (xiv). This response almost exactly misses the point. In addition to shifting back to talking about physical communities, Etzioni is describing precisely what worries people about the communitarian model: that people have a tendency to pull away from difference as much as possible, and to spend as much of their time as they feasibly can with people who think and behave the same way that they do. The concern is that communitarian theory entrenches that tendency.

In addition, there is something enraging about Etzioni's comment. African American slaves could not choose their work or residential communities; not everyone can simply pick up and move if they get irritated by their neighbors. Perhaps Etzioni does not, but I vividly remember people whose reaction to African Americans' complaints about segregation was, "If they don't like it, they can go back to Africa" and the "America: Love It or Leave It" bumper stickers directed at critics of U.S.

involvement in Vietnam. I was able to leave the politically reactionary community in which I grew up in order to move to the more comfortable Berkeley, but I still had to sign a state-mandated loyalty oath to work for the university. I could go on to teach in a fairly progressive community in Greensboro, North Carolina, but I would still receive a threatening letter from my university as to what would happen if I taught material that violated community standards. I can now teach in the liberal community of Austin, Texas, but I pay taxes to a state that executes minors and the mentally retarded.

Communitarianism has raised some interest in composition studies. As M. Jimmie Killingsworth remarks, "liberalism's stock is down" (110), and this makes communitarianism an attractive option. While not uncritical of communitarianism, Killingsworth does describe its attraction as a kind of middle ground.

> In liberalism, social organization depends upon two strong formations—the *individual*, who may enjoy a wide range of rights and freedoms at the possible cost of alienation and fragmentation, and the *nation-state*, which ensures the rights of individuals but, in its administration, tends toward faceless abstraction and bureaucracy. By contrast, communitarianism models social life on the organization of the village or small town; inhabitants share a face-to-face familiarity and a commitment to conversations among equals (based on dialogue, discourse, and communal trust). (110–11)

In contrasting communitarianism to "liberalism," of course, Killingsworth conflates the liberal political tradition with the liberal model of democracy. Still and all, it seems to me that his attraction to communitarianism is not unfounded—anything that speaks well of "community" is likely to be very attractive to rhetoricians. Yet, as has often been remarked, our own use of the term "community" is deeply flawed, as one can particularly see in regard to the notion of communities of discourse.

Compositionists' adoption of the notion of communities of discourse is usually traced through David Bartholomae, Kenneth Bruffee, and Patricia Bizzell back to Stanley Fish, Richard Rorty, and, ultimately, Thomas Kuhn. Often used interchangeably with the term "interpretive communities," the exact cause-effect claim implicit in the term is vague. For some theorists, it simply means something along the lines of "community-based norms that influence writing" (Beaufort 488) while for others it necessarily endorses a strong form of social construction of knowledge. Thomas Kent's definition is "our knowledge of others and of the world always will be relative to the particular conceptual schemes or communities in which we exist" (426). He connects this to "the claim that what we know is determined by or is relative to the community in which we live" (426). Thus, at one end of a spectrum, "communities of discourse" means little more than genre conventions, with the implication that people can move easily from one community to another; at the other end, the term becomes determinist, with the implication that communities of discourse shape one's knowledge to such a degree that discourse between communities is impossible—or "incommensurable" to use Kuhn's language.

Most of the criticisms of the notion of discourse communities involve that stronger form—the weaker cause-effect claim has been more or less ignored. The criticisms generally run along one of three lines. Some theorists (such as Myers, Joseph Harris, or Trimbur) argue that the concept tends to present students as people who must submit to the community—writing classes thereby become rites of passage into communities whose very nature students lack the ability to critique or change. Entering the community means conforming to its standards and preserving consensus, so that this approach to discourse communities is fundamentally (albeit unintentionally) conservative. A second, and closely connected, criticism is that the concept of a community of discourse overemphasizes agreement and uniformity, downplaying the tensions and disagreements that any community actually experiences (Cooper, Beaufort). The third criticism, one most effectively made by Kent, is that the epistemology at the very base of the notion is overdetermined and inaccurate.

The first two lines of criticism generally end with a call for a revision of the concept that would permit more conflict and somehow derail communities' rush toward consensus. John Trimbur, in his response to Kenneth Bruffee, suggests what amounts to something very similar to Gerald Graff's "teaching the conflicts": Rather than present a community of discourse (such as that of literary critics) as some kind of objective monolith, Trimbur encourages his students to see the community as constructed by conventions that are particular, fractured, and open to dispute. In making this argument, Trimbur significantly (in both senses of the word) shifts the meaning of Bruffee's central metaphor: negotiation.

The metaphor of negotiation recurs frequently in articles concerning communities of discourse, and it points to a central tension in the concept—the relation we imagine students have to the conventions of the community of discourse they are trying to enter. Bruffee has students negotiating "the rocks and shoals of social relations" ("Collaborative Learning" 403) whereas Trimbur has students negotiating "differences" (607). When a boat negotiates rocks and shoals, it does all the accommodating—the rocks and shoals will remain exactly where they began. This is essentially the liberal view of education and politics, that students are neophytes who must themselves change in order to enter a world of more or less stable judgments.

Trimbur's use of the metaphor of negotiation, however, assumes the kind of negotiation that occurs between people, both of whom are expected to make accommodations. This use of the negotiation metaphor may initially seem to be one that assumes more power on the part of students, but it too is problematic. While in theory negotiation may imply equality and reciprocally binding obligations, in practice, negotiation is often indistinguishable from bargaining. It is naive to think that students negotiate as equals with communities of discourse, or even that students have equal power when negotiating with one another. This latter point has been noticed, fundamentally the same as the criticism of communitarianism in politics, and critics of "communities of discourse" have expressed concern about the extraordinary pressure to conformity that peer groups can exert. I think this latter concern is often misunderstood or minimized, both among communitarians and compositionists, because it is so easy to fall prey to the mystique of progressivism.

Delores Schriner and William Rice, for instance, describe a situation in which a foreign student writes an extremely homophobic message to a class mailing list—advocating the death penalty for homosexuals, a practice that was, according to Schriner and Rice, "a practice common in his homeland" (477). They say that the instructor recommended on the list that "students who were offended by the discussion should feel free to ignore it and go on to other 'items'"—advice that was itself ignored by some students, so that the argument did continue. Schriner and Rice conclude:

> In the end, however, the students clearly had learned how to negotiate among starkly different sets of values in their community, and during class

meetings no hostile words or glances were directed to the dissenting student, who remained very much a part of the common enterprise. (477)

I find this story much more disturbing than Schriner and Rice seem to do because I think that they were paying attention to the wrong difference. In the first place, by negotiation, they seem to mean little more than that the students maintained American standards of civility in the classroom, and that is one problem with the concept of communities of discourse—that it is not at all clear what constitutes a successful "negotiation."[4] If a good community is assumed to be irenic and expressive, then simply maintaining the peace is sufficient, and this is a success story; if, however, one assumes that a good community should be agonistic or deliberative, then it is not.

Schriner and Rice present this incident as a narrative of successful negotiation of difference: but which difference? The foreign student was taking a minority stance on the mailing list, but one that is far from uncommon in American culture and that is dominant in his own. So he was only momentarily in the position of Other. For that student, being different in this regard is the anomalous situation. But what about a gay student? Chances are good that at least one student in the class was homosexual. For that student (or set of students) the "intense and lengthy exchanges on homosexuality" (477) were likely simply one more instance of hearing themselves demonized, pathologized, and threatened.

The community was likely one that reinscribed gay students' position as Other, reinforced difference, and diminished—if not trivialized—the experience. The instructor's advice that students ignore the exchange failed to distinguish between students who were simply offended by the notion that homosexuality is a crime that should be punished by death and those who feel themselves—and, to some degree, were and are—physically threatened by such an argument. Schriner and Rice refer to the "community" and "common enterprise," but to what extent were gay students ever part of that community, and to what extent did they feel a part of the common enterprise?

One can see a similar confusion in Schriner and Rice's comment about "the community's commitment to absolute freedom of expression" (477). Even ignoring the issue of whether or not the community actually had such a commitment—I assume the institution, if not the instructors, would have done something very quickly had someone started posting jpegs of child pornography—the fact that the instructors insisted upon the students having freedom from a certain censorship does not in any way ensure that students felt free to post what they really believed.

No community has absolute freedom of expression, either in the sense that the discourse is equally open to all points of view nor in the sense that the discourse has equal costs for all participants. There are different costs for a student who says, "some of my best friends are gay, and I do not think they should be executed" and a student who says, "I am gay, and I don't think I should be executed." The first is simply an argument in a class mailing list; the second is potentially a life-change. I would suggest that Chafe's argument regarding the mystique of progressivism's concealing inequalities and injustices similarly applies to an apparent commitment to absolute freedom of expression. Because there is a lot of discourse, we do not ask what kind it is. Because no one is excluded from the physical community, we fail to think carefully about other forms of exclusion. The discourse of community can obscure the discursive inequalities that really exist among members of that community.

Anyone who has used mailing lists or engaged in student-centered discussion has had experiences similar to a student arguing for execution of homosexuals. It is, in micro, the problem of any community that has someone in it who is committed to injustice. The problem is not that such arguments exist, nor even that people have trouble being polite in the presence of them; the problem is that theoretical pieces about communities of discourse—including ones like Trimbur's or Harris's that try to modify the concept—do not help instructors think through what is the best way to respond to this kind of situation.

The problem may well be in our own vague use of the term "community," and the problem that the distinction shared by many communitarians and many compositionists is the same (physical versus intellectual) is not the most useful. A more useful approach is the one used by Beiner, who is himself adopting a distinction made by Robert Paul Wolff: between "affective" and "rational" communities. "Affective communities" are defined by shared values and shared identities, by what Beiner critically refers to as "the raptures of *Gemeinschaft*" (33); they are what I would call irenic/expressive. "Rational communities" are defined by the need to make decisions together, "a shared world of political concerns that affect all in common" (33). As long as we are after the raptures of

gemeinschaft, civility is necessary, and significant difference is dangerous. If, however, our expectation is not to feel snug, but to make decisions along with the various people whom the decisions affect, then difference is necessary, and homogeneity is dangerous.

My criticism of communitarianism is that it does not provide any
protection of minority cultures; it does not protect against the tyranny
of the majority; it does not even ensure that members of more or less
mainstream cultures hear other points of view. It does not necessarily
complicate people's tendency to slip into enclaves, or stop them from
universalizing on the basis of experience that they do not even realize is
limited. It is easily seduced by the mystique of progressivism in its over-
emphasis on the need for consensus and its failure to theorize conflict.

It sits somewhere between liberal political theory and agonism. The
more that it assumes that difference is dangerous and avoidable, the more
it embodies the very flaws for which it condemns liberalism; the more
that it privileges agonistic and deliberative communities, the more it
shares the advantages and disadvantages of agonism and can slip into the
interest-based model.

I agree with Trimbur, Joseph Harris, and Jarratt that compositionists
evade conflict and that we need a model of teaching that makes conflict
not simply a preliminary step toward consensus but a "public space where
students can begin to form their own voices as writers and intellectuals"
(Harris 116). But it has to be a public space with rules. If all we strive
for is "a sort of teaching that aims more to keep the conversation going
than to lead it toward a certain end" (Harris 116), we can easily fall prey
to the mystique of progressivism—mistaking a lively discussion for a
place where people are actually learning about difference. We need to
imagine a public space where people do not simply speak to each other,
but one where they listen.

I want now to return to my deferred discussion of Kent's criticism of
communities of discourse—that it is tied to the social construction of
knowledge. Particularly since James Berlin's "Contemporary Composition," it is conventional in composition studies to assert that every pedagogy is implicitly connected to some epistemology—current-traditional
rhetoric to a positivism, expressivism to what is variously called Antinomianism or the myth of the autonomous, and the taxonomist's preferred pedagogy to some form of social constructivism. Despite articles

like Thomas Kent's or Reed Way Dasenbrook's, social constructivism remains hegemonic.

Yet, there are several striking things about the rhetoric of the hegemony. The first is that, as Eagleton remarks, it is made in service of an avowed pluralism and a politics that claims to be pluralistic, an interesting irony. Second, it is not so much that extraordinarily persuasive cases have been made *for* social constructivism, as it is that advocates have engaged in powerful critiques of the apparent alternatives. Berlin's New Rhetoric is contrasted to current-traditional and expressivist pedagogies, each of which is linked to an obviously untenable epistemology. Erika Lindemann contrasts knowledge-making pedagogies to process pedagogies and the belletristic tradition, each of which is identified as an earlier stage in the development of composition studies. Composition studies is not alone in setting up social constructivism as the only alternative to a dilemma presented by some form of positivism and some form of expressivism. Christopher Norris has described the same problem in theory:

> The whole debate is thus skewed to make it appear an issue of choice between, on the one hand, naive (subject-centered or "foundationalist") epistemologies and, on the other, an approach that takes its bearings from language and finds no room for such obsolete items of faith. (*Reclaiming* 48)

And, of course, the three-part taxonomy is far from exhaustive; earlier I remarked that Arendt's philosophy fits into none of the three categories, and one might also add the long philosophical tradition of skepticism (which is, as both Gage and Sloane have argued, especially important in the rhetorical tradition).

Norris's quote is especially useful since it points to what may seem counterintuitive. Both subject-centered epistemologies, such as the neo-Platonism of expressivism, and foundationalist epistemologies, such as the direct realism of positivism, assume the same model of knowledge. Whether knowledge is in the heart (in neo-Platonism) or in the world (in positivism), the models assume that perception can be unmediated by such characteristics as race, class, and gender. That assumption is precisely what postmodern thought has attacked; hence, it appears that some form of social constructivism is the only plausible alternative. But it is worth considering more closely just how that argument is made, particularly in regard to two points: first, exactly how the critiques of positivistic and subject-centered epistemologies apply to social constructivism itself; and second, the thoroughness and accuracy of the recurrent expeditio at the center of the argument.

Initially associated with Thomas Kuhn and philosophy of science, social construction of knowledge has been promoted in philosophy of mind by Richard Rorty, and in literary theory by Stanley Fish, both of whom draw on the authority of Kuhn. Kuhn and Rorty are somewhat different (especially as recent scholarship on Kuhn has shown), but both share the project of criticizing the naive realism, correspondence theory of truth, and autonomous self presumed by various traditions in Anglo-American philosophy. Berlin uses the term "epistemology," and compositionists have tended to follow suit. While far from incorrect, this usage is slightly different from that of philosophers, Kuhn being a philosopher of science and Rorty a philosopher of mind or pragmatist. Rorty calls what he does simply philosophy, as makes sense given that pragmatists tend to eschew intradisciplinary subdivisions.[5]

Social constructivism is simultaneously an epistemology and a model of the self. Rorty argues that it has beneficial consequences for culture (see especially *Achieving Our Country* and introduction to *Consequences of Pragmatism*), but he is primarily interested in arguing against philosophy's impulse to metaphysics. Rorty argues that the idea that the purpose of philosophy is to establish first principles about which one can be certain (which he attributes to Plato) both defines the philosophical community and wastes its time. In *Philosophy and the Mirror of Nature,* he follows out the inherent incoherence and destructive consequence of that impulse for the discipline of philosophy; in *Achieving Our Country,* he describes the political consequences and recommends that "the Left should put a moratorium on theory. It should try to kick the philosophy habit" (91). Attempts to get theory right simply paralyze us and are unnecessary:

> For purposes of thinking about how to achieve our country, we do not need to worry about the correspondence theory of truth, the grounds of normativity, the impossibility of justice, or the infinite distance which separates us from the other. For those purposes, we can give both religion and philosophy a pass. (97)

This quote points to several puzzling qualities about compositionists' appeals to social construction of knowledge. First, and the importance of this is hard to overstate, compositionists try to use Rorty to legitimate a project that he explicitly condemns—trying to get one's theory right. This does not mean that I think the goal of more arguments about theory is a bad one, but that the argument from authority for such a project is internally contradictory (the grounds on which foundationalism is rejected).

Second, the inference is usually drawn that social construction of knowledge means that one should not criticize dominant community practices (as in the controversy regarding postmodern and poststructural responses to female genital mutilation); yet, if that is the correct inference, it is not one that Rorty himself follows. He is neither pluralistic about nor deferential to the community of philosophers and their metaphysical impulse; he argues they are wrong, and that they should change. As with communitarians' attack on their community's dominant political philosophy, Rorty's refusal to defer to the community of philosophers is confusing, especially since he argues about foundations in order to say we should not argue about foundations. This is, essentially, a similar problem to his making theoretical arguments about how we should stop doing theory—are we to do as says, or to do as he does?

When Kuhn published *The Structure of Scientific Revolutions,* the dominant explanation of science, typified by Alexander Koyre, was that the history of science is teleological, that each generation of scientists builds on the previous one toward increasingly accurate and objective descriptions of reality. This teleology fits neatly with the positivist idea that the scientific way of knowing is the best, and that objectivity is both possible and desirable. The crudest versions of positivism assert that the mind can mirror nature, and language can mirror the mind, especially if an individual rejects tradition, prejudice, and authority to think for himself. This crude positivism was especially popular as a model of science, one that described a good scientist as someone who approached the facts without any prejudice. Manifest in the popular culture in forms like Sherlock Holmes or D. F. X. Van Dusen's "Thinking Machine," it remains in characters like Spock or Seven of Nine in *Star Trek.*

While Kuhn's brief is mainly against positivism, the basic notion that one should never rely on the perceptions of others, but should try to perceive and think for oneself, is shared with other traditions as well. In American culture, what has been known as the Antinomian strain also assumes that the ethical individual stands alone against society and social pressure (for more on this point see especially Lang). Knowledge of what is good and right comes directly to the individual from God (or

Nature). The same argument is promoted in "foundationalist" philosophy; Norris usefully defines a foundationalist as "a thinker whose ultimate appeal is to the subject construed as an absolute, transcendent, indubitable source of knowledge and truth" (*Reclaiming* 33). In social theory, this same concept has been described as "the mythic heroism of the social actor" with its assumption that

> the freedom of the self was conditional upon an antagonistic differentiation of the individual from his/her cultural and institutional webbing. Social relations and "traditions" became the "object"—the domain of constraint—in a subject-object duality. . . . It was the object in a subject-object, individual-against-society, antagonism from which the actor was impelled to be free. (Somers and Gibson 64)

I should here note that, while this naively realistic epistemology and the model of the autonomous self are often historically connected, there is no reason that they must be logically connected; one does not necessarily imply the other, so that one might have a model of the autonomous self without the direct epistemology, as with Rawls or Hannah Arendt.

Typically, expressivism (the term usually used in composition studies for subject-centered epistemologies) and positivism are critiqued on three grounds. First, it is argued that they are not accurate descriptions of how people genuinely think (e.g., Kuhn's *Structure of Scientific Revolutions*); second, it is argued that they are internally contradictory (e.g., Rorty's *Philosophy and the Mirror of Nature*); third, they are criticized on pragmatic grounds, as pedagogically or politically damaging (e.g., Berlin's criticism of expressivism, Rorty's *Achieving Our Country*). These three lines of argument lead to very powerful critiques; typically, one argues for a philosophy by showing that it is an accurate description of reality, is internally logical, and/or has attractive consequences.

It is worth considering, however, just what happens if one applies those three lines of criticism to social constructivism. In regard to the first, by its own argument, it cannot argue that it is more true than other philosophies, or else it lands itself in an important contradiction. Yet, social constructivists do, in fact, continually assert or imply that it is an accurate representation of how the mind works: "Like any brand of epistemological anti-realism, it consistently denies the possibility of describing the way the world is, and just as consistently finds itself doing so" (Eagleton 28). Something about social constructivism does seem right—

it does provide apt critiques of both positivism and expressivism. Yet, the very fact that it does so is the evidence that it is wrong. That is, the postmodern critiques of positivism and expressivism may well be right, but the affirmative case—its own epistemology and model of the self— is self-consuming. Dasenbrook has discussed this irony in regard to Thomas Kuhn's own assertion that theorists cannot claim to appeal directly to evidence; after all, that is exactly the stance that Kuhn himself does take:

> Kuhn does not present his observations of the history of science as ineluctably determined by his theories concerning scientific development; instead, he acts as if historical evidence is independently available and can be brought into the discussion in order to support his historical interpretations. . . . If Kuhn is right, he shouldn't be able to see and say the things he does. (555)

Even Rorty cannot help from making assertions about reality; in *Philosophy and the Mirror of Nature,* he argues that his readings of certain texts are more accurate than others, despite the cultural dominance of those inaccurate readings; in *Achieving Our Country,* he talks about what our political situation really is and how it can really be improved, as opposed to what people think it is and how it could be made better. His most common criticism of philosophies is that they cannot be true because they are internally inconsistent; while he does not ascribe to the correspondence theory of truth (although one might argue that it is implicit in *Achieving Our Country*), his criticism of philosophy does suggest something along the lines of a consistency theory of truth.

If social constructivism is preferable because it is more true, then especially the more extreme claims made on its behalf cannot be true. Even its claim to be more accurate than other philosophies of mind is problematic—how can one make that claim without appealing to some foundational, immanent, transcendent, or objective criteria for "true"? This paradox is not a fatal flaw for social constructivism (although it is for the crudest forms—the kind that Eagleton attacks in *Illusions of Postmodernism*), but it does mean that social constructivism, like positivism and expressivism, has its own problems with accuracy and internal consistency. Thus, the pragmatic argument becomes even more important.

In composition studies, social constructivism has been presented as an intelligent alternative to the incipient positivism of current-traditional rhetoric and the neo-Platonism of expressivism. As Berlin has argued, expressivism assumes that Truth is perceived individually and confirmed through writing. Within composition studies, expressivism has been criticized for its privileging of authenticity in writing, its assumption of learning as a private experience, and its epistemology. Perhaps one of the strongest criticisms has been on pragmatic grounds. That is, if one assumes the traditional defense of public education—that it prepares citizens for active and effective participation in public discourse—then the role of expressivism in this education is somewhat obscure. The topics preferred by expressivist pedagogies evade disagreement in favor of exploration. The main criticism is that such a pedagogy does little to prepare students to deliberate with people who have fundamentally different arguments (as opposed to express their own point of view in front of such people).

While this is an important point, the criticism is potentially unfair, at least when leveled from the perspective of a social construction of knowledge, because it is not clear that the latter epistemology is necessarily any more conducive to imagining communities in productive conflict. After all, Kenneth Bruffee speaks of "an *assenting* community of peers with whom we speak and to whom we listen in our heads" ("Writing" 573, emphasis added). And, as will be mentioned later, one of the main problems with social constructivism is that, while it claims to describe how people think, it cannot describe why people change their thinking; if knowledge is constructed by one's culture, then it is unclear how or why a culture would ever change.

Foundationalist epistemologies are as inaccurate and politically unattractive as expressivist ones. Underlying foundationalism is some version of the correspondence theory of truth, the idea that a proposition is true when it corresponds to reality. The obvious criticism of this theory is that it is not clear whether this is a claim that truth is an ontological quality, a perceptual one, or a discursive one. Is a sentence true whether or not we perceive it to be such? Can we always perceive the correspondence? Does a "true" sentence have more rhetorical power than one that is not? Is the degree or kind of assent given a proposition an indication of its correspondence to reality?

When the answers to these questions assert or assume a universal experience of truth, then the implicit epistemology is obviously false—the notion that somehow all people experience truth in the same way is quite obviously not true. Charles Lemert, who calls foundationalism the "strong-we" position (because it tends to include talk about what "we" believe), points out that the claims of such foundationalism "cannot be strongly asserted outside an enduring culture in which rival moral claims are incapable of compelling adherents of the strong-we position to doubt the universality of their convictions" (106), and no such culture has ever existed. As he says,

> While there are historical instances in which proponents of the strong-we position have enjoyed a virtual hegemony over legitimate moral claims in the realm, there are few instances where that hegemony was ever thorough enough to eliminate active, if ineffective, counter-claims. (106)

Michael Bernard-Donals and Richard Glejzer have put this claim even more strongly: "foundational notions of the human and natural sciences have been so discredited as to force us to consider what kind of anti-foundationalism gives us the most productive and perhaps emancipatory knowledge" (437).

Because of these pragmatic problems with expressivism and foun-dationalism, social constructivism may seem a better alternative in that, as Craig Calhoun has said, "it challenges at once the ideas that identity is given naturally and the idea that it is produced purely by acts of indi-vidual will" ("Social Theory" 13). It acknowledges the role of the social in the construction of thought, problematizes the assumption of easy universality, and points to the margins, but it too has its unhappy ethi-cal and political consequences. Norris has summarized one of the most pressing: "What is most to be feared is a wholesale levelling of the facul-ties which would deprive reason of its moderating role and thereby re-duce history, philosophy and politics to a mere force-field of contend-ing interests or rhetorical strategies" (*What's Wrong* 72). Rhetoric has long been defended as the alternative to force—if strong social constructivism is right, however, it is force all the way down.

A world where history, philosophy, and politics are simply arenas of conflict where the most powerful win is a world where dissent is nearly impossible. Martha Nussbaum, after watching Stanley Fish give a talk in which he repeatedly asserted a necessary connection between leftist politics and a rejection of traditional notions of rationality, and an equally necessary connection between a respect for rationality and reactionary politics, acidly remarked, "I am not sure what political position in

America does have a deep commitment to open public dialectic governed by traditional norms of rational argument and fair procedure, but I believe it is not the right" (*Love's Knowledge* 220–21). And, indeed, although the right has been extremely hostile toward postmodern and poststructuralist philosophy (e.g., Charles Colson's columns in *Christianity Today,* Roger Kimball's *Tenured Radicals,* Lynne Cheney's *Telling the Truth*), it has also been very quick to use the arguments from those philosophies. The Christian right immediately picked up the argument that foundational documents (e.g., the Constitution) are not neutral , but expressions of patriarchal and Judeo-Christian values, in order to argue that only Judeo-Christians can be trusted to enact democratic government. George W. Bush's defense of denying human rights to suspected terrorists was that such rights are not foundational or "natural," but constructed by legal entities and therefore only applicable to U.S. citizens.[6]

A recurrent argument against foundationalist epistemologies is that they are so closely allied with structural injustices. And, while can one point to such injustices, one can also point to liberating uses of foundationalism. One can point to the NAACP, the Declaration of Universal Human Rights, Amnesty International, the SNCC and see groups that have made real changes through foundationalist rhetoric. Can one point to similar moments for the social construction of knowledge? One can, oddly enough (given its implicit hostility to pragmatism), make a pragmatic argument for the Enlightenment model of self and politics; can one make a pragmatic argument for social construction of knowledge? In other words, as unattractive as are many of the pragmatic consequences of foundationalism, there are some positive ones; it becomes difficult, then, to argue that social constructivism is preferable on pragmatic grounds to foundationalism.

Proponents of the Enlightenment model are often accused of political naivete, ignoring the deeply ingrained structural inequalities and institutional forms of oppression, but the accusation applies even more strongly to proponents of the social construction of knowledge. Eagleton's *Illusions of Postmodernism* emphasizes this point:

> But in seeking to cut the ground from under its opponents' feet, postmodernism finds itself unavoidably pulling the rug out from under itself, leaving itself with no more reason why we should resist fascism than the feebly pragmatic plea that fascism is not the way we do things in Sussex or Sacramento. (28)

As Lester Faigley says, theorists have found it "extremely difficult . . . to find space for political agency in light of postmodern theory" (20). Its very strength is a weakness; postmodern theory's

> power to fold language back on itself makes postmodern theory at once an extremely powerful means for exposing the political investments of foundational concepts, but the same power prevents postmodern theorists from making claims of truth or emancipatory value for this activity. (43–44)

It may well be that social constructivism is not necessarily linked to political quietism, but one can hardly imagine it motivating political activism, especially on behalf of the rights of other people. Social change, such as ending slavery, extending the vote, changing working conditions, improving prison conditions, involves more than those directly interested; it requires getting people interested who could easily see themselves as unaffected. I fail to see how social constructivism could motivate people to engage in political action on behalf of others. In fact, it seems to me that it is most likely to do the opposite—how would a social constructivist defend King's behavior in Birmingham? He was from outside the community, he was rejecting the dominant and socially constructed values of segregation, as well as community standards regarding civility, and he was greatly disrupting communities. What is the social constructivist argument for Amnesty International? For sympathy strikes?

In short, there is a very strong pragmatic argument against social constructivism—it cannot make the world a better place; it cannot protect minority rights. While others have voiced this concern, and some postmodern thinkers have tried to respond (especially Lyotard and Rorty), there are serious problems with their arguments. As Robert Asen and Daniel Brouwer say,

> Lyotard calls . . . for a turn to dissension and heteromorphous local language games. But in renouncing terror—the threatened or actual elimination of a player from a language game—Lyotard appeals to the prescriptives, such as open access and debate, that he seeks to deny. (13)

It is the central criticism of social constructivism, as it means that there are serious problems with the only internally consistent argument for social constructivism—pragmatic consequences.

Thus, if one applies the three recurrent lines of criticism (accuracy, internal consistency, pragmatic consequences) to social constructivism, one has a troubling situation. It cannot argue it is true without falling into inconsistency. The assertions that other epistemologies are not true lead into internal inconsistencies. The pragmatic line of argument is no better than the argument that it is more true; it is precisely on pragmatic grounds that social constructivism is most disturbing. The pragmatic critique of expressivism is compelling—that it facilitates quietism because it makes political action nothing more than an expression of preferences—but that is exactly the same criticism that one can make of social constructivism. Apparently denying grounds for dissent, making political action a mere expression of preference, tending toward quietism or endorsing the use of force, the pragmatic consequences of social constructivism are deeply troubling. That leaves the major argument for social construction of knowledge the argument from authority, and even that is problematic.

Less common than argument by expeditio, but sometimes implicit, is an argument from authority (in which various authorities such as Kuhn, Rorty, and Foucault are asserted to have settled the issue). The problem with the former line of argument is that it relies on a false dilemma; the problem with the second is that it asserts a hegemony in the fields of philosophy of mind and philosophy of science that does not exist. The question of epistemology has not been settled in philosophy of mind, with naive realism (as a philosophy of perception, not cognition) a much stronger camp than the discourse in rhetoric and composition might lead one to believe (for an interesting recent defense of this position, see Hilary Putnam's *The Threefold Cord*). There remains a lively argument in fields like philosophy of mind, philosophy of perception, philosophy of language, and philosophy of science. We have taken part of that argument without ourselves taking part in it. That is, our own disciplinary discourse does not represent the full range of positions present in the disciplinary discourse from which we are borrowing. My intention is not to argue for realism in any form—were our only options social constructivism, positivism, expressivism, I would choose social constructivism—but to argue that there is an argument to be made, that the issue of epistemology is still an open one, with people of principle and intelligence (and various political agendas) on far more than three sides.

There are essentially two formulations of social construction. There is a strong form, the one advocated by Fish and Rorty, and there is a weaker form. The strongest form depends upon Kuhn's argument concerning "incommensurability"—the notion that different systems of thought are so different from one another that one can only move from one to the other through adopting an entirely new worldview. While many historians of science accept Kuhn's critique of essentially teleological histories (that the history of science is the history of increasingly unprejudiced men articulating increasingly objective and accurate theories in a steady progress toward truth), they balk at the notion of incommensurability. Certainly, Aristotelian and Newtonian physics are incommensurable, but Newtonian physics and quantum physics are not—in fact, students are taught Newtonian physics along the way to learning quantum physics. Were the strongest form of social construction right, that would be impossible.

The strong form of social construction of knowledge cannot explain why some individuals reject the values of their communities or are able to see flaws in dominant paradigms. The weaker form simply says that our thinking is strongly influenced by our social norms, that individuals do not have some kind of direct and easy access to an ontologically grounded truth, that determining the truth and accuracy of any proposition is extremely difficult and never assured. That line of argument is extremely common in the history of philosophy, even (as I argued earlier) among the very philosophers (like Locke, Plato, Popper, and Kant) who serve as foils for social constructivism. It is easy, and sometimes rhetorically desirable, to overstate the naivete of the epistemology proposed by Enlightenment philosophers. It is common to propose a skeptical and antifoundational epistemology by contrasting it to something that presupposes a brain in a vat; finding a major philosopher who proposes an easy and direct relation between mind and reality is a difficult task. Even among the more minor philosophers who do sometimes assert a direct epistemology, such as the New England Puritan theologians of the seventeenth century, one can find assertions regarding the importance of skepticism and self-reflection and the fallibility of human perception. As I have argued elsewhere, the problem is that their political actions (such as hanging Quakers and trying to enslave Amerindians) were not based in the skeptical epistemology they appeared to advocate but implied an uncomplicated and highly unskeptical estimation of their own ability to be certain.

The problem is that there are several very different attitudes that one might have toward the foundations of knowledge. One might assert that the foundations exist (a foundational ontology) and we can perceive them (direct epistemology) and we can know with certainty that we have done so (certainty) (e.g., Cartesianism). Social constructivism is most devastating against this view. Or one might assert that the foundations of knowledge exist and we can sometimes perceive them but we cannot be certain that we have done so (skepticism or fallibilism). Or one can assert that reality is foundational (foundational ontology) and that we can perceive this foundation with varying, but never complete, degrees of certainty depending upon the validity of the process whereby we gain and test our assertions (Popper). Social construction of knowledge has least to say about these last two views. Or one might say that one can know with certainty the foundations of knowledge do not exist (a self-contradictory argument). Or one can assert that the foundations of knowledge may or may not exist but what we call "knowledge" has little to do with them and cannot be made to do so. This list is not exhaustive: My intention is not to list all the possible combinations of various forms of ontologies and epistemologies, but to argue that the discourse in rhetoric and composition is impoverished to the extent that it presumes a foundationalist versus social constructivist dilemma insofar as it ignores the range of ontologies and epistemologies. Social constructivist attacks on expressivist and current-traditional pedagogies are very persuasive, because those pedagogies do tend to assert or assume a foundational ontology and direct epistemology, but there is more in the world than those philosophies dream of.

I am not claiming that no one has ever endorsed the kind of epistemology that social constructivism opposes. In fact, if one stops the person on the street to ask how s/he knows things, one is likely to get a very simplistic neo-positivistic direct epistemology. Although liberal political theorists from Mill to Rawls are some species of fallibilist, public discourse in liberal democracies often asserts that the truth is obvious. Much of American religion is dependent upon just that epistemology, innumerable political texts implicitly assume it, and I think Berlin is correct to connect certain pedagogies to it. But there is something odd about pretending that social construction of knowledge is the first or only philosophy of mind to point to the profound impact that *doxa* has on what we think we know. As Norris has said, social constructivism takes only one part in what has always been acknowledged to be a difficult balance:

> There is a failure to conceive how the subject could both exercise a power of autonomous, reasoned, principled decision and at the same time refer that decision to the wider community of knowledge-constitutive interests, of truth-claims, ethical judgments and evaluative priorities arrived at through the process of open participant debate. (Norris, *Reclaiming* 39)

There is a weaker form of social constructivism, one often associated with a weaker notion of communities of discourse—a term indicating that certain journals, disciplines, groups of friends, cultures, and media have different notions about what constitutes normal discourse. As Lindemann says,

> Each discipline advances its own understanding of what claims are worth asserting, what constitutes evidence, what sorts of proof may be offered, what aims and audiences are legitimate to address, what genres are appropriate. It is simply not the case that interpreting texts will help students gain confidence in interpreting the results of a chemistry experiment, a field experience in a psychology class, or a sculpture. These contexts all assume different kinds of interpretation. ("Freshman Composition" 315)

Lindemann uses this point as the basis for arguing that first-year composition classes should not be courses in literary criticism, but the implications go further. Regardless of the topic of the course, this is an important insight, as it shows the problems with English teachers' impulse to universalize from our own disciplinary conventions (or personal tastes). In my experience, college English teachers often abhor the passive voice, and I have found that they (I) encourage students to resist using it. This is extremely good advice for students going into some fields, or writing for some contexts, but extremely bad advice for others. One might make the same point about other writing conventions, such as use of MLA documentation methods, the practice of incorporating and analyzing quotes, inclusion of first-person pronouns, and the place of personal experience.

These are not merely conventions. Condemning certain prose styles as "voiceless" (Lanham 84) ignores that a strongly individualized prose style is a liability in some fields not simply because those fields want to be "most numinous, most impressive, most priestly" (Lanham 74). There are, as people like Lindemann or Bazerman have pointed out, epistemological issues manifesting themselves in different conventions. One could not simply take an article written within humanistic conventions and change a few aspects of its form in order to make it acceptable for publication in a physics journal. Different disciplines have different notions about what constitutes an important question, appropriate evidence, reliable authority, and a credible ethos.

These conventions are not necessarily incommensurable. Roy Bhaskar, Donald Davidson, and Habermas have, in different ways, argued that even very different approaches to discourse share certain fundamental practices. Norris, Andrew Collier, and Michael Bernard-Donals (in *The Practice of Theory*) have explicated and applied Bhaskar's concept that some disciplines provide the foundations for others; Thomas Kent has argued for grounding rhetoric and composition in Davidson's theory that all disciplines ultimately rely on similar ways of forming and answering questions (at least at a very abstract level). All of these theories point to ways out of the expressivism/positivism/social constructivism expeditio. I want to pursue Habermas's communicative action or what he sometimes calls universal pragmatics as an example of a philosophy of mind and discourse that is not foundationalist, expressivist, or social constructivist.

The basic insight is taken from John Austin and John Searle's speech act theory, which categorizes language use based upon the different things one might do with a proposition. These different actions (assert, promise, question, invoke) involve different kinds of truth-claims, as well as different speaker obligations. When making an assertion, one is expected to be accurate, but there is no sense that a question must be true. If one asserts that the meeting is over, one's hearer will expect that the meeting is over (or, at the very least, that the speaker sincerely believes it is); but, if one asks the question whether the meeting is over, there is not the same truth-claim being made. This is not to say that people never lie, but that we experience lies as failures and betrayals—if someone tells me the meeting has ended, and I discover it has not, I will be dismayed; if someone asks me if the meeting has ended, and I discover it has not, I will not have the sense that something went wrong with that communication.

Similarly, promises and assertions have different relations to reality. Searle once used the vivid example of a shopping list. If a housemate gives me a shopping list with three items, and I promise to get those items, and I return from the store with only two, that communicative interaction (the promise) is failed. But I can not redeem the promise by rewriting the list to have only the two items—my housemate will not feel that the interaction was suddenly made successful. I made a promise, and the list constitutes that promise; making the promise fit reality does not make the communication felicitous. In the speech act of promises, one is expected to make reality fit the speech. If, on the other hand, the list is not intended as a shopping list, but a list we're keeping for budget purposes, then crossing off an item I did not get would be appropriate. In fact, leaving the item on the list and apologizing profusely for failing to get it would likely be experienced by my housemate as dishonest. In assertions, the speech is expected to fit reality.

Questions are more complicated in that they are expected to fit reality only to the extent that there are assertions implicit in them. So, "Is the king of France bald?" implies something about reality (that there is a king of France) that might be judged as an assertion. In other ways, however, one does not speak of a question as true or untrue. Invocations (what Searle and Austin call performatives) are speech acts that change reality, as when the chair declares the meeting adjourned or the festivities begun, or someone with appropriate power proclaims a certain law to be in effect.

Searle claims that these speech acts are universal, not in the sense that all cultures enact every kind of speech (as not all cultures have promises, for instance) but that the obligations remain constant among those cultures that do have them. That is, while not all cultures have promises (although the number that do not is extremely small) all cultures that do have promises assume that promises involve obligations of sincerity. And all forms of communicative action (that is, action oriented to understanding)—whether promises, assertions, questions, or invocations—imply four claims, that the speaker is:

a. uttering something intelligibly,
b. giving (the hearer) something to understand,
c. making herself thereby understandable, and
d. coming to an understanding with another person. (Habermas "What Is Universal Pragmatics" 22)

These might be summarized as comprehensibility, communicability, accuracy, and sincerity. One can, of course, point to forms of speech that fail to fulfill one of the conditions: a drama that has a patently inaccurate premise, such as Einstein and Picasso meeting in a bar; a figure of speech that is ungrammatical or literally impossible; irony and satire. Searle generally categorizes such examples as indirect speech, whereas Habermas does not count them as communicative action. For Habermas, public discourse is necessarily communicative action, meaning speech that appeals to the obligations and assumptions involved in assertions.

Again, this does not mean that Habermas is so deluded as to think that public discourse never has people failing to fulfill their obligations; moral obligations are not laws of physics but are norms that have a powerful function in argument. He refers to people establishing morals "for a community in a convincing manner" ("Genealogical" 3, emphasis in original) and says that last phrase "means that the members of a moral community appeal to these norms whenever the coordination of action breaks down and present them as prima facie convincing reasons for claims and critical positions" (4). They are a kind of rhetoric that helps people to identify injustice. This is an important point about Habermas's philosophy, one that it seems to me is often overlooked: that morals, for him, are not universal prescriptions, but statements that have a specific function in public argumentation.

Perhaps one of the most challenging aspects of Habermas's thought is trying to understand exactly what he means by terms like "rational discourse" and "Reason." While it is difficult to be certain just what he does mean, it is clear what he does not mean, and he does not mean some relatively simplistic foundationalist, positivist, or materialist concept. Like Norris, Habermas notes that modern moral skepticism makes its case by rejecting a correspondence notion of truth;

> If one assumes that, in general, sentences can be valid only in the sense of being "true" or "false" and further that "truth" is to be understood as correspondence between sentences and facts, then every validity claim that is raised for a nondescriptive sentence necessarily appears problematic. ("Genealogical" 36)

In contrast to foundationalists, who would like to posit "a class of basic sentences whose truth is immediately accessible to perception or to intuition" ("Genealogical" 37), Habermas insists upon the importance of background understanding and argumentative context. A statement is true to the extent that it is justified through argumentative discourse:

"The truth predicate refers to the language game of justification, that is, to the public redemption of validity claims" (37).

Habermas grants that public argument is difficult in the absence of substantive norms, that there is a

> predicament in which the members of any moral community find them-
> selves when, in making the transition to a modern, pluralistic society, they
> find themselves faced with the dilemma that though they still argue with
> reasons about moral judgments and beliefs, their substantive background
> consensus on the underlying moral norms has been shattered. ("Genealogi-
> cal" 39, emphasis in original)

If they choose not to resolve the differences through bargaining or force, "their initial impulse is to engage in deliberation and work out a shared *ethical* self-understanding on a secular basis" (39, emphasis in original), a good summary of the impulse behind the communitarian movement. "But," says Habermas, "given the differentiated forms of life character-istic of pluralistic societies, such an effort is doomed to failure" (39). Instead, we should look to the act of communication itself, "on the 'neu-tral' fact that each of them [pluralistic societies] participates in some communicative form of life which is structured by linguistically medi-ated understanding" (40, emphasis in original). While he grants that such a basis is "rather meager" (41), he also makes a persuasive case for re-placing "appeal to moral content" with "a self referential appeal to the form of this practice" (41). Rather than appeal to the moral dicta of what-ever religious or cultural background we each happen to have—an ap-proach to argument that requires shared values—we appeal to the mor-als implicit in the act of arguing with one another.

Habermas lists two principles he sees naturally resulting from such an appeal, the "principle of discourse" and "the principle of universaliza-tion." The first, previously discussed, is that "Only those norms can claim validity that could meet with the acceptance of all concerned in practi-cal discourse" ("Genealogical" 41); the second is that

> A norm is valid when the foreseeable consequences and side effects of its
> general observance for the interests and value-orientations of each individual
> could be jointly accepted by all concerned without coercion. ("Genealogi-
> cal" 42)

Perhaps what makes Habermas's use of terms like "rational" and "Rea-son" so challenging is that he uses them to define contexts, not statements. That is, like his rejection of a correspondence notion of truth (which puts the truth or falsity of statement within the proposition) in favor of one that evaluates the truth of a statement on the basis of the process by which it is defended, so Habermas's definitions of rationality delimit a process. He summarizes his argument:

> Thus the rational acceptability of a statement ultimately rests on reasons in conjunction with specific features of the process of argumentation itself. The four most important features are: (i) that nobody who could make a relevant contribution may be excluded; (ii) that all participants are granted an equal opportunity to make contributions; (iii) that the participants must mean what they say; and (iv) that communication must be freed from external and internal coercion so that the "yes" or "no" stances that participants adopt on criticizable validity claims are motivated solely by the rational force of the better reasons. ("Genealogical" 44)

Habermas explicitly declines to specify exactly what constitutes better reasons, saying instead, "Of course, what counts as a good or bad argument can itself become a topic for discussion" (44).

Although Habermas argues that certain obligations are inherent to language, that does not mean he sees them as inevitable or irreversible historical processes, or that he thinks democracy does not need protection. After discussing the values necessary for the success of popular sovereignty, he says,

> Naturally, even a proceduralized "popular sovereignty" of this sort cannot operate without the support of an accommodating political culture, without the basic attitudes, mediated by tradition and socialization, of a population accustomed to political freedom: rational political will formation cannot occur unless a rationalized life world meets it halfway. ("Popular Sovereignty" 59, emphasis in original)

He is not making an empirical claim about how people behave, but about an always already present potentiality. Because it is a potential, it can be ignored.

The implications of this argument are interesting for teachers of composition. If we accept Habermas's view that all communities of public discourse share certain conventions, then we establish and enforce those conventions in our classes. The rules we establish for the communities of discourse would be relatively minimal: those implied in speech act theory, the principle of discourse, and the principle of universalization.

Students would be asked either to use good reasons as constituted by the communities they are trying to reach, or to make those communities' notions of reasons the subject of argument. What seems so extraordinarily powerful about this approach is that it suggests a productive response to the situation described by Schriner and Rice: a homophobic student who wants to argue from a substantive background not shared by the other students. In one of my favorite passages, Habermas says, "The equal respect for everyone else demanded by a moral universalism sensitive to difference thus takes the form of a nonleveling and nonappropriating inclusion of the other in his otherness" ("Genealogical" 40, emphasis in original). The central obligation the homophobic student must recognize is to make the argument from a perspective that a homosexual shares; he cannot make an argument based on premises that that student might share were he not homosexual, or otherwise deny the genuine differences. Similarly, of course, a student arguing for homosexual rights would need to argue from premises that the homophobic student shares.

My intention in all of this is not to argue for foundationalism or expressivism as preferable to social construction of knowledge. Social constructivism makes a compelling case against the recurrent impulse to metaphysics, and against any philosophy (of mind, language, or science) that assumes the correspondence theory of truth. But not all philosophies are metaphysics, and not all rely on the correspondence theory of truth. I am arguing against the notion that the expeditio of social constructivism, positivism, and expressivism exhausts our options. Nor am I arguing for a four-part expeditio, and suggesting that we should adopt Habermas's view because it is superior to expressivism, positivism, and social constructivism. Instead, my intention is to criticize the hegemony of social constructivism in rhetoric and composition by applying to social constructivism the criteria by which positivism and expressivism are rejected, and to argue that there are far more than three options.

Having included this discussion of Habermas in the chapter primarily devoted to communitarianism, I might have suggested that he is communitarian, and that is not my intention. He is clearly distinguished from communitarians by the thin but very clear line between those who describe democratic principles (such as the ones articulated by Habermas) as immanently present in all public discourse (a more or less Kantian position) and those who see their origin in particular sociohistorical trends (the communitarian position). People like Walzer do not disagree with Habermas as to the content of democratic principles, but simply their origins.

Without going into great detail on the relative strengths of the Kantian versus weak communitarian approach on this issue, I will mention a few of the implications for teachers of argument. While there are profound theoretical and even political consequences of these different narrations of the origins of democratic principles, there are not—it seems to me— enormous pedagogical differences. As I said, at least if one is following theorists like Walzer, one would not end up with a markedly different set of criteria for class discussion or student papers. The main difference would be how one explained the status of those criteria; a Kantian basis would mean that one would tell students that these are simply the obligations inherent in public discourse—a claim that might well have to be defended—whereas the communitarian basis would mean that one would tell students that these are simply the obligations inherent in public discourse in democracy as it is constituted here and now. While the latter course does raise the question of accuracy of our claims—it would be absurd for teachers of argument to say that this is how people really argue political questions—it might bring up the topic of utopianism in a productive way. There is no particular harm in instructors engaging in utopian teaching practices, as long as both we and our students are aware that we are doing so. But it does mean that instructors must be willing to have our utopianism the subject of argument, and it means that we will have to persuade students that our utopia is desirable.

There is not a single way to enact communitarian political principles in the classroom. In fact, the considerable differences among communitarians imply the possibility of very different communitarian classroom practices. If one accepts the argument that argument depends upon shared values, then one might break one's own class into various smaller communities of like-minded students, identify the values shared by the whole class (and restrict paper topics to ones that could be argued from those values), or use the class itself to enculturate students into what one perceives as the values necessary for democracy (or dominant in our culture). If the latter, then one has to wonder to what extent those values would themselves be up for argument. Sandel says that communitarianism (here called "republican theory") seeks

> to cultivate in citizens the qualities of character necessary to the common good of self-government. Insofar as certain dispositions, attachments, and commitments are essential to the realization of self-government, republican politics regards moral character as a public, not merely private, concern. In this sense, it attends to the identity, not just the interests, of its citizens. (25)

Lynch has argued that the Isocratean value suggests something similar, that we, as teachers of rhetoric, try to teach a culture of education and argument. And, to some extent, I agree—it seems to me that teaching argumentation requires creating a certain culture in class, one that is articulated in Habermas's communicative action. But it is important to remember that this is exactly the argument made in reactionary educational movements, ranging from English Only to conservative Christianity that wants school prayer. These practices are most likely to arise the more that one assumes versions of communitarianism that are closer to the irenic than agonistic side of the continuum (e.g., Etzioni, Taylor). The more that one adopted an agonistic form of communitarianism (e.g., Walzer, Beiner), the more one's practices would likely resemble agonistic ones, possibly with more argument about morals than might make someone like Arendt comfortable.

Whichever forms one adopts, and whatever ways one enacts them, it seems to me that an instructor would need to be both reflective and clear regarding such questions as whether one is looking for an affective, rational, physical, or intellectual community, whether one sees conflict as dangerous, what kind of agreement (if any) one hopes interlocutors to reach, and, as with any approach to argument, just what the ideal public sphere is supposed to look like.

5

LISTENING FOR DIFFERENCE

[Arendt] is surely right that thinking as a free citizen does
include these apparently incompatible requirements: forming
and following one's own judgment, and yet listening to and
respecting the opinions of one's fellow citizens.
                    —Hannah Fenichel Pitkin, *The Attack of the Blob:*
                              Hannah Arendt's Concept of the Social

Much of my criticism of various models of a democratic public
sphere rests on whether or not the model promotes a deliberative
versus an expressive public sphere. Yet I have not made the case for discussion. What makes discussion valuable? Why shouldn't people simply
vote without having to argue about anything first? Jon Elster lists nine reasons commonly given by political theorists that discussion is superior to
simply voting in terms of decision-making. Discussion in the public sphere

> reveals private information; lessens or overcomes the impact of bounded
> rationality; forces or induces a particular mode of justifying demands; legitimizes the ultimate choice; is desirable for its own sake; makes for Pareto-
> superior decisions; makes for better decisions in terms of distributive justice; makes for a larger consensus; improves the moral or intellectual qualities
> of the participants. (Introduction 11)

In the ideal liberal public sphere, people transcend the particulars of their
perspective to achieve some kind of perspective-free and completely
neutral conclusion. Proponents of deliberative democracy make an argument similar to Burke's and Kastely's—we cannot free ourselves of our
own perspective.

This insistence on the particularity of perspective may seem to invoke
the situation condemned by Jean Bethke Elshtain and others as saying
that individuals are locked in perspectival enclaves. But theorists of de-

liberative democracy like Young describe a process of listening to people with different perspectives through which people can enrich their experience. While we may not be able to enter those perspectives fully, we can do so to a large extent, and our resulting decisions will be better:

> Expressing, questioning, and challenging differently situated knowledge adds to social knowledge. While not abandoning their own perspectives, people who listen across differences come to understand something about the ways that proposals and policies affect others differently situated. . . . Such a more comprehensive social knowledge enables them to arrive at wise solutions to collective problems to the extent that they are committed to doing so. (Young, "Difference as a Resource" 403–4)

One is expected to move beyond one's own subjectivity, but not to free oneself of it entirely. The realm of public discourse is one where people try to share their personal experiences and specific perspectives—this means both that they try to present their own, and that they try to understand and adopt the experiences and perspectives of others (in Popper's terms, the second world).

Proponents of deliberative democracy continually emphasize this sense of reaching across one's own differences in order to understand another's. Joshua Cohen describes this process:

> In an idealized deliberative setting, it will not do simply to advance reasons that one takes to be true or compelling; such considerations may be rejected by others who are themselves reasonable. One must instead find reasons that are compelling to others, acknowledging those others as equals, aware that they have alternative reasonable commitments, and knowing something about the kinds of commitments that they are likely to have—for example, that they may have moral or religious commitments that impose what they take to be overriding obligations. ("Procedure and Substance" 100)

One's audience is not quite the hypothetical, counterfactual, and identity-free imagined audience of Rawls's original position. These are real people with compelling commitments that are different from one's own. This is, of course, exactly the advantage long posited about rhetorical training for public discourse: that it teaches rhetors to think about their argument from different perspectives (rather than striving for a perspective-free stance).

Proponents of deliberative democracy cite this encouragement to think rhetorically as a benefit of discussion before voting. They say that one of the consequences of that pressure is that people are more likely to argue that their desired policies are in the best interest of everyone.

> The presence of a plurality of social perspectives in public discussion helps frame the discourse in terms of legitimate claims of justice. Because others are not likely to accept "I want this" or "this policy is in my interest" as good reasons for them to accept a proposal, the need to be accountable to others with different perspectives on collective problems motivates participants in a discussion to frame their proposals in terms of justice. (Young, "Difference as a Resource" 403)

This is not simply out of the need to get the votes of other people; there is also a question of publicness embarrassing people who make self-interested arguments. As Fearon says, "even *majorities* commonly justify their actions in terms of the general public good rather than the narrow interest of the voting majority" (54).

There are, according to Elster's comparison of deliberation within two constitutional assemblies (the French Assemblée Constituante and the American Federal Convention), very real policy consequences of this need to make one's case in terms of general good. Bargaining—especially a kind in which people are not particularly concerned with making claims about the public good, but primarily with making their threats credible—was much more prevalent in the Federal Convention than it was in the public French Assemblée. Elster attributes this reliance on bargaining to the fact that the Federal Convention was private. He argues that the slave states insisted upon some protection of slavery not through any arguments that slavery was good (in fact, according to Gordon Wood, such arguments were rarely made at all until the nineteenth century) but through threats of pulling out of the convention altogether. Had they been forced to make the argument in public, Elster suggests, they would have had to argue from the topos of public good, and it is quite possible that they would have been unable to do so.

This framing of the argument in terms of justice and public good may be sheer sophistry (or simply rhetoric, as the political theorists tend to say), but its proponents claim that even then it is likely to have good consequence for the public as a whole. Gambetta says, "Hypocritical as such claims may be, they may lead to making concessions to the general interest or to the interests of other groups. Thus, deliberation can facilitate compromise, improve consensus, and, through consistency, disseminate principles in public life" (23). Fearon lists several of the potential benefits of even sophistic use of the public good topos: The psychological consequences of continually making that argument might cause even a very cynical person to believe it; such discourse will influence even the kinds of proposals put forward (so that they, too, must at least look like they are in the public good); having made arguments about public good makes it somewhat harder for representatives then to vote in favor of policies that are clearly self-interested. Earlier, I remarked on the importance of what might be called the outrage criterion: whether a model of the public sphere provides a rhetoric that can cause people to become outraged at injustice. Fearon's point that public discussion might reduce slopping at the public trough is somewhat similar—a politician gives voters a basis for outrage through his/her own arguments. Fearon does not claim that public discussion leads to altruistic public policies, but that it is more likely to do so than voting without any discussion, or at least that the policies are likely to be more altruistic than those that result from voting without discussion.[1]

Discussion, as Thomas Christiano says, means that "many more points of view will have to be debated to the extent that previously neglected sectors of society come to the fore" (249). While hostility to argument often comes from experience with unproductive forms of conflict, it is important to keep in mind the genuine dangers of some kinds of consensus. Dawes et al. comment that "group identity does not equal morality" (110). They cite the example of Rudolf Hoess who claimed to have participated in the Final Solution out of loyalty to the larger group, and at considerable self-sacrifice. Whether or not it was true in Hoess's case, observers of Adolf Eichmann's trial almost universally accepted Eichmann's claim that he participated out of a sense of duty and loyalty rather than individual conviction. It is a commonplace in group psychology that people will do things as members of groups that they would never do on their own. They are particularly likely to do them if they remain in enclaves. The public discourse surrounding the Final Solution was designed to ensure that people like Hoess and Eichmann never heard the Jewish arguments against it; similarly, group decisions to rape, riot, or lynch do not seem to occur after the group has listened to arguments from all perspectives—they are the result of enclave discourse:

> The best we can do toward achieving an understanding of justice and the common good is by means of a trial and error process wherein a diversity of points of view is always present to test any particular view. Hence, we ought not to be aiming at consensus on moral and political matters. As long as public discussion acts as a process of trial and error for excluding forms of

ignorance, it serves a useful purpose for individuals as well as for society while increasing the amount of disagreement in the community. (Christiano 250)

Discursive conflict benefits a community because it complicates and reduces the chances of the sort of consensus that results from discourse within an enclave.

The notion that discursive conflict benefits a community is essentially the argument that leads proponents of deliberative democracy to say that deliberation leads to better decisions, but it too has to be articulated carefully. Political theorists grant that there are many circumstances under which public discussion can lead to worse public decisions—when powerful interests manipulate the discussion, when pressure to social conformity silences dissent, when the discussion functions to rouse people to engage in unjust behavior (such as lynching). Thus, public deliberation leads to better and more just political decisions only if there is equal access on the part of people with genuinely different points of view, the opportunity to make arguments (rather than simply assertions), the time for exploration of different options, and a cultural milieu that values listening. These are the qualities that distinguish a deliberative from an expressive public sphere. One might easily imagine these being the goals of class discussion as well.

Some proponents of deliberative democracy suggest that deliberation creates the very environment it requires through a kind of cultural and intellectual bootstrapping. Fearon notes that a system dependent upon discussion rather than simply voting "would tend to result in the development of certain skills and perhaps virtues in the participants. The following come to mind as possibilities: eloquence, rhetorical skill, empathy, courtesy, imagination, and reasoning ability" (59). Fearon's list is largely supported by the history of rhetoric, which, as has often been noted, becomes a richer and more intellectual discipline in circumstances where public discourse genuinely contributes to public decisions and becomes a more technical and narrow discipline in other political circumstances. History suggests that there is a bootstrapping of rhetorical skill and public argument.

It is interesting to point out that one might draw similar conclusions regarding the role of rhetoric in public decisions by looking at research in composition studies. George Hillocks's *Ways of Teaching, Ways of Thinking* concludes that there is a close correlation between the kind of instruction given by instructors and the extent to which the classroom is monologic. Instructors who rely heavily on lecture and who do not permit class discussion to become a realm of inquiry on more or less open-ended questions are the most likely to teach writing as the inculcation of low-level technical competencies. Their method of class "discussion"— frontal and presentational—presumes that students do poorly because they do not know things that the teacher can simply tell them. This approach is the result and cause of such instructors' underestimating the intelligence and competence of their students. The consequence, according to Hillocks, is that the students' performance is worse than the performance of students whose instructors encourage a more deliberative class discussion. The latter kind of instructor seems to generate the kind of bootstrapping that Fearon speculates should occur; being in a public that values skills at discourse, the students become more skilled in discourse.

[margin note: what to avoid]

Not all discussion is good discussion. With each of the other models of the public sphere, I took some time to describe what happens when they go wrong. This is not a particularly interesting question in regard to deliberative democracy, which strikes me as an attempt to make the liberal model more agonistic. Thus, the more agonistic it is, the more it shares the potential pitfalls of agonism; the less agonistic, the more it is indistinguishable from the liberal model. The question is not whether or not it will go wrong, but whether or not it will go at all. Deliberative democracy makes high demands of citizens. We must treat one another with empathy, attentiveness, and trust; we must take the time to invent and continually reinvent our ideas in the light of informed disagreement; we must care enough about our own views to try to persuade others of them, but not so much that we are unwilling to change them; we must listen with care to people who tell us we are wrong; we must behave with grace when other views prevail; we must argue with passion but without rancor, with commitment but without intransigence.

[margin note: what to do]

Young summarizes the basic elements of a deliberative (or, in her terms, communicative) model of democracy:

> In a communicative interpretation of democracy, members of an institution or polity form a public in which they discuss issues. All are committed to this communication process and aim to agree on a mutually binding outcome. For outcomes to be legitimate, they must be clearly connected to the discussion process, and the social context of discussion should be free of domination or the possibility of threats. In the discussion situation all

issues and proposals are open to question, and participants are influenced only by the arguments, appeals, need expressions, meaning explanations, expressions of experience, and so on asserted in the public. ("Justice and Communicative Democracy" 129)

There are, as is appropriate, differences among proponents of deliberative democracy, and I will later discuss those differences in more detail. My major intention is to explore some of the implications for the teaching of argument of this model of democracy. While I understand the obligation to do more than critique teaching practices, I am also aware that it would be contradictory to spend so much time arguing for the need for people to deliberate with one another to find contingent solutions and then dictate acceptable enactments of deliberative democratic theory. Thus, I have not and will not describe the "deliberative classroom." Instead, I have tried to argue for deliberative democracy in the way I have made my own argument throughout this book: to be contentious and fair, to acknowledge weaknesses while still clearly advocating a policy, not to avoid conflict, but neither to rely on false controversy, and to interweave the personal and particular with more traditional notions regarding evidence.

At this point, instead of describing a single pedagogy, I will describe several different versions of deliberative democracy, pointing to different tensions in classroom practice. Like my categories of political theorists, these categories are neither exhaustive nor discrete; they are simply convenient groupings that enable me to talk about political controversies and productive arguments within and regarding the teaching of writing: James Fishkin's deliberative polls and the connected issues of representation; James Johnson's argument for single-peaked preferences and the problem of particular audiences; minimal discourse rules and the role of rationality.

Deliberative Polls

"Inclusive public sphere" is one of those god terms with which it is difficult for anyone to disagree; even the Federalists, whose political philosophy was fundamentally exclusive, had to argue that their Constitution enabled the true public interest to be represented, and thereby included all relevant interests (see especially numbers 10, 51, 84, 85). As early as 1642, Sir Edward Coke tried to argue that Parliament was truly representative, despite its already rotten boroughs and corrupt election system. The apparent agreement on the virtue of inclusion conceals just how much disagreement and even confusion remains regarding just what should be included. There has been substantial dissension concerning whether women, minorities, the poor, the apathetic, and so on should be physically included or can be virtually represented. In addition, what does it mean for anyone to be included. What, exactly, is included? One's ideas, one's body, one's arguments, one's point of view in all its complexity and hesitations, one's political agenda?

Inclusion is simply the other side of the question of representation. It is not possible, and probably not even desirable, for everyone to be physically present during political deliberations. Even the smaller Attic city-states had problems finding a site large enough for everyone to be present; any site that was physically large enough to hold all the people was too large for individuals to make their voices heard. Technology does not solve the problem: One might amplify voices, but then time becomes the limiting factor; there is not time for every person to speak once, let alone as often or as long as necessary for all views to be fully present. Moving to virtual presence, as in the Internet or Usenet, does not remove the time constraints—no individual could possibly read all the contributions it would be useful for every other individual to make—while it exacerbates the problem that it is unclear what must be present. Need one know what someone looks like in order to evaluate an argument? Need one know the gender of someone who makes an argument about gender, the ethnicity of someone who makes a generalization about an ethnicity, the personal background of someone who asserts an interpretation of a certain kind of experience? Should all disclosures be self-disclosures, or is some kind of biographical information so necessary that others who know the information are justified in exposing it if the author has chosen not to? Habermas's ideal speech situation posits a place where arguments are evaluated free of considerations of the status of the person who makes them, and Young's definition of communicative democracy emphasizes that the decision will be based on the *discourse* in which people engage, uninfluenced by the status, power, or identity of the people making the arguments. Yet, virtually all textbooks recommend that students consider the institutional status of the author when, for instance, evaluating Web pages. In an earlier chapter, I was highly critical of the interest-based model of discourse, but shouldn't a student know that, for instance, a page offering information on Israeli politics is put up by a neo-Nazi organization, and shouldn't that context be used to consider the credibility of the information? For composition teachers, then (or at least the authors of textbooks), the rationality of the argument cannot be assessed separately from the question of who is making it, and even Young elsewhere argues that a deliberative public sphere must include different sorts of people (suggesting that interlocutors should think about who makes the argument).

There is another problem with looking to the Internet or Usenet to provide the locus for perfect inclusion, and it is the paradox at the center of Habermas's *Structural Transformation of the Public Sphere:* that the more the public sphere became democratized, the less it could be an area of rational-critical argument. This is not to say that the masses are inherently irrational, or bovinely uncritical, but that ratiocination and participation are necessarily in conflict. By ratiocination, I do not mean simply an argument that moves through logically connected syllogisms to proof, but any process of reasoning in which one moves toward a conclusion through a series of connected arguments, whether those arguments are personal narratives, syllogisms, steps in a process of controversy, or even something like explication of complicated evidence. If the discourse group is very large, and everyone is to have a chance to contribute, then people can speak only very briefly, and only once. The former requirement means, as I said, that ratiocination is precluded, and the second means that people cannot indicate when they have additional questions, shifts in perspective, or hesitations. One necessarily has a public sphere where people express relatively simple ideas. It is unlikely that expressive discourse is tremendously persuasive, at least to people who had well-formulated positions before the discourse began, except insofar as they might note the sheer number of people who express a particular point of view.

For these reasons, political theorists as far back as Plato and as recently as Fishkin have insisted that one cannot have a mass democracy that engages in deliberation in a single locus *(Voice of the People).* The history of argument on Usenet, especially on social or political issues, suggests that this is the case. As newsgroups became increasingly large, there was a sense that one could not keep up with the arguments, and groups were split into smaller groups appealing to more specific topics (and tending to draw similar sorts of people). The move to a smaller group necessarily restricted the heterogeneity of the group; a newsgroup that discusses the philosophy of Ayn Rand will be less heterogeneous than a group that discusses whatever political and philosophical questions arise. Still, the sheer volume even on moderated and specific groups is simply overwhelming to many people who might otherwise be interested in participating in public argument. The volume—a natural consequence of becoming more inclusive—then inhibits the ability of the group to include everyone.

And there has been a correlated development; in *Structural Transformation,* Habermas describes the increasing commercialization of the public sphere, and one can see exactly that in regard to the Internet. It is questionable (to me, at least) whether the World Wide Web was ever a place of rational-critical argument, as it tended to be much more oriented toward an expressivist model of argument (one expressed one's views on a Web page). Very quickly, even such personal expressions were swamped by commercial pages. As the Web proliferated, users had to rely on commercial search engines, which themselves tend to favor commercial sites. The commercialization of Usenet followed a slightly different path. As public access to newsgroups increased, an increasing number of people came to use the newsgroups to promote products and services, either directly and explicitly through spamming, or more indirectly through appearing to participate in the discourse while actually selling a product or service. As I can say from personal experience, such commercialization reduced the capacity for the newsgroups to engage in perfectly inclusive argument; it necessitated moderation of some sort or another. Whether one advocates moderation or not, it is a step away from perfect inclusion; thus, in the public sphere (as in the classroom), a perfectly unconstricted and unmoderated public sphere, ironically enough, inhibits participation.

If one wants to avoid the problems of an expressive public sphere, then one is left moving toward smaller publics. If, however, there is not some attempt to ensure difference within those smaller groups, enclaves develop, with all their attendant damage. One resolution of this dilemma is to suggest that not everyone need be present, but the "interest" of the people. Thus, the Federalist Papers argue that the state legislature's appointment of senators will lead to a group of men who are capable of seeing beyond factionalized self-interest to the general interest and public happiness. The Senate will not be representative of the larger public in material ways (such as having the same ratio in regard to ethnicity, economic class, occupation, or region as the voting population). On the contrary, the Senate is explicitly *un*representative, given that the small and large states have the same representation (and, of course, the three-fifths compromise ensured that neither the House nor Electoral College fairly represented the voting population).

A different answer is that only people's views need be present. This is essentially the notion behind many defenses of public opinion polls, which are supposed to provide continual information to public figures as to how the public feels. Gerard Hauser's intelligent critique of public opinion polls lists numerous problems with the way that survey research "substitutes a *general populace* for an actively engaged *public* in framing political issues and shaping responses" (191, emphasis in original). Fundamentally, the problem with even the most accurate public opinion polls is that they are not deliberative; they are, to put it bluntly, the epitome of expressivist democracy. All that matters about a person's political philosophy is how s/he responds to an extremely constricted set of choices; there is no argument, no deliberation possible.

Yet another answer is that a representative body must have bodies materially like the people they claim to represent. Phillips discusses seven arguments why deliberative assemblies must include material considerations like race and gender; that is, why political bodies should have certain kinds of bodies in them (*Politics of Presence,* see especially 39–46). Her fifth is that, if certain kinds of groups are substantially disadvantaged (through small numbers, lack of education, lack of resources), then their concerns never even get onto the political agenda:

> The problem of representation is not just that preferences refuse to cluster around a neat set of political alternatives, or that the enforced choice between only two packages can leave major interest groups without any voice. There is an additional problem of the preferences not yet legitimated, the views not even formulated, much less expressed. (Phillips, *Politics* 44)

Phillips refers to research suggesting that the disadvantaged have low expectations, while the advantaged tend to have inflated expectations regarding what they are entitled to, so,

If we take the preferences that are expressed through the mechanism of the vote as the final word on what governments should or should not do, we may be condemning large sections of the community to persistently unjust conditions. It is no real justification for this to say that this is what people said they wanted. (44–45)

This point is the one that most highlights the potentially deliberative nature of assemblies; if assemblies are homogeneous (and they are always homogeneous to at least some degree), then some set of issues is never going to be raised. This is essentially the point raised by Young and Kastely mentioned earlier, and the one discussed by Mansbridge in terms of enclaves: Difference has a cognitive value. It is also, perhaps most famously, the argument John Stuart Mill uses to argue for liberty of opinion, that a community benefits when different (even wrong) points of view are aired. Even if we are not persuaded to change our own position by hearing another one, we are likely at least to understand our own better.

Thus, if one tries to solve the problem of the impossibility of deliberation in large groups by making smaller publics, one must somehow maintain difference within those smaller groups, or else one has a homogeneous group (an enclave), with all its attendant problems. Phillips and Young point to the importance that these groups have, more than symbolic representations of different groups, the need for members, especially of disadvantaged groups, to be present. This is not a question of justice, although it can be, but of pragmatic benefit. All students, by this argument, benefit by having a diverse student population because they hear from people with different experiences and perspectives, and they benefit in exactly the skills so often praised in university mission statements; if Mill, Young, and Phillips are right, then diversity helps students become better citizens. What I find compelling about this argument, even with the problems to be discussed below, is that it means that diversity in student populations is not simply a way to rectify past injustice or level the playing field—arguments that suggest that only the newly represented students benefit—but an educational good for all students.

One can see this especially clearly by thinking about classrooms as instances of what James Fishkin has called "deliberative polling":

The idea is simple. Take a national random sample of the electorate and transport these people from all over the country to a single place. Immerse the sample in the issues, with carefully balanced briefing materials, with intensive discussions in small groups, and with the chance to question competing experts and politicians. At the end of several days of working through the issues face to face, poll the participants in detail. (*Voice of the People* 162)

Fishkin maintains that this process represents not what citizens do think (which is what polls—at their best—do), but how they would think if they had the time and resources necessary to reach a genuinely informed decision. It is important, he says, that the experience is truly deliberative; he specifically rejected a model in which the participants would simply listen to experts present information. Deliberation requires discussion.

One can imagine doing something similar with classrooms—immerse the students in some issue or small set of issues with carefully balanced briefing materials, enable them to engage in intensive discussions, and then ask them to write papers. One could have a class spend a semester deliberating a single issue (as described in Lynch et al.), or a limited set of issues, but one could not have students all writing on different topics. What distinguishes this approach from many traditional ways of teaching argumentation is that the goal of the course is to teach students to engage in deliberation as a group, not simply to present their arguments in an effective way. A substantial part (almost all?) of the class time, then, would be discussion of the issue rather than instruction in the formal qualities of argument. Obviously, a deliberative classroom would not have the broad political consequences Fishkin predicts for deliberative polling (he hopes they would serve as public "cues," thereby influencing how the larger public views the issue). But they might still have a variety of positive political consequences, such as interesting students in political issues, enabling them to gain a better understanding of at least one (and possibly several) complicated issues, and enabling them to experience deliberation. The major flaw in shifting the context to the classroom is that one loses the representativeness of Fishkin's polls.

Fishkin's groups are carefully constructed to ensure that they are fully representative; classes are dependent on random chance, with the range of diversity restricted by the diversity of the larger student population. The diversity in writing classes, in my experience, is further restricted by such factors as whether (and by what majors) the course is required, what placement mechanism is used, how exemptions are granted. Of course, if Fishkin's project is to work as a cue, the groups must be fully representational. But, one might argue that full representation is also important for the project of teaching argument. If Young and Phillips are right, the ability of the class to engage in genuine deliberation can be seriously hampered if the students are not especially diverse.

But, of course, the problem arises as to just how one is to determine diversity. Phillips acknowledges the justice of Hannah Pitkin's argument (put forward in *The Concept of Representation*) that there is a "notorious slippery slope which stretches from women, ethnic minorities, and the disabled to take in pensioners, beekeepers, and people with blue eyes and red hair" (*Politics* 46). Phillips endorses Young's response to this problem, by saying that one need worry only about groups whose underrepresentation is both the consequence of and contributor to historical oppression. My problem with this argument is that it presumes precisely what is at question—who is oppressed, and how underrepresentation and oppression are (or are not) causally related. The rhetoric of the Ku Klux Klan has long appealed to a fantasy of oppressed and encircled white Protestants; that it is a fantasy is not to suggest it is insincere. Many religious radio stations carry a radio program whose very premise is that there is ubiquitous and substantial oppression of Christians; commentators will insist that this discrimination is worse than anything any other group faces. The notion that the rich are somehow oppressed and underrepresented goes at least as far back as Andrew Carnegie, who invokes it in "The True Gospel Concerning Wealth." As fantastical as these invocations of persecution may seem, I am convinced they are sincere. And I think they are worsened by the notion that one can win certain concessions or privileges by successfully playing the historical oppression card; Phillips and Young's line of argument (unintentionally) encapsulates that notion.

This is partially an argument about oppression. For the KKK, white Protestants are "oppressed" simply by having to treat Catholics, African Americans, and so on with equality. But, in addition, it is a question of what it means for a group to suffer discrimination. The "Focus on the Family Position Statement on Homosexual Rights," for instance, says,

> While the promoters of homosexual rights seek to place their demands within the context of the larger civil rights movement, several factors reveal this to be both misguided and duplicitous. First, homosexuals as a group do not demonstrate the characteristics which identity other disenfranchised classes such as racial minorities. They are not discriminated against in any

of the key areas considered by the courts: economical status, educational opportunity, or political representation. (Citizen Link 1)

Yet the Alliance Defense Fund, a Christian defense fund whose activities Focus on the Family formally endorses, describes certain activities as "Anti-Christian Discrimination" (1) such as a school not permitting a club to meet on campus during school hours and a public library not permitting a creationist group to use its "Constitution Room" for meetings, activities that are not instances of discrimination in any of the "key" areas noted in the statement on homosexual rights. Thus, the very definition of discrimination shifts when the group shifts from homosexuals to Christians. By the definition of discrimination in the Focus on the Family position statement on homosexual rights, Christians are not discriminated against; by the definition of the Alliance Defense Fund, homosexuals are. It seems, therefore, unproductive to hope to resolve the problem of homogeneous groups by referring to a criterion of oppression or history of oppression. That very criterion is itself part of what has to be argued.

The more conventional argument against ensuring fair representation is the "identity politics" argument—the argument that American politics has become balkanized into separate groups who claim special status for themselves (typically based upon some assertion of victimhood), which exempts them from claims of reciprocal responsibility or entitles them to special privileges. Elshtain refers to this move as a kind of retribalization:

> Any possibility for human dialogue, for democratic communication and commonality, vanishes as so much froth on the polluted sea of phony equality. Difference becomes more and more exclusivist. . . . Mired in the cement of our own identities, we need never deal with one another. Not really. One of us will win and one of us will lose the cultural war or the political struggle. That's what it's all about: power in the most reductive, impositional sort. (74)

While I disagree with Elshtain in many ways, I think her argument here has to be taken very seriously, and I think the Focus on the Family/Alliance Defense Fund instability regarding discrimination explains why. For them, it is significant discrimination for them not to be able to use schools and public libraries to meet; yet anyone sympathetic to gay and lesbians rights groups would likely say that such discrimination seems trivial compared to having one's children taken away or being physically threatened. *This* argument is about power in the most reductive, impositional sort.

Because those are legitimate criticisms, it has to be remembered that the goal of the kind of representation advocated by Phillips and Young is *not* to enable people to slink into enclaves, but for deliberative assemblies to include different voices. The question to ask, then, is whether the deliberations that led to the Focus on the Family statement included homosexual Christians. My guess is that they did not. Deliberative democracy does not promote people expressing themselves from within enclaves—it requires that people try to present their own arguments in ways that people who are very different might understand. The importance of this requirement cannot be overstated. If diversity is presented as a way of stabilizing an irenic public sphere, it will necessitate the creation of enclaves, thereby precluding the very goals of diversity, or worse. Dana Cloud remarks that "The down side of a cultural politics of recognition is that when it is undertaken in a context of material scarcity and inequality, it can take the form of violent scapegoating" (254).

Proponents of deliberative democracy hope that focussing on issues of presence will not lead to the pitfalls of identity politics because that they posit a very fluid sense of the relationship between groups and the self, as is typified especially in the work of Young and Phillips. Liberalism tries to bracket off inequality, to act as though it does not exist. As others have argued, though, this more often means that participants pretend that inequalities do not exist by ignoring them, declaring them irrelevant, or deciding that they are outside the realm of discussion. Thus, those whose very disadvantages inhibit their ability to participate in public discourse cannot even point to their own disadvantages. Proponents of deliberative democracy generally recommend instead that those inequalities be, in some way at least, made the object of discourse. Because there are inequalities between individuals, it is not possible to bracket off either the experiences or identities of individual interlocutors. Phillips argues, "the biggest mistake is to set up ideas as the opposite of presence: to treat ideas as totally separate from the people who carry them; or worry exclusively about the people without giving a thought to their policies and ideas" ("Dealing with Difference" 150). The answer, complicated as it must be, is to make the inequalities themselves the objects of argument.

The temptation, once we acknowledge that material conditions neither can nor should be bracketed off from public discourse, is to fall into some version of interest group politics by assuming a necessary connection between one's membership in a group and one's beliefs. This fall may be unintentional, but it can also be well-intentioned, as when students or teachers—trying to be inclusive—turn to another student in class discussion and ask how minorities/women/foreigners/poor people feel about the topic.

A woman student is not representative of women and should not be asked to speak for women. But a woman might have a different experience reading Sade, especially a woman who had been raped or threatened with rape. An environmentalist is not representative of all environmentalists, but s/he might indicate some of the reasons that environmentalists have for being environmentalist. The experiences of these students should not be denied, but neither should they be universalized. Their experiences both result from and result in their beliefs, and their experiences are likely to be influenced by their identities. As Carol Gould says,

> one needs to distinguish between the givenness of a characteristic and how this is taken or what is done with it. . . . This is not to say that individuals can always throw off a characteristic or change its significance by themselves. To do so may well require joint action over a period of time. (183)

What this leaves us is individuals.

But discussing individuals is complicated in several ways. First, the politics of identity has been criticized for assuming a necessary connection between identity and political agenda. While the liberal public sphere unintentionally privileges on the basis of class, it is no more liberatory to privilege on the basis of some assumption about essential identity or authenticity. As Gould has argued, "Essentialism with respect to groups is closely akin to abstract universality" (182). In both cases, one is denying difference—that individuals might be different from one another. Assuming, for instance, that women will necessarily have a certain reaction to a political proposal is a hidden normative statement; as it's virtually certain that at least one woman will not express that reaction, such an assertion of univocality will imply there is something wrong with her. Or, as Young has eloquently put it, "the attempt to define a common group identity tends to normalize the experience and perspective of some of the group members while marginalizing or silencing that of others" ("Difference as a Resource" 388).

The answer is, as Phillips says, that "there should be no privileging of some voices as more authentic than others, and no coercive imposition of a supposedly unified point of view" ("Dealing with Difference" 145–46). There are two separate issues in the quote from Phillips: that of the relative weight of various speakers' arguments (essentially, the question of whether ethos should matter in rhetoric), and that of essentialism. The former will be discussed in a later section; in regard to the latter, I have to point out that the reasonable rejection of essentialism can lead one to what Young has called "the dilemma of difference":

> On the one hand, any attempt to describe just what differentiates a social group from others and to define a common identity of its members tends to normalize some life experiences and sets up group borders that wrongly exclude. On the other hand, to deny a reality to social groupings both devalues processes of cultural and social affinities and makes political actors unable to analyze patterns of oppression, inequality, and exclusion that are nevertheless sources of conflict and claims for redress. ("Difference as a Resource" 389)

Young recommends that we resolve this dilemma by abandoning the tendency to see groups as necessarily entailing specific identities. Instead, they should be seen as relational: "Social processes and interactions position individual subjects in prior structures, and this positioning conditions who one is. But positioning neither determines nor defines individual identity" ("Difference as a Resource" 392). "Women" are characterized and categorized in certain structural relations; while one can discuss and critique those relations, one cannot draw conclusions about the experiences, beliefs, or commitments of any individual woman: "We are unique individuals, with our own identities created from the way we have taken up the histories, cultural constructs, language, and social relations of hierarchy and subordination, that condition our lives" ("Difference as a Resource" 392).

Unlike proponents of the liberal public sphere, who generally see group activity as necessarily fragmentary, proponents of deliberative democracy emphasize the contributions groups can make. In groups, people practice the skills necessary for participating in the larger public sphere; such "counterpublics" may even be, as Benhabib argues, the only real form the public sphere can take that is consistent with other principles of deliberative democracy. She argues that "a multiple, anonymous, heterogeneous network of many publics and public conversations" is "the chief institutional correlate" of deliberative democracy ("Toward" 87). And Fraser has argued that

> insofar as these counterpublics emerge in response to exclusions within dominant publics, they help expand discursive space. In principle, assumptions that were previously exempt from contestation will now have to be publicly argued out. In general, the proliferation of subaltern counterpublics means a widening of discursive contestation, and that is a good thing in stratified societies. (124)

Habermas himself has altered his position on this issue, moving from being hostile to subaltern counterpublics (in *Structural Transformation*) to describing a network of associations as something that helps make people accustomed to political freedom, subverts a univocal public sphere, and productively challenges convention ("Popular Sovereignty," see especially 58–63).

Mansbridge has argued for the importance of different kinds of publics, for people's oscillating "between protected enclaves, in which they can explore their ideas in an environment of mutual encouragement, and more hostile but also broader surroundings in which they can test those ideas against the reigning reality" ("Using Power" 57). Remaining entirely within enclaves is dangerous, as it never allows ideas to be tested, but having no access to enclaves is equally stultifying, in that it does not give people a place where they can explore their own partially articulated ideas. Elbow is partly right that people need a friendly and supportive place to think through ideas—an enclave—but it is actively dangerous if they do not have to think through those ideas with a hostile audience as well.

Single-Peaked Preferences

Deliberative democracy has ambitious goals for public discourse, and one does not achieve them through every kind of discussion; one must have a polis where people argue with one another, one with conflict. This is potentially uncomfortable for many teachers. As Jarratt says, the abandonment of public argument in composition studies is the result of resisting conflict. The feminist case is that women are set up to lose such arguments because the kind of conflict involved necessarily disadvantages the already disadvantaged. Thus, it appears that feminists must choose between conflict—which women will lose—and remaining in the enclaves that Mansbridge describes. This apparent dilemma results from assuming that conflict must be resolved, and it must be resolved through some kind of exertion of power. For liberal models of the public sphere, there is a tendency to see conflict as an aberration from the ideal, and this tendency is increased the more that one assumes a universal self who can perceive the truth. If everyone were to listen to this self, a community would achieve perfect agreement and the correct policies. Mouffe notes that the liberal model's mistrust of conflict is the result of hoping that there is some rational universal self that can dictate communal harmony; once one abandons that hope, one no longer sees conflict as harmful:

> Indeed it helps us to understand that conflict and division are to be seen neither as disturbances that unfortunately cannot be completely eliminated nor as empirical impediments that render impossible the full realization of a good constituted by an unreachable harmony, because we will never be completely able to coincide with our rational universal self. ("Democracy, Power" 254)

One does need to come to communal decisions, of course, but such decisions are always necessarily contingent and cannot be seen as ending the process, or permanently answering the question. The valuing of difference, which is central to deliberative democracy, necessitates a valuing of the kind of tension also promoted by agonistic rhetoric. Liberal political theory aspires to distribute off the areas of deepest disagreement; communitarianism assumes we must have consent on them; deliberative democracy should aspire to make such issues the subjects and objects of argument. Because deliberative democracy assumes that people are different, that no viewpoint is universal, then conflict among viewpoints is necessary.

This means that, while proponents of deliberative democracy do tend toward Kant in many ways, they should not, indeed logically cannot, make actual consensus a central political goal of discussion (Gaus comes to the same conclusion through a much more elegant argument in "Reason, Justification, and Consensus"). In terms of the matrix I presented in the introduction, deliberative democracy must be based on an agonistic and not irenic public sphere. If there is to be agreement, it must either be the kind of the highly contingent quality theorized by agonistic rhetoric, the extremely abstract argumentation implied by Habermas, or on single-peaked preferences as advocated by James Johnson. By this term, Johnson means simply that people who disagree on a tremendous number of things might find something on which they can agree; he argues that such moments of agreement are all we should hope for, not consensus on every point.

While I find this a sensible solution, and highly reminiscent of Perelman's discussion of particular audiences, I am concerned that there be some care that we do not slide back into bargaining or cynical alliances. The advantage of simply looking for single-peaked preferences is that it acknowledges that even very different groups of people can find agreement somewhere, as when some feminists and religious conservatives allied in order to write and promote antipornography legislation. That the groups came to the same policy goals (reducing the production and dissemination of pornography) from different principles is not necessarily a problem, if the alliance led to greater mutual understanding, or highlighted some previously dimly lit injustice, but there is no sign that it did. Instead, the alliance seems to have done nothing to reduce the mutual mistrust and misunderstanding of feminists and religious conservatives,[2] while it enabled critics like Irving to paint feminists with the brush of Puritanism, and even led to the possibilities of the legislation being used in antifeminist ways (there is considerable dispute as to whether or not this actually happened).[3]

I would suggest that the alliance between feminists and religious activists failed at least in part because it was based upon an evasion of principled difference, both about what is wrong with pornography and the consequences of antipornography legislation. While the feminist opposition to pornography resulted from seeing it as promoting a heterosexual patriarchy, the religious conservatives saw it as damaging to the patriarchal and heterosexual family. Religious conservatives assume that the consequence of such laws would be a return to more traditional and heterosexual mores regarding sex, marriage, and gender roles—that is, a reversal of current cultural trends. Feminists like MacKinnon and Andrea Dworkin, on the contrary, argue for such legislation as something that would sabotage traditional and heterosexual mores, as a continuation of the feminist trajectory. There should be no surprise, then, if the resulting legislation is used in ways never intended by MacKinnon and Dworkin, as any use that furthered the goals of the conservative Christians would be anathema to them (and vice versa). To put it another way, advocates of deliberative democracy insist that we give reasons that people from a different perspective will consider valid. The alliance between feminists and conservative Christians, however, was not based on such a discourse—they never agreed on reasons. That problematic alliance indicates the danger in making single-peaked preferences points of policy rather than points of principle.

The advantages and disadvantages of particularizing of argument are discussed by Perelman and Olbrechts-Tyteca. They say,

> Argumentation aimed exclusively at a particular audience has the drawback that the speaker, by the very fact of adapting to the views of his listeners, might rely on arguments that are foreign or even directly opposed to what is acceptable to persons other than those he is presently addressing. (31)

Perelman and Olbrechts-Tyteca emphasize the rhetorical disadvantages of this strategy—that an opponent might draw together the things one has said to these different audiences and show them to be incompatible or quote them in front of audiences for whom they were not intended— but there are other ones. The most obvious is simply that putting too much emphasis on finding arguments that work with particular audiences can inhibit the ability of interlocutors to achieve the larger goals of deliberative democracy.

To clarify this point, it is helpful to contrast deliberative democracy from mediation, an approach to discursive conflict with which it has many things in common. Mediation is generally very particular, working with finding common ground among whatever parties are immediately present. The problem with mediation is that it can often be indistinguishable from compromise, so that intransigence, or beginning with the more unreasonable position, are strategies that benefit a person. The end result of the mediation, then, is not necessarily dominated by whose position is more reasonable but may even be more influenced by who is being the least reasonable. Focusing on achieving agreement between the two particular people can easily mean that one loses track of what might be just.

One can also lose track of the larger context, and that larger context might be one in which a series of compromises have already been made. One might imagine a situation in which someone wants to develop a wilderness area. If each conflict is taken individually, and the solution is to mediate between the group that wants to preserve the wilderness and another that wants to develop it, then the median is likely to be developing half of it. When another developer wants to develop the remaining wilderness, focusing on the particular conflict will make it seem that the most reasonable way to mediate the conflict is, once again, to split the difference. Thus, the agreement to split off the national parks from the national forests and prohibit development in the parks was itself a compromise. Yet, recent talk of mining and oil exploration in parks is presented as a reasonable compromise between those who want to develop all land and those who want to preserve national parks in wilderness states, thereby ignoring the historical fact that this "compromise" has already been made.

The problem is that mediation tends to focus on simply finding something on which the interlocutors agree, regardless of what reasons any group is presenting. It is, then, a violation of the principle that conflicts will be settled on the basis of the discussion process. But this raises the question as to what reasons are. If deliberative democracy (or any model, for that matter) is going to enable people of genuinely different perspectives to reason together, then the very model of reason itself must be simultaneously normative (enabling people to reject some reasons as worse than others) *and* inclusive. A perfectly inclusive public sphere—one that never permitted any argument to be rejected—would not really be a deliberative one; there must be some standards by which arguments are identified as better and worse. But, as numerous theorists have argued, "majoritarian democracy also privileges what currently passes for common sense," so that something seems rational simply because the majority of people agree with it (Phillips, *Politics of Presence* 151).

James Johnson has remarked that many theorists of deliberative democracy underplay just how disruptive a genuinely open public sphere must be. Having abandoned the liberal model's fantasy that public discourse will lead to perfect agreement, theorists of deliberative democracy must acknowledge that people will find their most profound beliefs challenged. As he says,

> Once we relinquish the notion that deliberation ought to aim at, and is likely to generate, consensus, however complex, and see political disagreement as necessarily endemic to political debate and discussion, the extent to which we behave diplomatically or otherwise will not alter our ultimate aim. We

still will be challenging not just our opponent's values, interests, or preferences, but the broader understandings and commitments—in short, the
worldview—that sustain them. (167)

This seems to me a very apt criticism of much of the writing on deliberative democracy—a body of work that sometimes seems to imagine
that the resulting public sphere will be irenic. On the contrary, it must
be heavily—possibly even unpleasantly—agonistic.

The issue of offensive speech waxed with the rise of speech codes and
then waned when the University of Michigan code was declared uncon-
stitutional. It has waxed again, but in the context of hostile work and
educational environments. Some scholars are troubled by this development, seeing it as serious infringement on freedom of speech "that expresses ideas offensive to certain groups in order to make life easier or
more equal for members of those groups" (Volokh 326). Eugene Volokh
describes an incident at Santa Rose Junior College in which students had
organized a boycott over a sexist ad in the student newspaper; those students were verbally attacked to their faces, on an e-mail list, and elsewhere. He concludes that, although he has no doubt that the students
were upset by what was said to and about them,

> Especially on a college campus, such speech, warts and all, seems to be the
> sort of "uninhibited, robust, and wide-open" debate that we must expect when
> people debate issues that are important to them. Likewise, I had thought that
> people were free to criticize classmates who organize boycotts or file com-
> plaints against a newspaper, bulletin board, or a respected community fig-
> ure, even if the criticisms are unfair, personal, and intemperate. (314)

The conclusion reached by the U.S. Department of Education, according to Volokh, was to prohibit on-line speech that "'has the purpose or
effect of creating a hostile, intimidating, or offensive educational environment'" (315). While, unlike Volokh, I am not convinced with that
the U.S. Department of Education reached a poor decision in regard to
the original case, a statement like the above does seem troubling to me.
As Johnson says, people can react in a very hostile manner when their
deepest values are contradicted, and people are often offended by the
views proposed by others, and students can easily be intimidated simply by the rhetorical skills or depth of knowledge of other students. One
of the more alarming consequences of the hate-speech codes was the way
that they were used by white students against minority students. One

can easily imagine a similar consequence with rules like that suggested by the Department of Education, especially were they to apply to discourse on campuses in general. In a condemnation of the Harvard student newspaper's decision not to publish David Horowitz's antireparations ad and its retraction of (and apology for) an article that offended some students, columnist Stanley Kurtz refers to the campus demonstrations as "intimidation." When an anti-abortion demonstration that featured gruesome photos was countered by a pro-choice demonstration at my campus, the latter demonstration was shut down because it was deemed disruptive. In short, one should not imagine that any rules regarding offensive or intimidating speech will be used only to protect members of minority or traditionally oppressed cultures; like the hate-speech codes, they are quite likely to be used *against* such people.

The problem is that there is a subtle but important distinction between something that has the intention of being offensive, and something that has that effect. The only kind of situation in which people could be assured of never feeling intimidated or offended, or in which there is no hostility, would be an enclave of people who never experienced (or at least never acknowledged) conflict. There is no right not to be offended when it comes to a deliberative public sphere, but neither is there a right to be offensive.

Thus, there is a difference between discourse that is robust and discourse that involves personal threat. Uninhibited discourse (in the sense Volokh seems to mean it) is impossible—if students are free to threaten other students, then the discourse is inhibited. Some kind of inhibition is going to happen in any discussion; the central question is whether the inhibition will be by rules that can themselves be argued or if it will be de facto. This is particularly important in a classroom, as students have less ability to absent themselves from the classroom discourse than they do as citizens who may choose not to read a particular publication. If a particular radio commentator does nothing other than engage in hateful, inaccurate, misogynist, and racist attack, I can simply refuse to listen to him. The consequences of my refusing to listen to that commentator are trivial, at worst, and possibly even beneficial. A student does not have that option, without dropping the class, and that choice may have profound consequences for the student's education.

Having criticized the stance of neutrality, I may seem to be endorsing the argument that instructors openly advocate their own points of view, but I am not. While it is true that neutrality is a mask, so is the stance that the instructor's arguments have equal status in a classroom; the instructor's voice always carries more power, whether coming from authority or coercion. Some instructors, especially ones who are charming and charismatic, do manage to engage students in argument, but some also (and I count myself among these) have found that being forthright with one's point of view unhappily silences some students and can unproductively inhibit class discussion. The dichotomy of neutral versus advocate obscures the other options that instructors have, such as being fair.

"Neutral" is an epistemological term, describing how one thinks about something, but "fair" is a behavioral term, describing how one treats students. Whether one is neutral (even were such a stance possible) is not nearly as important as whether one is fair. That is, one can treat students with equal respect, one can articulate (and, if necessary, defend) a set of grading criteria that are applied to all students equally, and one can make the same discursive demands of all students. That last comment is important, as it points to what really matters in deliberative democracy: that there are rules of discourse. In a deliberative situation, we treat one another with respect, we care enough to disagree, we listen so well that we can articulate our oppositions' arguments in terms to which the opposition will assent, we do not try to offend and we try not to take offense, and we try to make arguments using reasons that people who disagree with us think are valid reasons.

Minimal Discourse Rules

Earlier I discussed Habermas's use of speech-act theory to argue for two rules of discourse. Bruce Ackerman has similarly argued for minimal discourse rules. Ackerman posits three rules that he (unhappily, I think) calls rationality, consistency, and neutrality. He defines rationality as: "Whenever anybody questions the legitimacy of another's power, the power holder must respond not by suppressing the questioner but by giving a reason" (4). In other words, conflicts will be resolved through discourse rather than through coercion (and might be better called the rule for discourse). The second rule is consistency: "The reason advanced by a power wielder on one occasion must not be inconsistent with the reasons he advances to justify his other claims to power" (7). That is, a person's discourse must be internally logically consistent. This represents a kind of minimalist rationality; Ackerman does not say that the arguments must follow rules of logic, be empirically verifiable, quantifiable, or universally applicable. The third rule is neutrality, which Ackerman explains:

> No reason is a good reason if it requires the power holder to assert:
> (a) that his conception of the good is better than that asserted by any of his fellow citizens, *or*
> (b) that, regardless of his conception of the good, he is intrinsically superior to one or more of his fellow citizens. (11, emphasis in original)

The term "neutrality" seems especially unfortunate to me, as it evokes the controversy regarding the ability of a person to be neutral, and that controversy has nothing to do with Ackerman's stance. Sunstein, like Ackerman, argues for "less ambitious" standards for neutrality. He mentions several, including "the requirement of neutrality is unobjectionable insofar as it is a call for internal consistency" (50). This rule is little more than the rule mentioned by Habermas, Young, and others that the status of a person should not enable someone to trump an argument.

While, on the whole, these three rules seem to me very powerful, and Ackerman's case is strong that they are probably adequate for a community to resolve conflicts (especially over resources), they raise the paradox earlier deferred: that even advocates of deliberative democracy indicate that there are times when the identity of the person making the argument matters. Young indicates such an assumption in her arguments that certain kinds of people must be represented in assemblies, and Habermas does through his own rhetoric, specifically his heavy reliance on argument from authority.

I want to consider two specific situations in which it would likely be quite reasonable to evaluate the rationality of an argument in light of the identity of the person who makes it: cases when such a context discredits the argument and cases when the strength of the argument is enhanced by considering the status of the author. The first situation is especially a problem when students have neither the time nor inclination to get immersed in the relevant material. If students (either individually or as a class) are familiar with dozens of sources, then any source or student text that has completely different information is likely to be an object of suspicion, whether or not the students are familiar with the author. Thus, this sort of situation is most likely to arise in the liberal public sphere classroom, where students look at a small number of sources (such as four) and other students do not have the expertise to catch anomalous sources because they are writing about completely different topics. I am not claiming that the problem is always solved by having students immerse themselves in a topic—students have lives, sometimes very complicated, and (regardless of what we ask) some of them will try to do a minimal amount of research.[4]

The second case is when one might be tempted to grant more credence to an argument because of its source. As the inconsistencies in Young and Habermas regarding status of the author indicate, this is more difficult. One assumes that a woman would know more than a man about what it is like to be a woman, but one might have to make exceptions. A woman from a very privileged background, for instance, might know less about what it is like to be a working class woman than a man who had extensively interviewed such women. Still and all, direct personal experience tends to have a strong persuasive force for me. I have discovered that students do not always share this perception, though, and the circumstances under which they do not are informative. My own experience listening to students confirms what Linda Alcoff says:

> In our society processes of socialization produce a situation in which there exists a presumption in favor of the views and arguments advanced by certain kinds of people over others. Thus men's views tend to be given more weight than women's, white's over nonwhite's, and persons of a professional-managerial class over persons of the working class. . . . In terms of general and universal claims, which philosophy understands itself most often to be making, although one might guess that the logic of the situation would dictate that anyone at all could have the right to make such claims, in fact discursive authority is accorded by class, race, sexuality, and gender. African Americans may be considered experts on African Americans but rarely will an African American politician be seen by whites as capable of understanding the situation of the whole community, whereas whites more often assume that white candidates can achieve this universal point of view. (68)

I have also been surprised by what kinds of personal experiences will discredit an author. The first time that I taught the Andrea Dworkin–John Irving debate, a graduate student (with considerable teaching experience at both the high school and college level) asserted that Dworkin's credibility was significantly damaged by her admission that she had been a prostitute. I was very surprised by that comment, as I thought Dworkin's direct personal experience, especially in contrast to Irving's, gave more credibility to her assertions as to what it is like to work in the sex industry and what motives women might have in doing so. But, for this student, Dworkin had thereby marked herself as a bad person.

The above, it seems to me, points to one set of problems regarding personal experience and indicates that we may need to work with our students to talk through preconceptions about ethos and what they mean when assessing credibility. The graduate student was, I think, probably closer in line with much traditional advice regarding ethos than was I. That advice, going at least as far back as Quintilian, suggests that one never admit anything shameful about one's self because, in John Quincy Adams's words, "The reputation of unsullied virtue is not only useful, as a mean of promoting his general influence, it is also among his most efficient engines of persuasion, upon every individual occasion" (1:352; see lecture 15 in general). But one can see how this perception of experience is at odds with a deliberative approach to personal experience. If the purpose of personal experience is just to enhance the credibility of the speaker through fundamentally liberal public sphere principles, as it is for John Quincy Adams, then the point of every narration must be to show that one has the ethos of a rational-critical autonomous individual capable of thinking with decorum. That is not Andrea Dworkin's intention. If, as it is for her, the intention is to provide a kind of evidence, then the standard one has to apply to it are the same standards one applies to any other argument from authority (or argument from example, as it often also is).

Another set of issues involves how the experience is presented. Earlier I mentioned that students were also offended by how Dworkin argued; they felt "put on the spot," as several students said. If we are going to be more flexible about genres in our argumentative writing classes, and I am persuaded we should be, we need to think carefully about certain genres function argumentatively. There are more and less deliberative ways of offering one's own personal experiences into the public realm. The technocratic and liberal models (and many conventional models of teaching composition) define the personal as nondeliberative. Because it presents personal experience as nonargumentative, the liberal model suggests that one cannot critique or disagree with someone's personal experience—one is moved or not. Teaching implicitly or explicitly grounded in the liberal model similarly draws a sharp line between personal experience and argumentation, contributing to the feminist and expressivist unwillingness to teach argument.

While I am completely in favor of pedagogical practices that enable and encourage students to connect the abstract and the personal, I am concerned that this be done in a way that facilitates deliberation; that personal narratives not simply be expressions of personal opinion. To offer one's personal experience as part of a deliberative process means not treating it as nonargumentative. In more positive terms, it means offering the experience as something with which people might disagree. Particular to oneself, it is not unique; of relevance and accessible to other people, it is not universal; indicative of one's perspective on an issue, it is an experience upon which one has reflected. Personal experience is not always presented in this way, nor is it always received this way. I have found, for instance, that readers have very strong reactions to the personal narrative with which Andrea Dworkin responds to John Irving ("Pornography and the New Puritans"), and those reactions are not always positive. Readers often have a similar reaction to the personal testimonies of women raped and molested by pornographers that Dworkin and MacKinnon include in *In Harm's Way*; while always finding them powerful, readers do not always find them powerfully persuasive. Rosa Eberly, who has noted a similarly hostile reaction to Dworkin's novel *Mercy,* suggests that it is at least partially a result of Dworkin's use of *ad personum,* her tendency to engage in a rhetoric of war. As Eberly says, this strategy tends to alienate everyone not already persuaded of Dworkin's point.

I want to extend Eberly's analysis somewhat, connecting it to my own arguments regarding interest-based democracy and identity. When I have had students (generally graduate students) read the Irving-Dworkin exchange, I have noticed that many of them get personally angry with Dworkin. It is not simply that they resent her personal attacks on Irving, but that they feel attacked themselves. And, in a way, they are.

While both Irving and Dworkin engage in personal attack and argument by insult, Irving insults and attacks Dworkin as someone who has advocated a particular policy (even as he misrepresents that policy), while Dworkin attacks Irving as A Man. Whereas Irving's central argument (and one of his many fallacies) is an analogy—Dworkin and MacKinnon are like people attempting to censor *American Psycho,* and like the conservatives who tried to ban *Our Bodies, Our Selves,* and they are all like the Puritans—Dworkin's central argument is a synecdoche—she, because of her experience, stands for all women victimized by pornography (which, by her argument, is all women), and Irving, because of his argument, stands for all pornographers. He stands for all pornographers not because he produces it or even uses it, but because he defends it; thus, any reader who finds the freedom of speech argument compelling is transformed into a pornographer. A fair number of the students in my classes have had experience with pornography or know people who enjoy pornography, and their experience, from their telling, is different from Dworkin's. What many readers—men and women—seem to resent is that Dworkin defines for them their true identity (pornographer) and tells them the meaning of their experiences while she is (justifiably) outraged at the way that others (including Irving) have tried to deny her right to define the meaning of *her* experience. The conventional way to think about the sort of argument in which Andrea Dworkin and Irving engage is that she is taking the illiberal position and he is taking the liberal one; I am arguing that they are both arguing from liberal premises. Both Andrea Dworkin and Irving rely on the liberal notion that one should argue from universals. He universalizes from his experience, and she universalizes from hers.

And their failure to further the argument points to the central problem of universalizing—it denies the difference of experience, as well as difference of interpretation. If there is a single meaning to the experience of pornography, but interlocutors articulate different ones, then someone must be told that their interpretation of their own experience is false. Because Dworkin has explicitly and repeatedly identified her argument with her self (as well as with her way of making her argument), then readers who wish to reject some part of her argument reject her. It is interesting that, in the course of doing so, they often fail to notice just how fallacious Irving's argument is. He cites a magician as an authority on law, misrepresents the Dworkin-MacKinnon proposal, argues that a policy is bad because one of its supporters has said something stupid about the Oscars, and, after ridiculing people for behaving as though fiction has significant impact on how people construct reality, cites a piece of fiction ("Endecott's Red Cross") as though it were real.

Although students had a tendency to say that they thought Irving was more persuasive, my suspicion is that readers were not actually persuaded by him. That is, he did not cause them to change their opinions, as they were generally very hostile to the Dworkin-MacKinnon project before reading the exchange. So nothing in the exchange persuades readers to change their position. It is not, then, that Irving persuades anyone, as much as it is that Dworkin fails to persuade. And she does so, it seems to me, because of a central assumption she makes about how public discourse is supposed to work; "Speech depends on believing you can make yourself understood: that a community of people will recognize the experience in the words you use and they will care" ("Portrait" 68). While that assumption does apply to enclave-based discourse, it is not true of speech in the midst of difference. In deliberative democracy, one must make one's argument understood in the words *others* use. While part of what makes narrative (especially personal narrative) so helpful in public discourse is its situatedness, it must speak to people in other situations: "Narrative also contributes to political argument by the social knowledge it offers of how social segments view one another's actions and what are the likely effects of policies and actions on people in different social locations" (Young, "Communication and the Other" 132). Young's description highlights the central requirement and the way that deliberative personal narrative acknowledges difference: It is an attempt to make a certain kind of experience comprehensible to people who have not had it.

My student wanted to dismiss Dworkin for her experience; an equally debilitating reaction (albeit less common) is to declare Dworkin's argument untouchable because she has described a narrative of personal tragedy. Disparagingly known as "playing the victim card," this strategy is less common than jeremiads about identity politics might suggest. Common or uncommon, it is a violation of Ackerman's "principle of neutrality," as well as Habermas's dicta that the very notion of good reasons has to be up for argument, and deliberative model proponents' insistence that argument and not speaker status should determine the discursive outcome. Playing the victim card (which Dworkin does not do) is not simply to describe an episode of personal tragedy but to invoke that experience as evidence that one has an exalted status (to put it in Ackerman's terms), that one's assertions cannot be disputed. It is an argument from authority, but one that simultaneously asserts the indisputability of that very authority (the authority is, so to speak, self-evident).

Despite Young and Habermas's explicit hostility to argument from authority (in their respective assertions that the states of the speakers should not affect the discourse), each of them complicates that dicta—Young by her argument concerning the need for physical presence of certain kinds of bodies, and Habermas through his own heavy reliance on argument from authority. Their own practice, then, suggests that there is nothing inherently debilitating in argument from authority. It becomes debilitating when argument from authority (like any other line of argument) is treated as a First Principle that one *must* accept.

And here we have returned to the issue of rationality. There are many different capacities that terms like "reason" and "rationality" might refer to—the ability to syllogize, instrumental reason, skill at mathematical formal logic, induction, the ability to think in abstract terms, dialectic. There is a tendency to take one of those capacities and declare it reason, either making other forms irrational, or pale versions (as the notion that rhetoric is an off-shoot rather than a counterpart to dialectic). One strong advantage in the rhetorical tradition is that it tends to be descriptive and eclectic, listing ways that people really do reason rather than how they should. Following this tradition, I want to suggest a minimalist definition of rationality: A line of argument is rational if the person using it applies it consistently, that is, if it is not rejected in other places in the argument and if s/he considers it a valid line of argument when used by an opposition. Thus, for instance, the Focus on the Family's simultaneous endorsement of the Alliance Defense Fund activities and position statement on homosexuality is irrational, not because they appeal to religious texts, and not because I disagree with them (although they do and I do), but because the line of argument regarding what constitutes discrimination is inconsistently applied.

A more deliberative, and more productively conflictual, approach to the teaching of writing necessitates changes in writing practices that complicate the already problematic mission of writing courses. I earlier mentioned that American rhetoric is Ramistic in its adoption of one half of a debate. One can trace this practice all the way to the American Puritans, whose sermons have the general structure of the five paragraph essay. The textbook *The Five Hundred Word Theme* describes (and promotes) this structure:

This paper makes just one main point: most car accidents on our highways result from human error. It's stated at the end of the introductory paragraph, preceded by a *blueprint* of supporting reasons. . . . Then, to convince the reader of the validity of the main point, the middle part of the paper explains the reasons in the same blueprint order as in the introduction, one in each of the three developmental paragraphs. The topic sentence of each paragraph restates a reason. (Martin and Kroitor 30, emphasis in original)

The five paragraph essay is regularly ridiculed among college teachers, so my using that example may see odd, but the distinction between it and the assignment to "write a letter to your congressperson" is obscure to me. Both presume that argument is a thesis-driven list of reasons—the only distinction is whether the introduction is a funnel paragraph and the number of paragraphs. This form of argument is appropriate to the liberal model of the public sphere because that model presumes that one's audience for public discourse is always the universal audience—members of which will evaluate one's reasons dispassionately and impersonally. It is also appropriate to the interest-based model of democracy, as that model assumes that one is never talking to one's opposition. Yet, if we want a more deliberative (or agonistic) discourse, it is worth considering our pedagogical reliance on this form more carefully.

It is an understatement to say that this form is unpersuasive to an intelligent and informed opposition audience, but it was never intended to be persuasive to such people—it was intended to inform and confirm the godly, to tell them something they more or less already knew, give them reasons they may or may not have previously heard, and end with a rousing exhortation.

As one can tell from reading British authors, this structure was never as dominant in British educational systems; it even has a somewhat odd relation to practice in the United States. Joseph Williams long ago showed that people read student writing with a different screen from the one they use for published writing—we read for error when we read student writing, and we are quite capable of ignoring error when we read an article in a journal ("The Phenomenology of Error"). Richard Braddock's study of the placement of topic sentences shows that our requiring students to have every paragraph begin with topic sentences bears no resemblance to the actual practice of writers ("Frequency and Placement"). I would suggest that we have a similar habit in regard to structures: we insist that students use a form we do not expect from other kinds of writers. Specifically, we insist that students put what we generally call "the thesis statement" at the end of their first paragraph, and we ask that this statement be supported by a list of reasons. Whether we ask for three reasons or twelve is irrelevant; whether the paper has five paragraphs or seven is a distinction without a difference; what matters is that we insist that students establish a certain kind of relationship with their audience. We ask that students *tell* their audiences things.

Furthermore, we typically make this highly problematic demand in the form of claim to reality, as when the *St. Martin's Guide to Writing* defines the thesis "as central informing principle of the essay" and asserts that "it is usually found in the form of a single-sentence declarative statement near the end of the introduction" (Axelrod and Cooper 204). On the contrary, as Ellen Barton has shown, the kind of writing to which our students aspire tends to have an introduction that problematizes a topic (see especially 756; see also Swales and Najjar).

All of this is lost on many composition instructors (and authors of textbooks) because so many people (at least in America) confuse the thesis and the partition. The thesis is the proposition the paper argues; it is the underlying principle. The partition is the statement of what the text will do—and the tense here is important. A partition establishes expectations about a text by saying what the topic will be and often how that topic will be handled—it may be a hypothesis, but it is not a thesis. In contrast to what *The St. Martin's Guide to Writing* (and a troubling number of textbooks) says, in most published writings, the thesis (if anywhere in the text at all) is stated at the end of the text, and it usually takes more than one sentence. In many texts, especially ones presented to students as models of good writing, there is no single thesis sentence. "Letter from Birmingham Jail," for instance, ends his introduction with a partition: "I want to try to answer your statement in what I hope will be patient and reasonable terms." His answer—his thesis—might be something like, all Judeo-Christians should support the SCLC's nonviolent direct action program, as the group's actions and goals are consistent with central legal and ethical principles. There is no single sentence in the text that says exactly that, but several sentences (in the eleventh, twenty-sixth, thirty-first, and thirty-third paragraphs) articulate some part of it. And that is typical of a text engaging in ratiocination.

There is very little published in composition studies about the thesis statement, and the very little that is published tends to be hostile. That hostility comes from the post-Ramistic notion that the thesis statement should precede both the process and product of a paper—a student should write one before writing the paper, and the paper itself should begin with one. Virginia Perdue remarks that, despite the ostensible adoption of "more flexible approaches," the major textbooks "continue to affirm the embodiment of the thesis in a single, arguable idea and its function to subordinate the rest of the essay's ideas within a hierarchical framework, thereby fulfilling readers' expectations" (136). This is not simply advice as to what a thesis is, but as to where it is; both the advice and Perdue's criticism of that advice conflate thesis and partition. Perdue's criticism of the practice of thesis statement, then—that it "assumes that ideas are static entities developed and defended by one person against the competing ideas of another" (138)—only applies to a practice that fails to distinguish thesis and partition. On the contrary, her criticism embodies exactly why one should carefully separate partition and thesis: "As a result, the requirement that a thesis argue for a central idea may close off exploration and questioning, encouraging students to value the security of clear answers over questions" (139).

Wilson Snipes's charming "Defense of Digressive Writing" recommends to students that "one way to really catch your reader's attention is through the potentially digressive thesis statement" (20). Of course, he does not mean thesis statement—that is, the central argument of a piece—but the partition—the statement that establishes readers' expectations for the piece. He begins his piece "I want to propose tongue-in-cheek, and in contrast to the epigraphical statement above, that every writer should digress right and left, back and forth, up and down, inward and outward at every opportunity" (19). This sentence—the first sentence in the article, leads the reader to expect a digressive and winsome exploration of the topic. Snipes's thesis is stated toward the end of the article, when he says,

> Modification of expression enables [the writer] to follow through verbally, imagistically, logically, associationally, to turn the screw on what he has previously thought and said, to turn not once but a series of turns; with each turn he also begins to anticipate the multiple expressive opportunities emerging in the discourse through which he may further develop and refine his thought. (23)

In short, separating the thesis and partition enables a writer to imagine discourse as a form of exploration. A continual immersion in such writing might help students (and teachers) imagine public discourse as a form of testing and exploration, rather than as a form of expression or aggression.

The notion that the introduction must clearly state the thesis is closely related to the idea that words carry a meaning to a reader. *The Five Hundred Word Theme,* which may be the strongest example of the thesis plus support approach to writing, not coincidentally exemplifies that model of communication:

> Effective *communication* is a three-way process involving (1) an information source (reality, books, knowledge), (2) a *message-sender* who processes information, and (3) a *message-receiver* who tries to understand the resulting end product or "*message.*" (9, emphasis in original)

So many composition theorists have criticized the "information-transfer" model that it may well seem that there is consensus that this is not how we want students to perceive knowledge largely because it "leaves little room for provisional or hypothetical thinking" (Penrose and Geisler 516); it reinforces "the adversarial, 'monologic' mode of argument that dominates academic discourse" (514). But requiring that students end the introduction with their thesis has exactly those consequences. There are, therefore, political consequences of thinking carefully about the distinction between thesis and partition.

I am belaboring this point not because it is tremendously important to deliberative discourse, but because it epitomizes several larger issues. First, my own taxonomies, especially connected to historical comments, might be taken to suggest a univocality to eras, and that is not the case. As Perdue argues, the thesis-driven approach to teaching, central to current-traditional rhetoric, co-exists with postmodern calls for less certainty and more deliberation, a goal with which it is incompatible. Second, there is always a slip between theory and practice. Current-traditional rhetoric is completely absent from composition journals, but, as shown by Hillocks's *Ways of Teaching,* and indicated in my own experience supervising composition programs, it is not only present but quite possibly dominant in practice. Third, there is a kind of inertia to practice. At a recent conference, Richard Fulkerson presented a very intelligent paper on the fundamental incongruity between composition textbooks' advice on reading and the research in reading. An author of one of the textbooks he criticized said this was not news to her, but the publisher insisted she include the hoary advice because teachers would not adopt the book otherwise. I have heard the same explanation for such atavistic practices as the inclusion of instructions on three-by-five cards or grammar worksheets.

It is easy, of course, for someone like me to criticize someone who fails to read the research on the futility of grammar worksheets, or who is resistant to changing lesson plans, but, given the unethical working conditions at many institutions, teachers' desires to minimize revision and their inability to keep current with new scholarship are quite reasonable. And, in many situations, assessment methods force teachers into outdated practices; state-mandated writing tests generally assess students' ability to write the five paragraph essay, and there is serious talk of assessing college writing the same way.

Finally, the example of thesis-driven writing points to a paradox of novice writing. Dominant educational practices in America do conflate the thesis and partition, do restrict student writing to simplistic points, do expect the first paragraph of a student paper to summarize the entire argument, and do not expect students to engage in deliberative writing. Mission creep, the notion that organizations tend to accumulate tasks in an unreflective manner, is present in college composition in the abundance of conflicting expectations regarding such courses—acculturating students to a broad range of academic discourses, teaching critical thinking, instilling habits of correctness, introducing students to research methods, providing instruction in computer proficiency, and refining the skills that enable students to be effective citizens in a democratic culture. If we do make the classroom more appropriate for a deliberative democracy, there are two consequences that will worsen the problem of fundamentally incompatible objectives in first-year composition. First, the only model of democracy that does not imply at least some inconsistency between acculturating students to academic discourses and refining their skills as citizens is the technocratic one. Because the technocratic model of democracy assumes that students will participate qua experts, focusing on increasing their expertise simultaneously hones the skills necessary for public discourse. But, the other models of democracy assist in preparing students for academic discourses at very fundamental levels, only to the extent that certain capabilities (effective reading, the ability to understand writings with which one disagrees, clarity in writing) are shared among disciplines and between academic and political discourse. While what is shared is far from trivial, it still leaves a large body of knowledge about writing that has to be taught somewhere other than first-year composition. This conflict is further exacerbated with deliberative democracy—at least as I suggest it be enacted—because it means not treating student discourse as novice discourse. While most are not yet members of the academic or professional communities that college enables them to join, almost all of our students already are citizens, and the rest will be citizens within a short amount of time. They already are members of the political community; they are our political peers, with the same quality and quantity of political rights and responsibilities that we have. Yet, as the research of Braddock and the elegant argument of Williams suggest, academic discourse treats student writing as novice writing, holding it to standards to which we never hold the writing of our peers. There is, then, likely to be an imperfect relation between what we expect of our students in first-year composition and what is expected of them in other courses. Our own tolerance regarding genre, the placement of thesis, and the interweaving of the personal is not likely to be replicated in all other academic writing situations.

The second consequence is the natural result of the deliberative model being, in most ways, a refiguring of the liberal model of the democratic public sphere. Like the liberal model, the deliberative model is unblushingly utopian. Neither I nor any other of its advocates suggest that an examination of the Congressional Record will unfailingly turn up examples of deliberation; on the contrary, one is most likely to see an expressivist public sphere. What we argue is that the public sphere *should be* deliberative, and, as with advocates of the liberal public sphere, our hope is that enabling students to experience that kind of discourse in a class will make them demand it in other places of the public. So, while they will not model their discourse on Jesse Helms, and they might not persuade Jesse Helms, at least they will try.

CONCLUSION

> Free citizenship presupposes the ability to fight—openly,
> with commitment, and about things that really matter—
> without fanaticism, without seeking to exterminate one's
> opponents. That ability contrasts both to the ruthlessness of
> *homo faber,* ready to eliminate whatever stands in his way
> (including people), and the spinelessness of the *animal
> laborans* and of the parvenu, so anxious to accommodate that
> he cannot bear open disagreement.
> —Hannah Fenichel Pitkin, *The Attack of the Blob:
> Hannah Arendt's Concept of the Social*

When Berlin published "Rhetoric and Ideology," he laid out a deeply problematic taxonomy, making a monolith of classical rhetoric, obscuring the distinction between models of perception and models of cognition, ignoring traditions like rhetorical humanism and pragmatism, and implying that practice and theory are necessarily connected. In a certain sense, none of those criticisms matter. His intention, almost certainly, was not to promulgate the taxonomy, but to raise the issue of the relation between epistemology and rhetorical practice. He therefore succeeded to the extent that people became more self-conscious about epistemological assumptions implicit in various practices (and vice versa), rather than to the extent that people used his categories. In my darker moments, however, I think he succeeded more in the latter than the former— that, for many people in rhetoric and composition, he settled the very question he was trying to raise, and his categories are set in stone.

My work might be usefully described as an attempt to revisit Berlin's question, but with political theory rather than epistemology the uncovering term, and my work is subject to the same criticisms. My taxonomy makes a monolith of each of the models discussed, obscures important distinctions, ignores various traditions, and implies a necessary connection between theory and practice. Needless to say, this is not my intention. My categories are arbitrary, and I can easily imagine someone usefully collapsing distinctions I have made and insisting on ones I have failed to make. The last thing I want is for my very ad hoc definitions to be reified. Nor do I believe that rhetoricians must simply get our theories straight and our practice will follow. As a very smart friend once said, ideas have consequences, but they do not have necessary consequences. Theory and practice have the potential to be mutually critical, but they also have the potential to exist independently. That is, one might (as I often have and probably still do) advocate a certain theory, while engaging in a practice that implies an absolutely contradictory one. Thinking carefully about the relation of theory and practice ought to enable me to see such contradictions and work to resolve them, either by revising the theory or practice—neither should be seen as the immutable foundation of the other.

In a perfect world, theories and practices engage in agon with one another, serving as critiques and countercritiques. If Burke is right, and there is no discourse without injustice, then the impulse to hierarchy in language similarly leads us to inherent hierarchies in rhetorical theory and practice. Our theories and practices are always unjust to someone or something. The task of the rhetorical critic, Burke says, is to argue for whatever has been dismissed. In terms of teaching, there is necessarily a similar hierarchy; the limited time we have means that we pay attention to some things and not others. The task of rhetoric is to argue for the value of those things to which we are not currently paying attention. If we choose the agonistic approach to public discourse, then we should try to hear at our backs the liberal model's insistence on universality. If we choose the liberal model, then we should hear the deliberative model's arguments for particularity.

A less agonistically based claim for the mutual critique of theory and practice is Fulkerson's, that combining different principles of composition leads to unreflective and muddled practice ("Four Philosophies"). His example is a teacher who gives expressivist assignments while using rhetorical grading criteria. It seems to me similarly confusing to tell students that interlocutors can and should evaluate proposals in a neutral fashion *and* that they should imagine their audience in terms of socio-economic interests, or that they write to a general audience *and* respond to peer reviews, or that a fact is a verifiable *and* noncontroversial statement that is not necessarily true, and so on. This is not to say that eclecticism is necessarily doomed; because my divisions are closer to the color spectrum than to a taxonomy of species, one might have a form of deliberative democracy closer to agonism, closer to communitarianism, or closer to liberal political theory. But some combinations enhance one another while others cancel one another out. Articulating which political theory we are using (as individuals, not as a discipline) should help us see when we are engaged in which kind of eclecticism.

That political theories are more like colors than species means that one cannot cogently list the advantages and disadvantages of the various theories. One has to talk in terms of tendencies. In regard to the traditional-universalist version of liberal political theory, the more beliefs designated self-evident (and thus beyond argument), the more narrow the cultural definition of "rational," the more that concepts like autonomy, universality, and neutrality are literalized, then the less critical and inclusive the ensuing public discourse. With the deontological model, the more narrow the concept of public reason, then the greater the disparity between how people actually make their decisions and how they can argue about them, and, hence, the more alien "public" argument must necessarily seem from what people really do. With either kind of liberal model, the more that individualism is emphasized over the commonality, then the more likely one will have the interest-based model of the public sphere; the more the interest-based model dominates conceptions of power, politics, and discourse, then the less argument can be an alternative to (rather than simply another form of) violence. The ability of the agonist model to provide a discourse oriented toward justice depends upon how inclusive it is or the extent to which it seeks foundations. If there is neither inclusion nor foundation, then it is simply the interest-based model. The more foundations, the more it looks like nothing more than an aggressive form of liberal rhetoric. If communitarianism is heavily irenic, it becomes indistinguishable from the traditional-universalist model and can only work to create enclaves; if it is agonist, then it starts to look more like deliberative democracy or agonism. There is not, then, some perfect model, regarding which I hope rhetoric and composition will reach normative agreement.

My primary intention is to persuade people involved in the teaching of argument that there are a variety of questions not yet settled, even though disciplinary discourse might suggest otherwise. Those questions—regarding political theory, philosophy of mind, models of the self, pedagogy—might be encapsulated in the one that inspired this book: *In what kind of public discourse do we want our students to engage?* My hope is not that we would resolve those questions, and all adopt one political theory, philosophy of mind, model of the self, and set of practices—I am enough of an agonist to mistrust consensus—but that we might begin to argue more productively about them.

The first step toward that goal is to acknowledge that there are arguments to be had. Concepts like autonomy, universality, neutrality, and realism are unpopular in rhetoric and composition (for good reason), but they are not untenable. There are pernicious versions of those concepts, but there are also potentially liberating ones—it is unclear to me, for instance, exactly how Giroux's concept of critical agency is significantly different from Kant's notion of autonomy. Universalism has demonstrably been associated with tyrannical and totalitarian political and pedagogical practices, but it has also been associated with criticism and emancipation. Must we abandon all search for universals, or could we at least argue about the relative merits of various versions of it—when is it critical, and when is it oppressive? Are there ways of recasting it (in Arendt's notion of the common world, in Chomsky's universal grammar, in Ackerman's principle) that facilitate critical discourse? Neutrality is never possible, but is it a desirable goal? If we abandon it as a goal, because, for instance, we want to ensure that people who are the outraged victims of injustice (and therefore hardly neutral) can participate, then on what grounds might we argue that tobacco companies might not be entirely credible sources of information regarding the consequences of smoking? Can we distinguish among kinds of interest?

I am not calling for consensus on our goals in teaching argument, but more argument about argument could be very helpful. In having that argument, our own discourse ought to model what we think we are teaching—if we are going to model inclusive discourse, we have to begin with the premise that people of principle and intelligence will be on various sides, that we will disagree with one another. Patricia Sullivan and Donna Qualley describe what happened when one battle in the culture wars hit composition, in the form of arguments about the University of Texas composition program.

> While few of us were surprised that an outsider and conservative like George Will would sound the liberal scare against academe and advocate a back-to-basics approach to a course he had never taught, many compositionists were taken off guard when their colleague, Maxine Hairston, an insider notably to the left of Will, sounded themes similar to his in a recent article in *College Composition and Communication.* (ix)

I would put the claim even more strongly; not only were people caught off guard, but Hairston was more or less subsequently ostracized. And why? Why was anyone caught off guard that someone would make the argument that Hairston did? While I disagree with it, it is not an absurd argument; in fact, it is exactly the argument that one would predict someone would make. Considering that compositionists acknowledge the pervasiveness of banking education, we ought not be surprised if someone worries about teachers imposing political views on students. If a teacher is going to pour information into students' heads and look to get it back in the papers, why assume that changing the nature of information from one topic to another will magically change the banking practice? (One might, of course, ask Hairston the same question—why does changing the topic to politics make any more likely the possibility that instructors will look to get their own opinions back on papers?)

I am, in short, concerned about rhetoric and composition behaving like an enclave. Van Eemeren et al. define argumentation as "not so much a process whereby a single individual privately draws a conclusion as it is a procedure whereby two or more individuals try to arrive at an agreement" (12). Everything might be an argument, but not everything is argumentation (or, to put it another way, everything is an argument, but not everything is a good argument): "For argumentation to occur, disagreement must be externalized, or at least externalizable: incompatible standpoints must be expressed and brought into confrontation with one another" (11). Hairston's argument was (and is), I suspect, more popular among composition instructors than one might infer from subsequent disciplinary discourse. There remains, I think, an argument to be had about the merits of political topics in composition classes, the dangers of instructors' imposing their points of view on students, and even the virtues of a uniform syllabus for a large class, but I am not convinced that this argument has been externalized.

I am convinced that there are very real dangers should rhetoric and composition become an enclave, but I am not at all clear what we should do about them. The more that we take certain positions for granted, the more that we are able to achieve that consensus by dismissing or ignoring alternate arguments, the more that our discourse assumes values and even terms at odds with the public, then the harder it will be for us to get the public to see the value of what we do. Then, the more we will see inappropriate policies imposed on us, resources denied us, unethical assessment methods mandated, and our own authority dismissed. But it is not possible for any group to be perfectly inclusive. Mansbridge describes the frustration that certain people felt in a leftist political organization that strived for inclusive, consociational, and completely democratic methods of decision making. As one person said, he simply got tired of having the same arguments over and over (*Beyond Adversary* 167; see also 164–65). I have the same feeling about the usage argument—there are moments that I think that I will start to scream if I have to explain, one more time, why a usage test will not assess a student's ability to write an effective paper. I am tired of having that argument, and I want to move on. A perfectly inclusive public sphere, however, means that one must be willing to have that argument as many times as there are others who assert the self-evident connection between performance on certain tests and writing ability.

Van Eemeren et al. describe four stages in argumentation:

> (1) identifying disagreements; (2) establishing agreements between two parties as to the means by which the disagreement will be settled; (3) providing for indefinite exploration of the merits of the competing positions, as needed; and (4) ending with either a resolution of the disagreement or a mutual recognition that no agreement is (currently) attainable. (26)

Van Eemeren et al. assert that resolution is necessarily the goal of argument, and I take issue with that assertion. Certainly, it is for certain kinds of policy deliberations, as there will ultimately be some kind of policy written or not written, but that seems less the case for philosophical, political, aesthetic, and disciplinary arguments. In such cases, simply identifying the disagreements seem a useful beginning as well as even an end. And that is the intention of this book.

Another rhetoric and composition debate that, I think, has not been externalized concerns argument. I know that there is hostility to teaching argument, but, appropriately enough, many of the people who feel that way do not themselves make arguments as to just what is wrong with argument. There is not a raging controversy within composition journals as to whether or not we should be teaching public argument. Instead, the people who dislike it simply evade or minimize it. My sense is that there is considerable hostility to the teaching of argument because there is reasonable discomfort with certain approaches to it. Some instructors mistrust the liberal public sphere's aspirations for neutrality and rationality; some instructors want no part of enabling students to succeed in interest-based discourse; some instructors dislike the uncertainty and conflictual nature of agonism. My hope is that identifying the disagreements regarding the public sphere will help such instructors understand that they can reject specific models of public argument without rejecting argument altogether.

And some instructors evade argument because they think that argument is ineffective, that it does not really persuade anyone. In many ways, they are right. That is, certain advice that we give students, and much of what they are presented as models to emulate, does not describe practice that will enable intelligent and informed people to engage in argumentation. Not only does it not tell students how to persuade someone; it does not even help students engage in the sort of open-ended, recursive, and reciprocally critical argumentation described by Eemeren et al. Hillocks's *Ways of Teaching* describes teachers who engage in ineffective teaching practices; rather than take the ineffectiveness as evidence for changing the practice, such teachers interpret their failures as confirmation about their own fatalism regarding teaching. This behavior of Hillocks's nonoptimistic teachers may look absurd, as other people's self-fulfilling prophecies generally do, but, throughout this book, I am suggesting that we engage in a similarly fatalistic practice in regard to public argument. We are in the position described by Hillocks in regard to nonoptimistic teachers, but many of us are nonoptimistic about rhetoric itself. While Ramism (at least in the guise of current-traditional rhetoric) has been attacked in many ways, the dominant approaches to argumentation continue to assume that participating in public argument means stating one's opinion on policy issues and listing one's reasons.

Ramistic rhetoric does not actually persuade an intelligent and informed opposition audience; it was never intended to, as Ramism denied the very existence of such an audience. Rather than let the continued rhetorical failure of that form cause us to rethink our approach to rhetoric, we have come to rely even more heavily on it, just as lecturing teachers lecture even more. If public argument is bad, perhaps there is something wrong with the teaching of public argument. Instead of replicating exactly the practice that leads to the consequences we dislike, we can reflect on it, and try to enact a practice that might get us the kind of public discourse we would like to see.

NOTES
WORKS CITED
INDEX

Notes

Introduction

1. There are problems with the phrase "public sphere," ranging from its overuse to the underlying suggestion that the region of public discourse is somehow autonomous. I've opted to use it, regardless of those legitimate criticisms, partially because it is the term used so often, but also because it evokes biospheres. Thinking of areas of public discourse as similar to biospheres suggests an area of mutual dependence, something often forgotten in discussions of public argument.

2. It is not only communitarians who make that criticism. I'm indebted to one of the SIU Press readers for pointing out that this is J. B. MacPherson's criticism of liberal political theory, that it has always had the bad seed of possessive individualism.

3. The distinction may seem confusing. As has often been noted, many metaphors for persuasion involve images of triumph, domination, and war—people win an argument, knock down an opposition's argument, undermine someone else's position (Lakoff and Johnson). Less often noted is that metaphors for public discourse are often expressive—they involve images of people speaking without listening, and they assume that deliberation is separate from discourse. We often talk about taking a stand in public, having one's say, speaking one's mind, expressing one's point of view, stating one's case; the public sphere is an area where people go in order to express the things they have deliberated elsewhere. Deliberation is a silent process in which individuals engage before or after public "debate," and that "debate" consists of people expressing different (and often unconnected) points of view. Our metaphors rarely suggest a public sphere where people deliberate through disagreement—where people might behave like interlocutors engaged in dialectic. The liberal model (like, I will argue, the interest-based and communitarian models) ends up endorsing this expressivist approach to public discourse, what James Fishkin has called "democracy without deliberation" ("Beyond Teledemocracy" 55). In such a democracy, one might choose to incorporate a previous speaker's point in one's own (in order to build on or contradict it), but there is no sense that one is obligated to do so. There is also no sense that one is obligated

even to listen carefully to any of those other points of view. Such is the expressivist public sphere.

4. In current discourse, the great opponent of reason is assumed to be emotion, but liberal political theorists such as Kant, Locke, or Mill tend to contrast reason and tradition. Emotions were generally described as handmaids to reason, or irrelevant to reason, but aids to the will. When defined in opposition to deference to authority, "rational thinking" is nearly synonymous with current notions of critical thinking (see, for instance, Dewey, *Individualism* 77, 78, 81). Since the Enlightenment, the definition of "rational" has narrowed to mean instrumentalist scientism (at least in the Anglo-American tradition), and religion has come to represent the epitome of irrational behavior.

5. Ironically enough, many Christian attacks on science rely on this same strict definition of rationality, and the most extreme attacks make the same move of lumping all nonrational beliefs into the irrational category. For instance, anti-evolutionists will often point to disagreements among scientists, or recently discarded theories, or even the inherently speculative nature of many aspects of scientific theories as "proof" that science is not rational. It is, they then conclude, no more rational than creationism.

1. Politics Without Argument

1. John Silber similarly uses "he" when talking about what the liberal does (and he identifies himself as a liberal). This usage marks the traditional-universalist assumption that certain stances are neutral and universal at the same time, that "he" includes everyone. With Silber, it also marks the liberal tendency to play up the individual's conflict with conformity—when he talks about ideologues, he uses "they," as though ideologues always operate as a group while liberals are autonomous individuals (see 204). Allan Bloom also always uses "he" and "man" and "men." With the exception of a "girl" who likes Ayn Rand, Bloom's hypothetical examples are exclusively male.

2. To that degree, liberal political theory remains subversive, especially among people like Jerry Falwell, James Dobson, or Pat Robertson, who are deeply threatened by the secular/sacred distinction; it was not simply a slip of the tongue that made Falwell include the ACLU among the groups that caused the terrorist attack—he sees such organizations as satanic.

3. As these examples suggest, part of what gets buried in that rockshelf—and, thus, beyond the realm of public argument—is just what that tradition is. As will be discussed in regard to education, this means that a particular set of texts is assumed to be the traditional canon, when it is actually quite recent. Since *Brown v. Board of Education* is often marked as the beginning of judicial activism, and the decision is now fifty years old, the judicial philosophies behind such "judicial activism" are now the tradition; reactionary judges are, despite their rhetoric, in the position of activists going against tradition.

4. As will be discussed later, liberal political theory is constantly accused of privileging individual autonomy at the expense of community. This sense of "neu-

tral"—that one must consider one's arguments from the perspectives of others, and that one cannot make arguments that are only in one's own best interest—serves as an important corrective to that isolating tendency in autonomy.

5. Enlightenment philosophies of mind and politics are not quite as hostile to emotions as they are sometimes accused of being (as in, for instance, Suzanne Clark). It is a convention in Enlightenment texts (in philosophy as well as rhetoric) to distinguish between the affects and the passions (e.g., Kant), or the sentiments and passions (e.g., the Scottish school of moral sense), or habits and passions (e.g., John Quincy Adams). Sentiments like benevolence, empathy, and desire for honor are beneficial to society and appropriate bases for persuasion. Passions like anger and hatred, however, are corrupting for individuals as well as communities because passions last longer, rouse one more, and more thoroughly derange the reasoning capacities.

6. To some extent, this distribution of disagreements is absolutely necessary if public discourse is always policy discourse. If the two are the same, then arguments about transcendent issues always imply that some policy would result—a condition that, as Fraser has said, has considerably muckled feminist critiques of, for instance, pornography.

7. This advice strikes me as very similar to Elbow's discussion of the writing process. It also matches much advice regarding what students should do in regard to their own research: While textbooks on research papers often advise that students contemplate the things they have read in the course of doing research (perhaps even free-writing or journalizing about them), it is uncommon for textbooks to recommend that students argue about them.

8. Oddly enough, the reverse is not true—while there has been serious discussion of making president someone with no experience in government but considerable experience in business, it would never be suggested that success in governance is, *ipso facto,* indicative of competence in business, that a successful senator with no previous business experience be made a CFO of a major corporation. The implication is that politics is a subset of business, rather than the two being equivalent practices. The notion of politics as a subset of public behavior is connected to the assumption that politics is something that one can avoid, or, even, that one should avoid. As Held says, to say that a statement is political is to bring it into disrepute (295).

9. It is also the process that reactionaries like Kimball, Dinesh DiSouza, and Bloom bemoan, waxing nostalgic for a moment whose universal agreement was the result of exclusive admissions practices (for more on this point, see Martha Nussbaum's review of Bloom's *Closing of the American Mind*).

10. The more that a political theory assumes the self-evidence or universality of certain points of view, the more it posits an expressivist public sphere. This criticism of liberal political theory should not be taken as an endorsement of strict antifoundationalism; one also gets an expressivist public sphere by assuming that arguments have no rational, reasonable, or cognitive foundations (as in the interest-based public sphere).

2. Autonomous Selves, Liberally Educated

1. Similarly, one can take issue with Eagleton's attack on postmodernism in that he rarely quotes from Rorty, Lyotard, and so on. He defends that decision on the grounds that he is most concerned with the nearly hegemonic version of postmodernism—the kind that one hears in faculty meetings and at conferences. And, certainly, one *does* hear the kinds of arguments he attacks in those places. The sense of self advocated or assumed by Locke, Kant, Plato, or Popper is not the essentialized and ahistoric self that Giroux and others attack, but one can hear it advocated or assumed in faculty meetings, at conferences, in the paper, and so on. Beiner has noted this problem in regard to liberal political theory: While the major theorists of liberal political theory do not favor the unencumbered self, the practice of liberal democracies almost always does. He says it is not clear whether this means that one should criticize the theory for the apparently attendant practice or criticize the practice for not living up to the theory.

2. Autonomy initially meant the ability of a polis to make its own laws. The long history of nationalism and resistance to imperialism—a history that includes non-Western cultures—shows a deep-seated preference for autonomy in some sense. Resistance to slavery coexists with slavery, even in cultures in which education relentlessly promoted slavery as morally right. That people were willing to risk extraordinary dangers for freedom suggests that there really is a distinction between autonomy and slavery, even if one of degrees. There is something ultimately insulting to slaves to suggest that there is no difference between slaves and masters, even if neither is fully free.

3. Because I remarked on Holmes's and Silber's use of "he" as the universal pronoun, connecting it to their accepting the liberal model's universal/masculinist subject position, I should be fair to Gerald Dworkin and explain this his use of "he" at this point is not such an indication. Dworkin's book alternates pronoun use from one chapter to the next, and this list happens to be in a chapter in which he was using "he."

4. And the more likely, I think, one is to find oneself in contradictions. Thus, for instance, Bloom continually uses critical thinking in a way similar to Kant's autonomy—critical thinking is a rejection of authority and tradition—*and* he insists upon a deeply respectful attitude toward traditional texts and pieces of music. For him, only some rejections and criticisms of tradition are critical thinking, or, perhaps more accurately, only some traditions can be considered critically.

5. The power of facts is shown by the extraordinary lengths to which propagandists will go to silence them. Propagandists attack those who "insist on talking about facts or events that do not fit the image" ("Truth and Politics" 255) as much as they do the putative enemy. In times of conflict, "the main effort of both the deceived group and the deceivers themselves is likely to be directed toward keeping the propaganda intact" ("Truth and Politics" 255). Whether claims are true matters less than whether they fit preexisting notions.

6. The distinction between the good and the right is more than a little confusing, especially because American political discourse tends to make everything a ques-

tion of right (which, one might note, points to a problem with a philosophy that insists that only the right is an appropriate basis for governmental intervention; the likely consequence is that questions of good get recast as questions of justice).

7. But participants in exploratory discussions may make statements, pose questions, and pursue lines of reasoning in which they have no stake. They do not assume such statements or lines could be proved valid for all people because they are themselves unsure whether or not they believe the statements to be true. Hence, Böhler's assertion excludes the possibility of argumentation being essentially exploratory—that people might engage in an argument in order to discover or pursue knowledge through discursively experimenting with different arguments.

8. Pick a topic about which you care deeply, and write a letter of 1,000–1,250 words to your congressperson arguing for or against some specific policy concerning that topic. You should make certain that, at some point in your paper, you consider the opposition's argument. You must use at least four sources.

9. It appears that certain positions (rather than how they are articulated) are more or less sophisticated for Fishman, an attitude that necessitates the distinctly peculiar assumption that faith in free will, autonomy, or individuality are inherently unsophisticated positions—thereby making people such as Augustine, Erasmus, Arendt, and Popper unsophisticated thinkers. While I don't agree with all of them, would that I were so unsophisticated.

3. Closing My Eyes as You Speak

1. Jon Elster, Jurgen Habermas, Bohman and Rehg, and Seyla Benhabib use the term "pluralist" for this model, but I have found this usage somewhat confusing. As Gary Chapman pointed out to me during a conversation, almost all models of democracy after Mill accept the fact of a pluralistic society. Thus, what distinguishes this model is not that it assumes what Robert Dahl calls a polyarchy, but how it theorizes what causes the different points of view, whether they can be reconciled, and how discourse functions both internally (whether people are ever persuaded by discourse) and externally (what makes one piece of discourse better than another).

2. Even Dahl is a problematic example, not only because he very quickly moved toward a much more complicated view of polyarchy, but also because he never endorsed a completely laissez-faire public sphere.

3. With some justice, one might make a similar criticism of Brodkey's. Perhaps because her piece is primarily an expression of her side, it does not directly respond to some of the arguments raised by critics of the program, such as Maxine Hairston's argument that the course permitted if not encouraged instructors to grade students on the extent to which they shared the same interpretations of the material.

4. One might imagine that a community has a common area for grazing cattle, and that the common area can best support ten cattle. If there are ten cattle, then each cow will gain ten pounds; if there are eleven, then each cow will only gain nine pounds; if there are twelve, then each cow will only gain eight pounds, and so on. One can see that ten cattle is the optimum for the community, in that there

is a total weight gain of one hundred pounds, but only ninety-nine at eleven, and so on. The problem is that an individual deciding whether or not to put an additional cow on the commons will conclude that doing so is beneficial if s/he looks only at what is his/her narrow best interest. A person with one cow on the common will get a weight gain of ten pounds, but two cows—even if that puts the total up to eleven cows—will get a weight gain of eighteen pounds. In other words, it is in the short-term best interest of each individual to do what is obviously going to damage the larger community.

Unfortunately, the tragedy of the commons is an apt simile for many political decisions. The most obvious analogies are to environmental issues—it is in the narrow best interests of individuals, individual companies, and even individual communities to pollute, especially if they can do so in ways that will harm some other individual, community, or generation. Dumping waste into water that will affect downstream communities, using up resources that future generations will need, and extinguishing species are all strategies that can enhance the prosperity of a small group of people at least for the short term. There are other examples—promoting tobacco use in other countries can benefit U.S. companies, thereby increasing the prosperity of U.S. citizens without increasing our health care costs; supporting tyrannical governments in other countries can give access to resources at cheap costs for U.S. businesses; prohibiting immigrants from access to emergency medical care can reduce costs on American taxpayers; refusing to support local schools once one's own children have finished their schooling will reduce one's taxes. All of these policies are bad only if one considers oneself a citizen of the world, as having obligations to future generations, or as bound by rules of reciprocal conduct—in other words, if one thinks beyond one's own narrow self-interest.

Of course, one can argue—as have proponents of pluralist democracy—that one's self-interest must include long-term self-interest because of the behavior of other individuals (this is the kind of pluralism imagined by Dahl, for example). If, that is, I put another cow on the commons, so will all my neighbors, and the commons will become so overgrazed that all cattle will starve; thus, a thoughtful consideration of what is in my best interest will cause me to refrain. There are two problems with this argument. The first is that I will only worry about current competitors for the commons. Because future generations cannot retaliate, in that their actions cannot possibly harm me, I need not worry about them. This argument ignores, second, that the very system encourages me to think about what will benefit me, so my reaction to these potential negative consequences of everyone adding cattle to the commons is most likely to be to try to find some way that I can increase my use of the commons without other people increasing theirs. It would be easy for me to limit others' use of the commons if I have the ability to threaten other people in the community or the power of the government behind me (as is almost literally what happened in the case of the enclosures). I may even find a way to get help from my neighbors in forbidding some people's access to the commons if those people are members of some minority and disadvantaged group. In other words, a central assumption of interest-based democracy—that a lot of people looking out for their own best interest will result in the best policies for the community as a whole—is wrong.

5. Of particular interest is what Page and Shapiro conclude causes public opinion to change. While change in "life circumstances" (some of which might be considered interests) is important, so are other factors such as level of education, world events, changes in media. The shift from an agricultural to industrial economy, for instance, has eroded support for policies that benefit farmers, possibly because fewer people saw it in their interests (or the interests of their constituents) to maintain such practices. But, support for civil rights, the authors suggest, resulted as much from a generally more educated populace (and the connection between education and tolerance is generally well established.)

6. One reason people get uncomfortable with the sort of advice given in Fisher and Fisher is that it seems to hearken back to the liberal model's assumption that one can transcend the personal. If we give up the notion that beliefs and identity are connected, then aren't we back to argument having to do with impersonal (and, ultimately, false) universalism and neutrality? That is the dilemma if and only if "personal" and "identity" are assumed to be synonymous. The problem with the interest-based model is that it posits a clear causal relation between beliefs and identity—that socioeconomic identity causes belief—without acknowledging that the relation is actually far more complex, an issue that is discussed at greater length in regard to deliberative democracy. The problem is that one must somehow avoid the motivism of the interest-based model without falling into the false universalism of the traditional-universal model of liberal democracy.

7. In fairness to advocates of ideal normative agreement, I think that what they might mean is something closer to my example of a teacher believing that students who knew everything about writing instruction at a college would agree with his/her policies. Still, the problem, it seems to me, is that one ends up denying someone's knowledge—in that example, I make my knowledge perfect knowledge. (It is, after all, cognitively impossible to make any decision on the basis of knowledge other than what I have.) On a practical level, it does not work to ignore what my students know about writing, even when I disagree with it. College students come to us as not as empty slates but as adults who have had twelve years of writing instruction. If we are teaching at a selective institution, then they know how to get good grades. If I do not acknowledge that knowledge, if I fail to recognize the legitimacy of their own knowledge (perhaps especially when I think it no longer applies, as in the case of students who *know* that, regardless of what their teacher says, they can start a paper the night before), then I have no credibility with them. In addition, I am quite likely to universalize my own personal and disciplinary preferences unless I listen to what they know about writing in their own lives and disciplines.

8. An interesting question is to what extent people in a totalitarian system can themselves choose to engage in authority-based practice, or at what cost. Earlier, I mentioned my instrumental/normative acquiescence in regard to decisions of the Composition Committee. I always thought the committee's decisions facilitated good practice, just not what I always considered ideal practice for me personally.

I often disagreed with the decisions, but I never found them repellent or unethical. Had they reached decisions that led to bad practice, my situation would have been very different. Arendt's ideal, as Pitkin argues, is the action of the French Resistance, so her implicit answer to the dilemma of what to do in a totalitarian system is that one must resist, with potentially very high costs.

4. What Angels of Our Nature? Communitarianism, Social Constructivism, and Communities of Discourse

1. And, in fact, part of his argument against liberalism is that it fails to acknowledge the depth of some commitments (see his discussion of Lee in *Democracy's Discontent,* 15–16).

2. In fact, a consistent reliance on such research would end up generating a very different platform: A recent study concluded that the reduced crime rate was the result of certain kinds of women getting abortions; it is hard to imagine that the authors of the platform would use such a study to conclude that the government should encourage poor single mothers to terminate their pregnancies.

3. When I took over as secretary in a homeowners' association, I read the file of correspondence of the previous boards. It had numerous letters indicating overzealous board members, ones who took the time to chastise neighbors for not having their children put away toys, not getting their grass mowed often enough, or leaving sand piled at the ends of their driveways. This was in a neighborhood that was heavily wooded, so none of these infractions was visible from public areas. During the period that board members were taking the time to write letters like these, the community sewer plant was in near-constant violation of EPA regulations, and therefore polluting a local stream and putting the homeowners' association at risk for considerable fines. I was very troubled by the priorities that people had, and the experience comes to mind when I read communitarians make cheerful assessments about where communities will and will not interfere.

4. One sees the same high regard for simple politeness in Fishman and McCarthy, who also describe the continued "civility" (their term) in the North Carolina class as an achievement, despite the controversial issues discussed. Having spent some time teaching in North Carolina, I am convinced that such civility is not particularly noteworthy; I generally found discursive disagreement among students much more difficult to achieve.

5. This means that the tendency to say that one should not criticize social construction of knowledge on pragmatic grounds, or as a moral system, is deeply problematic. To make that argument, one must either posit such intradisciplinary categories as ontologically grounded (in which case one is making a foundationalist defense of antifoundationalism), or one must reject the self-descriptions of the very people who are cited as authorities on the subject—Rorty et al.

6. This is *not* to say that postmodernism or poststructuralism caused such arguments; they long predate postmodernism. After all, the whole point of Frederick Jackson Turner's *Significance of the Frontier in American History* is to argue against the notion that only white Anglo-Saxon Protestants can enact democracy, and the

argument that human rights are restricted to citizens was central to Nazi procedures regarding Jews (see Arendt's discussion of Jew's "statelessness" in *Eichmann in Jerusalem*). My point is that the right has found such arguments to be very useful.

5. Listening for Difference

1. As unrealistic as this last assertion might seem, there is empirical support for it. Robyn M. Dawes, Alphons J. C. van de Kragt, and John M. Orbell summarize their consistent findings that decision-making without discussion tends to lead to a large number of subjects deciding purely on the basis of self-interest, while discussion increases cooperation and group identity:

> That generalization has held true over the last ten years for 27 different no-discussion conditions with 1,188 subjects in 178 groups, and for 12 different discussion conditions with 637 subjects in 97 groups. All 39 variations we have developed lead to the same conclusion: with no discussion egoistic motives explain cooperation; with discussion, group identity—alone or in interaction with verbal promises—explains its dramatic increase. (109)

2. I was surprised to hear the host of a Christian radio program directed at women assert that the two main projects of feminists in the last twenty years had been the promotion of abortion and lesbianism. I thought that, given the alliance of at least some feminists and some Christian activists, the commentator might have acknowledged action against pornography, but she did not, and her call-in listeners seemed to agree with her assessment of feminists.

3. While Irving and others maintain that this is the case, MacKinnon and Andrea Dworkin counter that Canadian antipornography seizures were not the result of the antipornography legislation they supported but exemplified long practice (see <http://www.igc.org/Womensnet/dworkin/OrdinanceCanada.html>).

4. The classic advice is to have students look critically at their source material, and that seems to be relentlessly sensible, but we have to be careful how we define looking critically. I am not convinced that the advice concerning the status of the author is tremendously helpful; some sources, for instance, suggest that students give more credibility to pages that have a university sponsor, but that seems bad advice on two grounds. The more trivial is that this advice is given in the spirit of trying to direct students to scholars, but it may just as well direct them to the projects of other students. More important, being a scholar and having spent a lot of my life around scholars, I am not personally persuaded that we are necessarily more knowledgeable than other people. This approach to "critical thinking" is not, it seems to me, critical thinking at all, but obedience to authority. And it is not the kind of deference to authority implicitly praised by Arendt—we are not saying that students should defer to people who are more knowledgeable than they about a topic (a perfectly appropriate piece of advice)—but that students should assume that someone is more knowledgeable without asking that it be demonstrated.

WORKS CITED

Prepared with the assistance of Heather Grassmick

Ackerman, Bruce A. *Social Injustice in the Liberal State.* New Haven: Yale UP, 1980.

Adams, John Quincy. *Lectures on Rhetoric and Oratory.* 2 vols. Cambridge: Hilliard, 1810.

Alcoff, Linda. "How Is Epistemology Political?" *Radical Philosophy: Tradition, Counter-Tradition, Politics.* Ed. Roger S. Gottlieb. Philadelphia: Temple UP, 1993. 65–85.

Alliance Defense Fund. "Equal Access Project Protects Christians' Rights." 6 Mar. 2001. <www.alliancedefensefund.org.>

Annas, Pamela, and Deborah Tenney. "Positioning Oneself: A Feminist Approach to Argument." *Argument Revisited; Argument Redefined.* Ed. Barbara Emmel. Thousand Oaks: Sage, 1996. 127–52.

Arendt, Hannah. "The Crisis in Education." *Between Past and Future: Eight Exercises in Political Thought.* By Arendt. Harmondworth, Eng.: Penguin, 1968. 173–96.

———. *Eichmann in Jerusalem: A Report on the Banality of Evil.* Harmondworth, Eng.: Penguin, 1984.

———. "Heidegger the Fox." *Essays in Understanding.* Ed. Jerome Kohn. New York: Harcourt, 1994. 361–62.

———. *The Human Condition.* 2d ed. Chicago: U of Chicago P, 1958.

———. *Lectures on Kant's Political Philosophy.* Ed. Ronald Beiner. Chicago: U of Chicago P, 1982.

———. *The Life of the Mind.* New York: Harcourt, 1978.

———. *On Violence.* New York: Harcourt, 1969.

———. *The Origins of Totalitarianism.* New York: Harcourt, 1973.

———. "Truth and Politics." *Between Past and Future: Eight Exercises in Political Thought.* By Arendt. Harmondworth, Eng.: Penguin, 1968. 227–64.

———. "What Is Authority?" *Between Past and Future: Eight Exercises in Political Thought.* By Arendt. Harmondworth, Eng.: Penguin, 1968. 91–142.

Asen, Robert, and Daniel Brouwer. Introduction. *Counterpublics and the State.* Ed. Asen and Brouwer. Albany: State U New York P, 2001. 1–34.

Axelrod, Rise B., and Charles R. Cooper. *The St. Martin's Guide to Writing*. 6th ed. Boston: Bedford-St. Martin's, 2001.

Ayer, A. J., ed. *Logical Positivism*. New York: Free, 1959.

Barbour, Ian G. *Religion and Science: Historical and Contemporary Issues*. San Francisco: Harper, 1997.

Baron, Dennis. *The English-Only Question: An Official Language for Americans*. New Haven: Yale UP, 1990.

Bartholomae, David. "Writing with Teachers." *Cross-Talk in Comp Theory: A Reader*. Ed. Victor Villanueva Jr. Urbana: NCTE, 1997. 479–88.

Barton, Ellen. "Evidentials, Argumentation, and Epistemological Stance." *College English* 55 (1993): 745–69.

Bazerman, Charles. "An Interview with Charles Bazerman." By Crawford T. Hugh and Kary D. Smout. *Composition Studies/Freshman English News* 23 (1995): 21–36.

———. *Shaping Written Knowledge: The Genre and Activity of the Experimental Article in Science*. Madison: U of Wisconsin P, 1988.

Beaufort, Anne. "Operationalizing the Concept of Discourse Community: A Case Study of One Institutional Site of Composing." *Research in the Teaching of English* 31 (1997): 486–529.

Becker, Carl. *The Declaration of Independence: A Study in the History of Political Ideas*. New York: Knopf, 1942.

Beiner, Ronald. *What's the Matter with Liberalism?* Berkeley: U of California P, 1995.

Benhabib, Seyla. "Models of Public Space: Hannah Arendt, the Liberal Tradition, and Jürgen Habermas." *Habermas and the Public Sphere*. Ed. Craig Calhoun. Cambridge: MIT P, 1992. 73–98.

———. *The Reluctant Modernism of Hannah Arendt*. Thousand Oaks: Sage, 1996.

———. "Toward a Liberal Model of Democratic Legitimacy." *Democracy and Difference: Contesting the Boundaries of the Political*. Ed. Seyla Benhabib. Princeton: Princeton UP, 1996. 67–94.

Bentham, Jeremy. *The Principles of Morals and Legislation*. Amherst: Prometheus, 1988.

Bercovitch, Sacvan. *The American Jeremiad*. Madison: U of Wisconsin P, 1978.

Berlin, Isaiah. "The Pursuit of the Ideal." *The Crooked Timber of Humanity*. By Berlin. Princeton: Princeton UP, 1990. 1–19.

———. "Two Concepts of Liberty." *Four Essays on Liberty*. By Berlin. Oxford: Oxford UP, 1969. 118–72.

Berlin, James. "Contemporary Composition: The Major Pedagogical Theories." *The Writing Teacher's Sourcebook*. 3rd ed. Ed. Gary Tate, Edward P. J. Corbett, and Nancy Myers. New York: Oxford UP, 1994. 9–21.

———. "Rhetoric and Ideology in the Writing Class." *Cross-Talk in Comp Theory: A Reader*. Ed. Victor Villanueva Jr. Urbana: NCTE, 1997. 679–700.

Bernard-Donals, Michael. *The Practice of Theory: Rhetoric, Knowledge, and Pedagogy in the Academy*. Cambridge: Cambridge UP, 1998.

Bernard-Donals, Michael, and Richard Glejzer. Introduction. *Rhetoric in an Anti-Foundational World: Language, Culture, and Pedagogy.* Ed. Bernard-Donals and Glejzer. New Haven: Yale UP, 1998. 1–30.

Berubé, Michael. *Public Access: Literary Theory and American Cultural Politics.* London: Verso, 1994.

Bhaskar, Roy. *A Realist Theory of Science.* London: Verso, 1997.

Blackburn, Simon. "Self-evident." *The Oxford Dictionary of Philosophy.* Oxford: Oxford UP, 1994. 345.

Bloom, Allan. *The Closing of the American Mind.* New York: Simon, 1987.

Böhler, Dietrich. "Transcendental Pragmatics and Critical Morality: On the Possibility and Moral Significance of a Self-Enlightenment of Reason." *The Communicative Ethics Controversy.* Ed. Seyla Benhabib and Fred Dallmayr. Cambridge: MIT P, 1990. 111–50.

Bohman, James, and William Rehg. Introduction. *Deliberative Democracy: Essays on Reason and Politics.* Ed. Bohman and Rehg. Cambridge: MIT P, 1997. xi–xxx.

Booth, Wayne C. *The Company We Keep: An Ethics of Fiction.* Berkeley: U of California P, 1988.

———. *Modern Dogma and the Rhetoric of Assent.* Chicago: U of Chicago P, 1974.

Braddock, Richard. "The Frequency and Placement of Topic Sentences in Expository Prose." *On Writing Research: The Braddock Essays, 1975–1998.* Ed. Lisa Ede. New York: Bedford-St. Martin's, 1999. 29–42.

Brandt, William J. *The Craft of Writing.* Englewood Cliffs: Prentice, 1969.

Brodkey, Linda. "Making a Federal Case of Difference: The Politics of Pedagogy, Publicity, and Postponement." *Writing Theory and Critical Theory.* Ed. John Clifford and John Schilb. New York: MLA, 1994. 236–61.

Brody, Miriam. *Manly Writing: Gender, Rhetoric, and the Rise of Composition.* Carbondale: Southern Illinois UP, 1993.

Bruffee, Kenneth A. "Collaborative Learning and the 'Conversation of Mankind.'" *Cross-Talk in Comp Theory: A Reader.* Ed. Victor Villanueva Jr. Urbana: NCTE, 1997. 393–414.

———. "Writing and Reading as Collaborative or Social Acts." *A Sourcebook for Basic Writing Teachers.* Ed. Theresa Enos. New York: Random, 1987. 565–74.

Brutus. "Essays." *The Anti-Federalist Papers and the Constitutional Convention Debates.* Ed. Ralph Ketcham. New York: Mentor, 1986. 269–308.

Burke, Kenneth. *Language as Symbolic Action: Essays on Life, Literature, and Method.* Berkeley, U of California P, 1973.

Burstein, Andrew. *Sentimental Democracy: The Evolution of America's Romantic Self-Image.* New York: Hill, 1999.

Calhoun, Craig C. "Nationalism and the Public Sphere." *Public and Private in Thought and Practice: Perspectives on a Grand Dichotomy.* Ed. Jeff Weintraub and Krishan Kumar. Chicago: U of Chicago P, 1997. 75–102.

———. "Social Theory and the Politics of Identity." *Social Theory and the Politics of Identity.* Ed. Craig C. Calhoun. Oxford, Eng.: Blackwell, 1994. 9–36.

Calhoun, John. *The Papers of John C. Calhoun.* South Caroliniana Society, 1959. Ed. Robert L. Meriwether. Columbia: U of South Carolina P, 1991.

Cappella, Joseph N., and Kathleen Hall Jamieson. *Spiral of Cynicism: The Press and the Public Good.* New York: Oxford UP, 1997.

Carnegie, Andrew. "The True Gospel Concerning Wealth." *Our Nation's Archive: The History of the United States in Documents.* Ed. Erik Bruun and Jay Crosby. New York: Black Dog, 1999. 452–57.

Carpenter, C. C. J., et al. "Public Statement by Eight Alabama Clergymen." *Audiences and Intentions: A Book of Arguments.* Ed. Arthur Quinn and Nancy Bradbury. New York: Macmillan, 1994. 42–43.

Caygill, Howard. *A Kant Dictionary.* Oxford, Eng.: Blackwell, 1995.

Chafe, William. *Civilities and Civil Rights: Greensboro, North Carolina, and the Black Struggle for Freedom.* Oxford: Oxford UP, 1981.

Chambers, Simone. *Reasonable Democracy: Jurgen Habermas and the Politics of Discourse.* Ithaca: Cornell UP, 1996.

Cheney, Lynne. *Telling the Truth: Why Our Culture and Our Country Have Stopped Making Sense—And What We Can Do about It.* New York: Simon, 1995.

Christiano, Thomas. "The Significance of Public Deliberation." *Deliberative Democracy: Essays on Reasons and Politics.* Ed. James Bohman and William Rehg. Cambridge: MIT P, 1997. 243–78.

Citizen Link: A Web Site of Focus on the Family. "Focus on the Family Position Statement on Homosexual Rights." 6 Mar. 2001. <www.focusonthefamily.org>.

Clark, Gregory. "Response." *College Composition and Communication* 45 (1994): 386–88.

Clark, Gregory, and S. Michael Halloran. *Oratorical Culture in Nineteenth-Century America: Transformations in the Theory and Practice of Rhetoric.* Carbondale: Southern Illinois UP, 1993.

Clark, Suzanne. "Rhetoric, Social Construction, and Gender: Is It Bad to Be Sentimental?" *Writing Theory and Critical Theory.* Ed. John Clifford and John Schilb. New York: MLA, 1994. 96–108.

Clifford, John. "The Subject in Discourse" *Contending with Words: Composition and Rhetoric in a Postmodern Age.* By Clifford. New York: MLA, 1991. 38–51.

Cloud, Dana. "Doing Away with Suharto—and the Twin Myths of Globalization and New Social Movements." *Counterpublics and the State.* Ed. Robert Asen and Daniel Brouwer. Albany: State U of New York P, 2001. 235–63.

Cmiel, Kenneth. *Democratic Eloquence: The Fight over Popular Speech in Nineteenth-Century America.* Berkeley: U of California P, 1990.

Cohen, Joshua. "Deliberation and Democratic Legitimacy." *Deliberative Democracy: Essays on Reason and Politics.* Ed. Seyla Benhabib, James Bohman, and William Rehg. Cambridge: MIT P, 1997. 67–92.

———. "Procedure and Substance in Deliberative Democracy." *Democracy and Difference.* Ed. Seyla Benhabib. Princeton: Princeton UP, 1996. 95–119.

Collier, Andrew. *Critical Realism: An Introduction to Roy Bhaskar's Philosophy.* London: Verso, 1994.

Conley, Thomas M. *Rhetoric in the European Tradition*. New York: Longman, 1990.

Connelly, Paul. "Exploratory Writing to My Colleagues." *Pre/Text* 11 (1990): 77–82.

Cooper, Marilyn. "The Ecology of Writing." *College English* 48 (1986): 364–75.

Dahl, Robert A. *Democracy and Its Critics*. New Haven: Yale UP, 1989.

———. *On Democracy*. New Haven: Yale UP, 1998.

———. *A Preface to Democratic Theory*. Chicago: U of Chicago P, 1956.

———. *Who Governs? Democracy and Power in an American City*. New Haven: Yale UP, 1961.

Daniel, Neil, and Christina Murphy. "Correctness or Clarity? Finding Answers in the Classroom and the Professional World." *The Place of Grammar in Writing Instruction: Past, Present, Future*. Ed. Susan Hunter and Ray Wallace. Portsmouth, Boynton, 1995. 225–42.

Dasenbrook, Reed Way. "Truth and Methods." *College English* 57 (1995): 546–61.

Daümer, Elisabeth, and Sandra Runzo. "Transforming the Composition Classroom." *Teaching Writing: Pedagogy, Gender, and Equity*. By Daümer and Runzo. Albany: State U of New York P, 1996. 45–62.

Dawes, Robyn M., Alphons J. C. van de Kragt, and John M. Orbell. "Cooperation for the Benefit of Us—Not Me, or My Conscience." *Beyond Self-Interest*. Ed. Jane Mansbridge. Chicago: U of Chicago P, 1990. 97–110.

Dewey, John. *Individualism Old and New*. Amherst: Prometheus, 1999.

———. *The Public and Its Problems*. Athens: Swallow, 1954.

Diggins, John Patrick. *The Rise and Fall of the American Left*. New York: Norton, 1992.

Downs, Anthony. *An Economic Theory of Democracy*. New York: Harper, 1957.

Dworkin, Andrea. "Portrait of a New Puritan—and a New Slaver." *Life and Death: Unapologetic Writings on the Continuing War Against Women*. By Dworkin. New York: Free, 1997. 67–72.

Dworkin, Gerald. *The Theory and Practice of Autonomy*. Cambridge: Cambridge UP, 1988.

Dworkin, Ronald. "Women and Pornography—Only words by Catherine A. MacKinnon." *New York Review of Books* 21 Oct. 1993: 36–41.

Eagleton, Terry. *The Illusions of Postmodernism*. Oxford, Eng.: Blackwell, 1996.

Eberly, Rosa. *Citizen Critics*. Urbana: U of Illinois P, 2000.

Ede, Lisa, and Andrea Lunsford. "Audience Addressed/Audience Invoked: The Role of Audience in Composition Theory and Pedagogy." *On Writing Research: The Braddock Essays*. Ed. Lisa Ede. Boston: Bedford-St. Martin's, 1999. 156–71.

Elbow, Peter. "Being a Writer vs. Being an Academic: A Conflict in Goals." *Cross-Talk in Comp Theory: A Reader*. Ed. Victor Villanueva Jr. Urbana: NCTE, 1997. 489–500.

———. "Closing My Eyes as I Speak: An Argument for Ignoring Audience." *The Harcourt Brace Sourcebook for Teachers of Writing*. Ed. Patricia Roberts. Fort Worth: Harcourt, 1998. 51–71.

———. *Writing Without Teachers*. London: Oxford UP, 1973.

Elshtain, Jean Bethke. *Democracy on Trial.* New York: Basic, 1995.

Elster, Jon. "Arguing and Bargaining." Unpublished ms. in English. Published in French as "Argumenter et negocier dans deux assemblees constituantes." *Revue Francaise de Science Politique* 44 (1994): 187–256.

———. Introduction. *Deliberative Democracy.* Ed. Elster. Cambridge: Cambridge UP, 1998. 1–18.

———. "The Market and the Forum: Three Varieties of Political Theory." *Deliberative Democracy: Essays on Reason and Politics.* Ed. James Bohman and William Rehg. Cambridge: MIT P, 1997. 3–34.

Etzioni, Amitai. Introduction. *The Essential Communitarian Reader.* Ed. Etzioni. Lanham: Rowman, 1998. ix–xxiv.

Faigley, Lester. *Fragments of Rationality: Postmodernity and the Subject of Composition.* Pittsburgh: U of Pittsburgh P, 1992.

Farrell, Thomas. *Norms of Rhetorical Culture.* New Haven: Yale UP, 1993.

Fearon, James. "Deliberation as Discussion." *Deliberative Democracy.* Ed. Jon Elster. Cambridge: Cambridge UP, 1998. 44–68.

Fiedler, Leslie. *Love and Death in the American Novel.* Revised ed. New York: Dell, 1966.

Fish, Stanley. *Doing What Comes Naturally: Change, Rhetoric, and the Practice of Theory in Literary and Legal Studies.* Oxford, Eng.: Clarendon, 1989.

Fisher, Roger, and William Ury. *Getting to Yes: Negotiating Agreement Without Giving In.* New York: Penguin, 1991.

Fishkin, James. "Beyond Teledemocracy." *The Essential Communitarian Reader.* Ed. Amitai Etzioni. Lanham: Rowman, 1998. 55–60.

———. *The Voice of the People: Public Opinion and Democracy.* New Haven: Yale UP, 1995.

Fishman, Stephen M., and Lucille Parkinson McCarthy. "Teaching for Student Change: A Deweyan Alternative to Radical Pedagogy." *College Composition and Communication* 47 (1996): 342–66.

Fraser, Nancy. "Rethinking the Public Sphere: Contribution to the Critique of Actually Existing Democracy." *Habermas and the Public Sphere.* Ed. Craig Calhoun. Cambridge: MIT P, 1992. 109–42.

Freehling, William F. *The Road to Disunion: Secessionists at Bay, 1776–1854.* New York: Oxford UP, 1990.

Freire, Paulo. *Pedagogy of the Oppressed.* New York: Continuum, 1988.

Fukuyama, Francis. "The End of History?" *The National Interest.* 16 (1989): 3–18.

Fulkerson, Richard. "Four Philosophies of Composition." *The Writing Teacher's Sourcebook.* 3rd ed. Ed. Gary Tate, Edward P. J. Corbett, and Nancy Myers. New York: Oxford UP, 1994. 3–8.

———. *Teaching the Argument in Writing.* Urbana: NCTE, 1998.

Gage, John T. "The Reasoned Thesis: The E-Word and Argumentative Writing as a Process of Inquiry." *Argument Revisited: Negotiating Meaning in the Composition Classroom.* Ed. Barbara Emmel et al. Thousand Oaks: Sage, 1996. 3–18.

———. *The Shape of Reason: Argumentative Writing in College.* Boston: Allyn, 2001.

Gambetta, Diego. "Claro! An Essay on Discursive Machismo." *Deliberative Democracy.* Ed. Jon Elster. Cambridge: Cambridge UP, 1998. 19–43.

Gaus, Gerald. "Reason, Justification, and Consensus: Why Democracy Can't Have It All." *Deliberative Democracy: Essays on Reason and Politics.* Ed. James Bohman and William Rehg. Cambridge: MIT P, 1997. 205–42.

Giroux, Henry. *Disturbing Pleasures: Learning Popular Culture.* New York: Routledge, 1994.

Gitlin, Todd. *The Sixties: Years of Hope, Days of Rage.* New York: Bantam, 1993.

———. *The Twilight of Common Dreams: Why America Is Wracked by Culture Wars.* New York: Holt, 1995.

Gould, Carol. "Diversity and Democracy: Representing Differences." *Democracy and Difference: Contesting the Boundaries of the Political.* Ed. Seyla Benhabib. Princeton: Princeton UP, 1996. 171–86.

Graff, Gerald. *Beyond the Culture Wars: How Teaching the Conflicts Can Revitalize American Education.* New York: Norton, 1992.

Gross, Alan G. "Does Rhetoric of Science Matter? The Case of the Floppy-Eared Rabbits." *College English* 53 (1991): 933–43.

Gruen, Erich. *The Last Generation of the Roman Republic.* Berkeley: U of California P, 1995.

Gutmann, Amy, and Dennis Thompson. "Democratic Disagreement." *Deliberative Politics.* Ed. Stephen Macedo. New York: Oxford UP, 1999. 243–80.

Habermas, Jürgen. *Between Facts and Norms: Contributions of a Discourse Theory of Law and Democracy.* Cambridge: MIT P, 1996.

———. "A Genealogical Analysis of the Cognitive Content of Morality." *The Inclusion of the Other: Studies of Political Theory.* By Habermas. Cambridge: MIT P, 1998. 3–48.

———. *Legitimation Crisis.* Boston: Beacon, 1975.

———. *On the Pragmatics of Communication.* Cambridge: MIT P, 1998.

———. *Philosophical-Political Profiles.* Cambridge: MIT P, 1983.

———. "Popular Sovereignty as Procedure." *Deliberative Democracy: Essays on Reason and Politics.* Ed. James Bohman and William Rehg. Cambridge: MIT P, 1997. 35–66.

———. "'Reasonable' versus 'True,' or the Morality of Worldviews." *The Inclusion of the Other: Studies of Political Theory.* By Habermas. Cambridge: MIT P, 1998. 75–104.

———. *The Structural Transformation of the Public Sphere: An Inquiry into a Category of Bourgeois Society.* Cambridge: MIT P, 1992.

———. "Three Normative Models of Democracy." *The Inclusion of the Other: Studies of Political Theory.* By Habermas. Cambridge: MIT P, 1998. 239–52.

———. "What Is Universal Pragmatics?" *On the Pragmatics of Communication.* Ed. Maeve Cooke. Cambridge: MIT P, 1998. 21–104.

Hairston, Maxine. "Diversity, Ideology, and Teaching Writing." *Cross-Talk in Comp Theory: A Reader.* Ed. Victor Villanueva Jr. Urbana: NCTE, 1997. 659–76.

Halloran, S. Michael. "On the End of Rhetoric, Classical and Modern." *Landmark*

Essays in Rhetorical Invention. Ed. Richard E. Young and Yameng Liu. Davis: Hermagoras, 1994. 79–90.

Hamilton, Alexander, James Madison, and John Jay. *The Federalist Papers.* Ed. Clinton Rossiter. New York: Mentor, 1961.

Harkin, Patricia, and John Schilb. Introduction. *Contending with Words.* Ed. Patricia Harkin and John Schilb New York: MLA, 1991. 1–10.

Harris, Muriel. "Collaboration Is Not Collaboration: Writing Center Tutorials vs. Peer-Response Groups." *College Composition and Communication* 43 (1992): 369–83.

Harris, Joseph. "Negotiating the Contact Zone." *Journal of Basic Writing* 14 (1995): 27–42.

———. *A Teaching Subject: Composition since 1966.* Upper Saddle River: Prentice, 1997.

Hauser, Gerard. *Vernacular Voices: The Rhetoric of Publics and Public Spheres.* Columbia: U of South Carolina P, 1999.

Held, David. *Models of Democracy.* Stanford: Stanford UP, 1996.

Herman, Edward S., and Noam Chomsky. *Manufacturing Consent: The Political Economy of the Mass Media.* New York: Pantheon, 1988.

Hillocks, George, Jr. *Research on Written Composition.* Urbana: NCRE, 1986.

———. *Ways of Teaching, Ways of Thinking.* New York: Teachers College P, 1999.

Hirsch, E. D. *Cultural Literacy: What Every American Needs to Know.* Boston: Houghton, 1987.

Holmes, Stephen. *The Anatomy of Anti-Liberalism.* Cambridge: Harvard UP, 1993.

———. *Passions and Constraints: On the Theory of Liberal Democracy.* Chicago: U of Chicago P, 1995.

hooks, bell. *Outlaw Culture: Resisting Representations.* New York: Routledge UP, 1994.

Horner, Winifred. *Nineteenth-Century Scottish Rhetoric: The American Connection.* Carbondale: Southern Illinois UP, 1993.

Howell, Wilbur Samuel. "The Declaration of Independence and Eighteenth-Century Logic." *William and Mary Quarterly* 18 (1961): 463–84.

Hurlbert, Claude Mark, and Michael Blitz. *Composition and Resistance.* Portsmouth: Boynton, 1991.

Ignatieff, Michael. "Human Rights: The Midlife Crisis." *New York Review of Books* 20 May 1999: 58–62.

Irving, John. "Pornography and the New Puritans." *New York Times Book Review* 29 Mar. 1992.

Jamieson, Kathleen Hall. *Eloquence in an Electronic Age: The Transformation of Political Speechmaking.* New York: Oxford UP, 1988.

———. *Everything You Think You Know about Politics: And Why You're Wrong.* New York: Basic, 2000.

Jarratt, Susan C. "Feminism and Composition: The Case for Conflict." *Contending with Words: Composition and Rhetoric in a Postmodern Age.* Ed. Patricia Harkin and John Schilb. New York: MLA, 1991. 105–23.

Jefferson, Thomas. *Autobiography. Thomas Jefferson: Writings.* Ed. Merrill Peterson. New York: Library of America, 1984. 1–101.

———. "Letters." *Thomas Jefferson: Writings.* Ed. Merrill Peterson. New York: Library of America, 1984. 509–1518.

———. *Notes on the State of Virginia.* Ed. William Peden. Chapel Hill: U of North Carolina P, 1982.

Johnson, James. "Arguing for Deliberation: Some Skeptical Considerations." *Deliberative Democracy.* Ed. Jon Elster. Cambridge: Cambridge UP, 1998. 161–84.

Johnson, Nan. *Nineteenth-Century Rhetoric in North America.* Carbondale: Southern Illinois UP, 1991.

Justman, Stewart. *The Autonomous Male of Adam Smith.* Norman: U of Oklahoma P, 1993.

Kagan, Jerome. *Three Seductive Ideas.* Cambridge: Harvard UP, 1998.

Kant, Immanuel. *Groundwork for the Metaphysics of Morals.* Ed. Mary Gregor. Cambridge: Cambridge UP, 1997.

———. *Logic.* Trans. and ed. Robert S. Hartman. New York: Dover, 1988.

———. *The Metaphysics of Morals.* Trans. and ed. Mary Gregor. New York: Cambridge UP, 1996.

Kastely, James L. *From Plato to Postmodernism: Rethinking the Rhetorical Tradition.* New Haven: Yale UP, 1997.

Kennedy, X. J., et al., eds. *The Bedford Guide for College Writers: With Reader, Research Manual, and Handbook.* 4th ed. Boston: Bedford-St. Martin's, 1996.

Kent, Thomas. "On the Very Idea of a Discourse Community." *College Composition and Communication* 42 (1991): 425–45.

Kerouac, Jack. *On the Road.* 1955. New York: Penguin, 1991.

Killingsworth, M. Jimmie. "Discourse Communities—Local and Global." *Rhetoric Review* 11 (1992): 110–22.

Kimball, Roger. *Tenured Radicals: How Politics Has Corrupted Our Higher Education.* Chicago: Dee, 1998.

King, Martin Luther, Jr. "Letter from Birmingham Jail." *Audiences and Intentions: A Book of Arguments.* Ed. Nancy Mason Bradbury and Arthur Quinn. New York: Macmillan College, 1991. 48–62.

Kleiman, Mark. "Drug Abuse Control Policy: Libertarian, Authoritarian, Liberal, and Communitarian Perspectives." *The Essential Communitarian Reader.* Ed. Amitai Etzioni. Lanham: Rowman, 1998. 217–26.

Kolodny, Annette. *The Lay of the Land: Metaphor as Experience and History in American Life and Letters.* Chapel Hill: U of North Carolina P, 1975.

Kuhn, Thomas. *The Structure of Scientific Revolutions.* Chicago: U of Chicago P, 1970.

Kurtz, Stanley. "P.C. Hits Anchorage." Guest comment. *National Review Online.* 2 Apr. 2001. <http://www.nationalreview.com/comment/comment-kurtz040201.shtml>.

Lakoff, Sanford. "Autonomy and Liberal Democracy." *Review of Politics* 52 (1990): 378–97.

Lakoff, George, and Mark Johnson. *Metaphors We Live By.* Chicago: U of Chicago P, 1980.

Lang, Amy. *Prophetic Woman: Anne Hutchinson and the Problem of Dissent in the Literature of New England.* Berkeley, U of California P, 1987.

Lanham, Richard. *Revising Prose.* 3rd ed. New York: Macmillan, 1992.

Lassner, Phyllis. "Feminist Responses to Rogerian Argument." *Rhetoric Review* 8 (1990): 220–32.

Lazere, Donald. "Ground Rules for Polemicists: The Case of Lynne Cheney's Truths." *College English* 59 (1997): 661–85.

———. "Teaching the Political Conflicts: A Rhetorical Schema." *College Composition and Communication* 43 (1992): 194–213.

Lemert, Charles. "Dark Thoughts about the Self." *Social Theory and the Politics of Identity.* Ed. Craig Calhoun. Oxford, Eng.: Blackwell, 1994. 100–130.

Lind, John. *An Answer to the Declaration of the American Congress.* 5th ed. London: T. Cadell, 1776.

Lindemann, Erika. "Freshman Composition: No Place for Literature." *College English* 55 (1993): 311–16.

———. "Three Views of English 101." *The Harcourt Brace Sourcebook for Teachers of Writing.* Ed. Patricia Roberts. Fort Worth: Harcourt, 1998. 3–17.

Locke, John. *An Essay Concerning Human Understanding.* 1693. New York: Dover, 1959.

———. *A Letter Concerning Toleration.* 1689. New York: Prometheus, 1990.

———. *Some Thoughts Concerning Education and of the Conduct of the Understanding.* 1693. Ed. Ruth W. Grant and Nathan Tarcov. Indianapolis: Hacketty, 1996.

Loewen, James. *Lies My Teacher Told Me: Everything Your American History Textbook Got Wrong.* New York: New, 1995.

Lynch, Dennis. "Teaching Rhetorical Values and the Question of Student Autonomy." *Rhetoric Review* 13 (1995): 350–70.

Lynch, Dennis, Diana George, and Marilyn Cooper. "Moments of Argument: Agonistic Inquiry and Confrontational Cooperation." *College Composition and Communication* 48 (1997): 61–85.

MacIntyre, Alasdair. *After Virtue.* 2d ed. Notre Dame: U of Notre Dame P, 1984.

MacKinnon, Catherine A., and Andrea Dworkin, eds. *In Harm's Way: The Pornography Civil Rights Hearings.* Cambridge: Harvard UP, 1997.

———. "Pornography: An Exchange—Comment/Reply." *New York Review of Books* 21 Oct. 1993: 36–42.

Mansbridge, Jane. *Beyond Adversary Democracy.* Chicago: U of Chicago P, 1983.

———. "A Deliberative Theory of Interest Representation." *The Politics of Interests: Interest Groups Transformed.* Ed. Mark P. Petracca. Boulder: Westview, 1992. 32–57.

———. "The Rise and Fall of Self Interest in the Explanation of Political Life." *Beyond Self-Interest.* By Mansbridge. Chicago: U of Chicago P, 1990. 3–24.

———. "Using Power/Fighting Power: The Polity." *Democracy and Difference:*

Contesting the Boundaries of the Political. Ed. Seyla Benhabib. Princeton: Princeton UP, 1996. 46–66.

Martin, Lee J., and Harry Kroitor. *The Five Hundred Word Theme.* New York: Prentice, 1980.

McCormick, Kathleen. "On a Topic of Your Own Choosing . . ." *Writing Theory and Critical Theory.* Ed. John Clifford and John Schilb. New York: MLA, 1994. 33–52.

McFague, Sallie. *Metaphorical Theology: Models of God in Religious Language.* Philadelphia: Fortress, 1982.

McNeil, Linda. *Contradictions of Control: School Structure and School Knowledge.* New York: Routledge, 1988.

Mill, John Stuart. 1859. *On Liberty.* Ed. Currin V. Shields. Indianapolis: Bobbs-Merrill, 1956.

Miller, Richard. "Fault Lines in the Contact Zone." *College English* 56 (1994): 489–508.

Miller, Robert. *The Informed Argument.* 5th ed. Fort Worth: Harcourt, 1998.

Miller, Thomas. *The Formation of College English: Rhetoric and Belles Lettres in the British Cultural Provinces.* Pittsburgh: U of Pittsburgh P, 1997.

Mouffe, Chantal. "Democracy, Power, and the 'Political.'" *Democracy and Difference: Contesting the Boundaries of the Political.* Ed. Seyla Benhabib. Princeton: Princeton UP, 1996. 245–56.

———. "For an Agonistic Pluralism." Introduction. *The Return of the Political.* By Mouffe. London: Verso, 1997. 1–8.

———. "Pluralism and Modern Democracy: Around Carl Schmitt." *The Return of the Political.* By Mouffe. London: Verso, 1993. 117–34.

———. "Radical Democracy: Modern or Postmodern?" *The Return of the Political.* By Mouffe. London: Verso, 1993. 9–22.

Muir, William. *Legislature: California's School for Politics.* Chicago: U of Chicago P, 1982.

Myers, Greg. "Reality, Consensus, and Reform in the Rhetoric of Composition Teaching." *Cross-Talk in Comp Theory: A Reader.* Ed. Victor Villanueva Jr. Urbana: NCTE, 1997. 415–38.

Nagel, Thomas. "What Is It Like to Be a Bat?" *Mortal Questions.* By Nagel. Cambridge: Cambridge UP, 1979. 165–80.

Nicholson, Linda. "Ethnocentricism in Grand Theory." *Radical Philosophy: Tradition, Counter-Tradition, Politics.* Ed. Roger S. Gottlieb. Philadelphia: Temple UP, 1993. 48–64.

Nie, Norman H., et al. *Education and Democratic Citizenship in America.* Chicago: U of Chicago P, 1996.

Norris, Christopher. *Against Relativism: Philosophy of Science, Deconstruction, and Critical Theory.* Oxford, Eng.: Blackwell, 1997.

———. *Reclaiming Truth: Contribution to a Critique of Moral Relativism.* Durham: Duke UP, 1996.

————. *What's Wrong with Postmodernism: Critical Theory and the Ends of Philosophy.* Baltimore: Johns Hopkins UP, 1990.

Nussbaum, Martha C. *Love's Knowledge: Essays on Philosophy and Literature.* New York: Oxford UP, 1990.

————. "Patriotism and Cosmopolitanism." *For Love of Country: Debating the Limits of Patriotism.* Ed. Joshua Cohen. Boston: Beacon, 1996. 3–17.

————. "Undemocratic Vistas." *New York Review of Books.* 5 Nov. 1987.

Ohmann, Richard. *English in America: A Radical View of the Profession.* Middletown: Wesleyan UP, 1996.

Olson, Gary, and Sidney I. Dobrin, eds. *Composition Theory for the Postmodern Classroom.* Albany: State U of New York P, 1994.

Ong, Walter. *Fighting for Life: Contest, Sexuality, and Consciousness.* Amherst: U of Massachusetts P, 1981.

Orwell, George. *As I Please, 1943–1945.* Boston: Nonpareil Books, 2000. Vol. 3 of *The Collected Essays, Journalism, and Letters.*

Page, Benjamin I., and Robert Y. Shapiro. *The Rational Public: Fifty Years of Trends in America's Policy Preferences.* Chicago: U of Chicago P, 1992.

Paine, Thomas. "Common Sense." 1776. *The Thomas Paine Reader.* Ed. Michael Foot and Isaac Kramnick. London: Penguin, 1987. 65–115.

Penrose, Ann M., and Cheryl Geisler. "Reading and Writing Without Authority." *College Composition and Communication* 45 (1994): 505–20.

Perdue, Virginia. "Authority and the Freshman Writer: The Ideology of the Thesis Statement." *Writing Instructor* 11 (1992): 135–42.

Perelmen, C. H., and L. Olbrechts-Tyteca. *The New Rhetoric: A Treatise on Argumentation.* Notre Dame: U of Notre Dame P, 1969.

Peterson, Linda. "Writing Across the Curriculum and/in the Freshman English Program." *Writing Across the Curriculum: A Guide to Developing Programs.* Ed. Susan McLeod and Margot Soren. Newbury Park: Sage, 1992. 58–65.

Phelps, Louise Wetherbee. "A Constrained Vision of the Writing Classroom." *ADE Bulletin* 103 (1992): 13–20.

Phillips, Anne. "Dealing with Difference: A Politics of Ideas, or a Politics of Presence?" *Democracy and Difference: Contesting the Boundaries of the Political."* Ed. Seyla Benhabib. Princeton: Princeton UP, 1996. 139–52.

————. *The Politics of Presence.* Oxford, Eng.: Clarendon, 1995.

Pitkin, Hannah Fenichel. *The Attack of the Blob: Hannah Arendt's Concept of the Social.* Chicago: U of Chicago P, 1998.

————. *The Concept of Representation.* Berkeley: U of California P, 1967.

Popper, Karl. "Knowledge and the Shaping of Reality: The Search for a Better World." *In Search of a Better World: Lectures and Essays from Thirty Years.* By Popper. London: Routledge, 1994. 3–29.

————. "The Logic of the Social Sciences." *In Search of a Better World: Lectures and Essays from Thirty Years.* By Popper. London: Routledge, 1994. 64–81.

————. *Objective Knowledge: An Evolutionary Approach.* New York: Oxford UP, 1972.

———. *The Open Society and Its Enemies: The High Tide of Prophecy: Hegel, Marx, and the Aftermath.* Vol. 2. Princeton: Princeton UP, 1971.

———. "Public Opinion and Liberal Principles." *In Search of A Better World: Lectures and Essays from Thirty Years.* By Popper. London: Routledge, 1994. 151–60.

Porter, Roy. *English History in the Eighteenth Century.* New York: Penguin, 1990.

Putnam, Hilary. *The Threefold Cord: Mind, Body, and World.* New York: Columbia UP, 1999.

Ramage, John D., and John C. Bean. *Writing Arguments: A Rhetoric with Readings.* 4th ed. Boston: Allyn, 1998.

Rawls, John. "The Idea of Public Reason." *Deliberative Democracy: Essays on Reason and Politics.* Ed. James Bohman and William Rehg. Cambridge: MIT P, 1997. 93–130.

———. *Political Liberalism.* New York: Columbia UP, 1993.

———. *A Theory of Justice.* Cambridge: Harvard UP, 1999.

Reid, Thomas. *Inquiry and Essays.* Ed. Ronald E. Beanblossom. Indianapolis: Hackett, 1983.

"The Responsive Communitarian Platform: Rights and Responsibilities." *The Essential Communitarian Reader.* Ed. Amitai Etzioni. Lanham: Rowman, 1998. xxv–xxxix.

Rich, Adrienne. "Conditions for Work: The Common World of Women." *On Lies, Secrets, and Silence: Selected Prose.* By Rich. New York: Norton, 1979. 203–14.

Roberts-Miller, Patricia. *Voices in the Wilderness: Public Discourse and the Paradox of Puritan Rhetoric.* Tuscaloosa: U of Alabama P, 1999.

Rorty, Richard. *Achieving Our Country: Leftist Thought in Twentieth-Century America.* Cambridge: Harvard UP 1998.

———. *Consequences of Pragmatism.* Minneapolis: U of Minnesota P, 1982.

———. *Philosophy and the Mirror of Nature.* Princeton: Princeton UP, 1979.

Rottenberg, Annette. *Elements of Argument.* 5th ed. Boston: Bedford, 1997.

Rousseau, Jean-Jacques. "On the Social Contract, or the Principles of Political Right." 1762. *The Basic Political Writings.* Ed. and trans. Donald A. Cress. Indianapolis: Hackett, 1987. 141–227.

Sandel, Michael. *Democracy's Discontent: America in Search of a Public Philosophy.* Cambridge: Belknap-Harvard UP, 1996.

———. *Liberalism and the Limits of Justice.* 2d ed. Cambridge: Cambridge UP, 1998.

Schriner, Dolores K., and William C. Rice. "Computer Conferencing and Collaborative Learning: A Discourse Community at Work." *College Composition and Communication* 40 (1989): 472–78.

Schumpeter, Joseph A. *Capitalism, Socialism, and Democracy.* New York: Harper, 1950.

Searle, John. "The World Turned Upside Down." *New York Review of Books* 27 Oct. 1983: 74–79.

Sears, David O., and Carolyn L. Funk. "Self-Interest in Americans' Public Opinions." *Beyond Self-Interest.* Ed. Jane Mansbridge. Chicago: U of Chicago P, 1990. 147–70.

Selznick, Philip. "Foundations of Communitarian Liberalism." *The Essential Communitarian Reader.* Ed. Amitai Etzioni. Lanham: Rowman, 1998. 61–72.

Siegel, Fred. "The Loss of Public Space." *The Essential Communitarian Reader.* Ed. Amitai Etzioni. Lanham: Rowman, 1998. 3–14.

Silber, John. "Procedure of Dogma: The Core of Liberalism." *The Betrayal of Liberalism: How the Disciplines of Freedom and Equality Helped Foster the Illiberal Politics of Coercion and Contra.* Ed. Hilton Kramer and Roger Kimball. Chicago: Dee, 1999. 189–206.

Sloane, Thomas O. *Donne, Milton, and the End of Humanist Rhetoric.* Berkeley: U of California P, 1985.

———. *On the Contrary: The Protocol of Traditional Rhetoric.* Washington, D.C.: Catholic U of America P, 1997.

Smith, Henry Nash. *Virgin Land: The American West as Symbol and Myth.* New York: Vintage, 1957.

Smith, Jeff. "Students' Goals, Gatekeeping, and Some Questions of Ethics." *College English* 59 (1997): 299–320.

Snipes, Wilson. "A Modest Proposal: In Defense of Digressive Writing." *Freshman English News* 17 (1998): 19–24.

Somers, Margaret R., and Gloria D. Gibson. "Reclaiming the Epistemological 'Other': Narrative and the Social Construction of Identity." *Social Theory and the Politics of Identity.* Ed. Craig Calhoun. Oxford, Eng.: Blackwell, 1994. 37–99.

Strauss, Leo. "Liberal Education and Responsibility." *Liberalism, Ancient and Modern.* By Strauss. Chicago: U of Chicago P, 1968. 9–25.

———. "What Is Liberal Education?" *Liberalism, Ancient and Modern.* By Strauss. Chicago: U of Chicago P, 1968. 3–8.

Sullivan, Patricia, and Donna Qualley, eds. *Pedagogy in the Age of Politics: Writing and Reading (in the Academy).* Urbana: NCTE, 1994.

Sunstein, Cass R. "Neutrality in Constitutional Law (with Special Reference to Pornography, Abortion, and Surrogacy)." *Columbia Law Review* 92 (1992): 1–52.

———. "Preferences and Politics." *Philosophy and Public Affairs* 20 (1991): 3–34.

Swales, John, and Hazem Najjar. "The Writing of Research Article Introductions." *Written Communication* 4 (1987): 175–91.

Tannen, Deborah. *The Argument Culture: Stopping America's War of Words.* New York: Ballantine, 1998.

Taylor, Charles. *Philosophy and the Human Sciences.* Cambridge: Cambridge UP, 1985.

———. *Sources of the Self: The Making of the Modern Identity.* Cambridge: Harvard UP, 1989.

Timmons, Mark C. "Objective rightness." *The Cambridge Dictionary of Philosophy.* 2d ed. Ed. Robert Audi. Cambridge: Cambridge UP 1999. 624–25.

Trimbur, John. "Consensus and Difference in Collaborative Learning." *College English* 51 (1989): 602–16.

Urquhart, Brian. "Mrs. Roosevelt's Revolution." *New York Review of Books* 26 Apr. 2001: 32–34.

Van Eemeren, Frans, et al. *Reconstructing Argumentative Discourse.* Tuscaloosa: U of Alabama P, 1993.

Volokh, Eugene. "The Constitution under Clinton: A Critical Assessment: Freedom of Speech, Cyberspace, Harassment Law, and the Clinton Administration." *Law and Contemporary Problems* 299 (2000): 299–335.

Weintraub, Jeff, and Krishan Kumar. "The Theory and Politics of the Public/Private Distinction." *Public and Private in Thought and Practice.* Ed. Jeff Wientraub and Krishan Kumar. Chicago: U of Chicago P, 1997. 1–42.

Wells, Colin. *The Roman Empire.* Stanford: Stanford UP, 1984.

Wells, Susan. "Rogue Cops and Health Care: What Do We Want from Public Writing?" *College Composition and Communication* 47 (1996): 325–40.

Will, George F. "Consciousness Raising on Campuses." *The Leveling Wind. Politics, the Culture and Other News.* By Will. New York: Penguin, 1994. 121–22.

Williams, Joseph. "The Phenomenology of Error." *College Composition and Communication* 32 (1981): 152–68.

Wills, Garry. *Inventing America: Jefferson's Declaration of Independence.* New York: Vintage, 1979.

Wood, Gordon S. *The Radicalism of the American Revolution.* New York: Random, 1993.

Young, Iris Marion. "Asymmetrical Reciprocity: On Moral Respect, Wonder, and Enlarged Thought." *Intersecting Voices: Dilemmas of Gender, Political Philosophy, and Policy.* Princeton: Princeton UP, 1997. 38–59.

———. "Communication and the Other." *Democracy and Difference: Contesting the Boundaries of the Political.* Ed. Seyla Benhabib. Princeton: Princeton UP, 1996. 120–36.

———. "Difference as a Resource." *Deliberative Democracy: Essays on Reason and Politics.* Ed. James Bohman and William Rehg. Cambridge: MIT P, 1997. 383–406.

———. "Justice and Communicative Democracy." *Radical Philosophy: Tradition, Radical Tradition, Politics.* Ed. Roger S. Gottlieb. Philadelphia: Temple UP, 1993. 123–43.

———. *Justice and Politics of Difference.* Princeton: Princeton UP, 1990.

Young-Bruehl, Elisabeth. *Hannah Arendt: For Love of the World.* New Haven: Yale UP, 1982.

Zaret, David. "Religion, Science, and Printing in the Public Spheres in Seventeenth Century England." *Habermas and the Public Sphere.* Ed. Craig Calhoun. Cambridge: MIT P, 1992. 212–35.

INDEX

Ackerman, Bruce, 23, 66, 67, 77, 207–8, 213, 224

Adams, John Quincy, 29–30, 210

Adventures of Huckleberry Finn, The, 25, 42

adversarial model. *See* self-interest

agonistic public sphere (agonism), 18, 121–25; and communitarianism, 160; definition of, 5; discourse in, 152, 158; fact in, 124–26, 134–35; and interest-based argument, 114, 121; and irenic public sphere, 12–13; and liberalism, 127–28; and liberty, 89, 126–38; minorities in, 136; rhetoric, 124–27, 131, 143. *See also* composition classroom; deliberative public sphere; difference; enclave; heterogeneity; individual; normative agreement; rationality; universality; utopia

Alcoff, Linda, 29, 33, 209

Amnesty International, 24, 168–69

Arendt, Hannah, 18, 30, 32, 34, 36, 40, 54, 75, 88, 98, 120, 121–28, 130–41, 143, 161, 164, 181, 182, 224, 235 9, 237–38n. 8

argument: by authority, 170, 208, 213–14; and enclave-based discourse, 110; and ethos, 210; by expiditio, 162, 170, 174, 179; hegemonic, 170; and identity, 113–16, 237n. 6; objectivity in, 73; personal experience in, 209–11; universal validity of, 43–47, 83–84. *See also* composition pedagogy; deliberative public sphere; logic; public debate

assessment: standardized, of composition, 219, 226

audience, general, 82, 223; and composition pedagogy, 84–87, 99–100, 118–19, 215; in public debate, 81–87

audience, particular, 52, 81–83, 84–85, 202–3

audience, universal, 81, 84, 215

autonomy, 24; in American literature, 61–62; and composition pedagogy, 59–60, 63, 90; and "concept of freedom," 66–67, 234n. 2; and critical thinking, 234n. 4; definition of, 59, 64–65, 67–68; individual conscience in, 67–68; individual versus community, 148, 153–55; and isolation, 68; in liberalism, 21–23, 58–60, 64–65, 67–68, 71, 143, 144–45; 232–33n. 4; myth of, 61–63, 69–71; origins of, 67; in universalism, 65. *See also* determinism; fact; normative metaphor; political theory; pornography; rhetoric; women

bargaining: in public sphere, 101; right to, in liberalism, 52

Bartholomae, David, 59–60, 64, 69, 89–90, 151, 155

Benhabib, Seyla, 28, 51, 123, 135, 137, 143, 199

Bercovitch, Sacvan, 55–56

Berlin, Isaiah, 49, 70–71, 88–90, 94

Berlin, James, 40, 60, 63, 64, 72, 88, 90, 160–62, 164, 165, 172, 221

Patricia Roberts-Miller, an associate professor in the Division of Rhetoric and Composition at the University of Texas at Austin, is the author of *Voices in the Wilderness: The Paradox of the Puritan Public Sphere.* She has also served on the faculty (and directed first-year composition) at the University of North Carolina at Greensboro and the University of Missouri at Columbia.